THE MESSAGE OF THE PROPHETS

GERHARD VON RAD

The Message of the Prophets

HARPER & ROW, PUBLISHERS
New York, Evanston, San Francisco, London

A translation of the German
Die Botschaft der Propheten
Siebenstern-Taschenbuch 100/101,
published 1967 by Siebenstern Taschenbuch Verlag,
Munich and Hamburg

The German edition is a revised version of material from
Theologie des Alten Testaments
made by Eduard Haller in collaboration with the author.

The complete English edition
Old Testament Theology (Vols. I and II)
is published by Oliver & Boyd Ltd, London and Edinburgh,
with whose permission the present edition appears.

Translated by D. M. G. Stalker.

THE MESSAGE OF THE PROPHETS Copyright © 1962, 1965 by Oliver and
Boyd Ltd. All rights reserved. Printed in the United States of
America. No part of this book may be used or reproduced in any
manner whatsoever without written permission except in the case of
brief quotations embodied in critical articles and reviews. For
information address Harper & Row, Publishers, Inc., 10 East 53rd
Street, New York, N.Y. 10022.

ISBN: 06-068929-3

LIBRARY OF CONGRESS CATALOG CARD NUMBER: 72-183633

CONTENTS

Contents

PUBLISHER'S NOTE

IN 1967, the sections of Gerhard von Rad's *Theologie des Alten Testaments* dealing with the prophets were reprinted in paperback form by the Siebenstern Taschenbuch Verlag under the title *Die Botschaft der Propheten*. The present book is a straight translation of that edition.

For the paperback version, Dr von Rad and his assistant Eduard Haller have worked through the original text in order to make it more readable for non-theologians. Most of the footnotes have been deleted, and technical expressions and foreign words have been paraphrased as far as possible. In some places additions have been made, and one section, that on apocalyptic, has been rewritten completely.

The English text is reprinted from the translation of the *Old Testament Theology* by D. M. G. Stalker, with the kind permission of the publishers, Messrs Oliver and Boyd. Mr Stalker has been responsible for translating additional material and has also taken this opportunity of making alterations to his original translation. The material printed here originally appeared as *Old Testament Theology*, Vol. I pp. 64-8; Vol. II, pp. 33-321. Substantial additions or alterations to the original text may be found on pp. 13f., 42f., 45, 52f., 238-40, 259, 267-74, 284.

December 1967

1 Introduction

B Y the time those men to whom we give the regrettably well-worn title 'the prophets' appeared on the scene, Israel could already look back on a long history with her God. Many generations had shared in writing the stories of the patriarchs, the revelation on Sinai, the entry into the land of Canaan, the time of the Judges and of David, and had given literary form to experiences of God which were (inevitably!) almost confusing in the variety of their form and background. The tremendous religious heritage of these experiences was a point of reference which the prophets could use when talking to their contemporaries, but it had already become somewhat strange to these contemporaries because of the manifold political and religious influences to which they were exposed. True, they had not irreligiously neglected the ancient traditions of the 'mighty works of God' (Acts 2.11), and they still worshipped and prayed to their God in the cult as they had always done. But apart from specifically religious activities, Israel – which had meanwhile become a state – had learnt to look after her own social and political affairs and to arrange them at her own discretion. The history books show a few places where counter-movements, e.g. the Levites, had developed in opposition to this religious emancipation. But what would have become of the faith of Israel if its defence had been left to these scattered and perhaps not particularly influential endeavours!

Here we come upon the most astonishing phenomenon in the whole of Israel's history: at a time when Yahwism was being increasingly undermined, and indeed was not far short of disintegration, it was able once again to re-emerge, with almost volcanic force, in a completely new form – in the message of the prophets. As the historian looks back, he sees the emergence of the prophets very closely connected with four features of long standing. The first was the degeneracy of Yahwism because of syncretism. The second was of a political nature, the systematic emancipation from Yahweh and his offer of protection brought about by the formation of the state. Through her armaments and her alliances – in other words, through her political tactics – Israel had thrown off Yahweh's guiding hand and become politically autonomous. The third lay in the economic and social developments which both kingdoms had undergone. The state with its taxation and its civil service had brought about a further disintegration of the old social order within the tribes of Israel. In this connection, the transference of the focal point of the economy to the towns was a particular blow. The great landowners, who already lived in the towns, gained control over the country people, and the result was severe social injustice. Because of the burden of taxation, the peasant, economically weak, became less and less able to remain a free man on his own land – his old influential and honourable status in the time of the ancient Israelite amphictyony as a free man liable for military service dwindled away, and ownership of land came more and more into the hands of a small number of capitalist town-dwellers. The country people became increasingly part of a proletariat (Isa. 5.8; Micah 2.1f.).

The last feature, apart from which we cannot conceive the great prophets, was of a different kind: it was not a false development within the state itself, but denoted a shift in political power in the realm of general history. This was the rise of Assyria to the summit of her power and the threat which she directed against Palestine from the eighth century onwards. We have to recognize that it was only a period of weakness in the great world empires which allowed the Israelites to conquer Palestine and create a state there at all. About 1200 BC, Egypt finally had to give up its old political claims to dominate Palestine. At roughly the same time the Hittite empire in the north succumbed to the attack of the 'sea peoples'. Assyria had certainly achieved the rank of a great power before the eighth century, but this first prominence under Tukulti Ninurta I (1235-1198) was followed by a period of sharp decline. Admittedly, her final display of power began as early as the ninth century, but this new expansion was not at first felt in Palestine. It was only with Tiglath Pileser III that Assyria's land-grabbing policy was systematically directed against Palestine, and this was the time of Hosea, Amos, and Isaiah. From then on, the political independence of Israel and Judah was at an end – it was only a question of time, and of Assyria's tactics, until the death-blow fell. About 733 BC, Tiglath Pileser seized the northern provinces of the kingdom of Israel (II Kings 15.29f.); Samaria fell about 721, and with its fall the whole northern kingdom was incorporated into Assyria's provincial organization. About 701, Sennacherib forced Jerusalem to capitulate (II Kings 18.13-16), and about 664 Asshurbanipal actually set foot in Thebes, the capital of Upper Egypt. The rapid decline of Assyria, which started in the middle of the seventh century, and its final collapse in about 612, brought Palestine no alleviation of political pressure, for the neo-Babylonians, rapidly coming to power, gave effect to Assyria's last political will and testament for Palestine under Nebuchadnezzar: between 597 and 587 what remained of the state of Judah was demolished. This was the time of the prophets Zephaniah, Habakkuk, Jeremiah, and Ezekiel.

What is the common factor in the message of these prophets? The first characteristic is that they have their roots in the basic sacral traditions of the early period. Certainly, there are very great differences in the way in which the individual prophets draw upon the old traditions. One has only to compare the extremely different, though contemporary, prophets Hosea and Isaiah, the former of whom takes his stand on the old Israel-Covenant tradition, while the latter does not even seem to have had knowledge of this, and appeals exclusively to the Zion-David tradition. A careful examination of each prophet is needed to see their versatility and their different ways of appealing to the old election traditions: there are many problems of detail here. It was obviously of the essence of a prophet to be thus rooted in the religious tradition – without it his office was inconceivable. Indeed, as their polemic makes clear, this was a much more real and fundamental thing for the prophets themselves than it was for their contemporaries. They work away, using the most extraordinary means, to convince their hearers of the binding force and undiminished validity of ordinances from which the latter had long broken away, and of which they were perhaps indeed no longer aware. In this appeal to the old uncorrupted Yahwistic traditions, the prophets' work had a thoroughgoing element of reformation. It is, of course, striking that the prophets are often very arbitrary as they bring the old material to bear upon their own day: that is, they do not always do justice to its old form as they restate it, but apply it as they understand it. This often enough means that they boldly make it more radical. We need only think of the way in which Amos or Isaiah proclaimed the demands of the old divine law.

Another characteristic of the prophets is their equally intensive view into the future. For in the complexities of world history, especially in the appearance of the Assyrians, the neo-Babylonians,

and the Persians on the horizons of Palestine, they see – in the near
future – Israel and Judah encountering a completely new action of
Yahweh in history. These proclamations of the prophets are, of
course, by no means just the result of an intelligent estimate of the
political situation, for they designate this threatened disaster as one
brought about by Yahweh to punish the sins of his people. Thus
for the prophets there was not the slightest ambiguity in the events
taking shape on the political horizon: the foreign peoples who
were approaching Israel were regarded without exception as the
instruments of the divine wrath, and were of no interest apart from
this task laid upon them. The reason why the military and political
aspects of the situation are left in the background is, of course, the
fact that the prophets believed that in the imminent disaster Israel
was being led to a completely new confrontation with Yahweh. It
was therefore Yahweh himself whose uprising was being heralded
in the turmoil of history. It was he whom the prophets saw coming
and descending upon the high places of the earth, 'because of the
transgression of Jacob and because of the sins of the house of Judah'
(Micah 1.2-5).

What is absolutely new here is the fact that, beside the dealings
of Yahweh with Israel and his meetings with her which the old
traditions recounted, the prophets announce other dealings, and
another meeting, which were in store for her, which in importance
and significance stand absolutely on a par with those handed on in
the sacral tradition. Indeed, in so far as they mark the irrevocable
end of all Yahweh's history with Israel until now, they even surpass
the old in relevance. The prophets proclaimed Yahweh's sentence
of death upon Israel: what is more, in so far as their message made
Israel's obduracy still stronger, they actually joined the band of
executioners. But another thing which made the prophets' proclamation something absolutely new and hitherto unheard-of in Israel
was that, even in the very act of proclaiming judgment, they made
known the beginnings of a new movement towards salvation. When
the kingdom of Judah, too, had been destroyed and every political
prop completely smashed, Deutero-Isaiah then delivered his message of comfort amongst those in exile, and, faced with the new
situation, which he regarded as already very close at hand, broke
out into a jubilation which was strangely out of keeping with the
dreary realities both before and after the Return. In this way the
prophets broke off and destroyed the existence which Israel had
hitherto had before Yahweh, and with increasing enthusiasm traced

out the outlines of a new salvation for her and even for the nations.

The history of the study of the prophets is not a long one. Prophecy, as an independent religious phenomenon, was not discovered until the nineteenth century, when a whole new area of the Bible was brought to light – an unusual event in the history of biblical interpretation! From the start, this discovery had an influence on its time which extended far beyond the bounds of specialist scholarship. The greatest factor to affect this new understanding of prophecy was the detaching of the message of the prophets from the 'Law', which was thought to have preceded them.[1] It was possible to approach the prophets in a new way as soon as the results of source criticism made it no longer necessary to assume that they were acquainted with the later (and the latest) traditions of the Pentateuch. All at once the prophets emerged from the shadows which had obscured their real significance.

The pendulum, however, swung too far in the other direction. The prophets were not as original, as personal, as immediate to God as they were then thought to be. We can now see how from time to time they are dependent on ancient traditions which they interpret and present anew. We even see the need to restore to the prophets their share in the 'Law'. The corrections to the picture of 'the classical study of the prophets' which have become necessary have far-reaching implications. In the first joy of discovery, the essential character of the prophet was thought to be his spiritual independence and his religious immediacy. Today, however, it has become quite clear that these are the very points at which modern ideas of the freedom and spirituality of the religious personality have influenced the interpretation of the prophets. Scholars have since shown that the prophets' involvement in ancient Eastern ideas, in cult and myth, indeed even in primitive 'magic' ideas (as they were then called) was much greater than had been supposed. Furthermore, this involvement in the traditions and general religious ideas of their environment was by no means just a peripheral one: it extended to the centre of their message.

Now once that is granted, any definition of the prophet as a brilliant religious personality, standing close to God, falls to the ground. So, too, does the whole concept of 'prophetic religion', which was set up as a spiritual counter-balance to 'the priestly

---

[1] The view that the prophets were interpreters of the law of Moses was maintained in Protestantism from Luther to the middle of the nineteenth century.

religion of the cult'. The more scholars leave aside psychology, personality and idealism in their portrayal of the prophets, however, the more difficult it becomes to say just what was the *new* element in the message of these men. The very recognition of the links between the prophetic message and tradition has in effect thrown scholars back on the old question from which they began. On the basis of their new insights, they must seek to redefine the specific characteristics of the 'prophetic'. If the origin of the message of the prophets cannot be derived from their immediate religious experience, it must be explained in other terms. What is the theological context of their unique independence and religious authority?

If we are to answer these elementary questions, it is essential for us to see the message of the prophets as it developed through history.[2]

[2] It is impossible here to go into the question of 'pre-classical' prophecy. For discussion, the reader is referred to my *Old Testament Theology* II, (1965), pp. 6-32. Other accounts of the prophets may be found in: T. H. Robinson, *Prophecy and the Prophets in Ancient Israel* (1923); C. Kuhl, *The Prophets of Israel* (1961); E. W. Heaton, *Old Testament Prophets*; J. Lindblom, *Prophecy in Ancient Israel* (1962).

2 The Traditions of the Prophets

ABOUT a century after Elijah, Amos, Hosea, Isaiah, and Micah appeared on the scene. If the source material for them is compared with that available for their predecessors, we find that in the eighth century a new factor has emerged. The narrative form of report, which is the only kind of source we have for Elijah and Elisha, markedly diminishes, and its place is taken by collections of dis-connected sayings, speeches, poems. This difference in the way in which the account of the prophets' activity has been handed on forces us to give some consideration to the literary 'form' in which the memory of their work and preaching has ultimately come down to us, for upon this largely depends the theological evaluation of later ages.

Like the historical tradition, the prophetic corpus lies before us in what are, to some extent, very shapeless collections of traditional material, arranged with almost no regard for content or chrono-logical order, and apparently quite unaware of the laws with which we are familiar in the development of European literature.[1] Ezekiel is the first to give us the benefit of an arrangement according to a chronology based on the time at which the oracles were delivered. Nevertheless, within this vast body of material a differentiation, at once simple and at the same time of great theological importance, is immediately forced upon the reader's notice. This is the dis-tinction between passages in poetry and passages in prose. While there are exceptions, the prophets' own way of speaking is, as a rule, in poetry: that is to say, it is speech characterized by rhythm and parallelism. In contrast, passages in which they are not them-selves speakers but are the subjects of report, are in prose. There are thus two ways in which the prophets made their contribution

---

[1] On the confusing impression which the literary legacy of the prophets makes on the uninitiated, Luther says: 'They (the prophets) have a queer way of talking, like people who, instead of proceeding in an orderly manner, ramble off from one thing to the next, so that you cannot make head or tail of them or see what they are getting at.' *Works*, Weimar Edn. Vol. XIX, p. 350.

to the literature of the Old Testament, or at any rate to the traditions contained in it; on the one hand there are narratives or collections of narratives which tell of what they did, and on the
other oracles or collections of oracles which they themselves delivered. Accordingly there are two reasons why they attracted the
attention both of their own contemporaries and of those who came
after them. One was the content of their preaching; the other was
the circumstances of their appearance, the conflicts in which they
were involved, the miracles they performed, and their particular
encounters with particular people. In cases where both what a
prophet himself said and what was reported about him are preserved, it is obviously not always possible to harmonize the
accounts, for the point of view of a narrator who sees the prophet
involved in the tensions and dramas of public life may be different
from that of a group of disciples whose sole interest was to record
in correct form oracles whose historical context had been forgotten.
This explains, for example, the marked dissimilarity between the
picture of Isaiah given in the stories told about him (Isa. 36-39) and
that conveyed by his own oracles. The former is much closer to
the popular estimate of him, and scarcely gives any indication of
the enormous intellectual sweep of his preaching as reflected in
the oracles. It must also be self-evident that of these two forms
of prophetic literature, that of the report is the earlier. Time, some
degree of familiarity with the phenomenon of prophecy itself, and
some education into a more spiritual outlook were all needed before it became possible to collect only the prophets' bare words,
and to view them in detachment from their historical context, and
evaluate them on their own intrinsic merits.

1. The first stage was undoubtedly that stories were told about
the prophets,[2] and in this respect the stories about Elisha give the
impression of coming from a distant past. On the other hand, the
very considerations just noticed should warn us against allowing
these popular miracle stories to lead us into forming too naïve a
picture of this prophet as he really was. He gave formal lectures
to disciples (II Kings 4.38; 6.1). If we had a collection of his lectures
or his sayings, our picture of him might well be different. The same
would be true of Elijah. By the time of Amos, however, people had
learned to take a prophet's words by themselves and to write them

[2] The stories, too, can be separated into accounts of prophetic acts (e.g.
I Kings 17.1-7, 8-16, 17-24) and accounts of prophetic words (e.g. I Kings
21.17-20; II Kings 1.3f.).

down. This meant that the centre of gravity in the prophetic tradition now moved from the story told about the prophet to the collection and transmission of his sayings. This development did not, however, lead to the disappearance of the custom of telling stories about the prophets, or indeed, to any decline in such a practice. This literary category still remained influential, for when she came to a more spiritual understanding of prophecy, Israel never went so far, in the interest of reducing the prophetic message to its ideal truths, as to sever it from its original roots in concrete events. On the contrary, she never ceased to see each of the prophets in his own historical situation, either as one who initiated historical movements or as one who was crushed to powder in the conflicts of history. The largest number of stories about a prophet is to be found in the book of Jeremiah, which is comparatively late.[3] When we come to it, we shall have to consider the importance of these as a supplement to Jeremiah's own oracles.

In reading the prophets today we must, of course, realize that what chiefly interests us, biographical detail, imports into these stories a viewpoint which is foreign to them themselves. Even the idea of 'prophetic personalities' which so readily comes to our minds is very far from being what the sources themselves offer us. In all probability, the writers were much less concerned than we imagine to portray a prophet as a 'personality', that is to say, as a unique human being who possessed special qualities of mind and spirit. The same is true of interest in biographical detail. We can even feel that the sources are opposed to any attempt to write 'lives' of the prophets. Had the writer of Amos 7. 10ff. had any intention of giving information about Amos's own life, he would never have ended his account as he does, and have failed to inform the reader whether or not the prophet complied with the deportation order. If the story is to be read as a fragment taken from a biography, the only possible verdict on such an ending is 'unsatisfactory'. Amos is here only described from the point of view of his being a prophet, that is to say, as the holder of an office, and because of this the writer had no interest beyond describing the clash between the bearer of a *charisma* and the high priest, and recording the oracle of doom to which this gave rise.

The stories about Elijah, Elisha, and Isaiah also provide examples

[3] In connection with the so-called Temple address in the year 609, the tradition contains the prophet's words (Jer. 7.1-15) and independently a story which describes the incident (Jer. 26).

both of a similar lack of interest in biographical detail and of a concentration upon how a prophet acted in virtue of his calling. A change comes about with Jeremiah. Jeremiah the man and his *via dolorosa* are now really described for their own sake. This, however, is closely connected with the fact that with Jeremiah prophecy entered upon a critical phase of its existence, and that a new concept of a prophet was beginning to appear. Probably the first to realize that suffering was to be regarded as an integral part of a prophet's service was Baruch. There was more to being a prophet than mere speaking. Baruch saw a completely new aspect of the office. Not only the prophet's lips but also his whole being were absorbed in the service of prophecy. Consequently, when the prophet's life entered the vale of deep suffering and abandonment by God, this became a unique kind of witness-bearing. Yet even this does not mean that in narrative portions of Jeremiah the account of the prophet's life is given for its own sake. It is given because in his case his life had been absorbed into his vocation as a prophet, and made an integral part of the vocation itself. But, as I have already stressed, this insight was only reached after some time and must therefore be dealt with at a later stage.

2. Prophecy ultimately employed the 'messenger formula' as the most direct means of expressing its function. But since from its very first appearance in Israel there were more kinds of prophecy than one, it is practically impossible to point to any single basic 'form' of prophetic speech and to identify it, from the point of view of form criticism, as prophecy's original starting-point.[4] Yet, even though the 'messenger formula' cannot be taken as this, it should be considered first, since it persists as a constant factor in all OT prophecy from Elisha to Malachi, and is, too, the most consistently used of all the many different prophetic literary categories.

As everyone knows, it was a common custom in the ancient world for a messenger with some announcement to make to discharge his errand when he came into the recipient's presence, by speaking in the first person, the form in which the message had been given to himself; that is to say, he completely submerged

---

[4] An old form, perhaps one of the oldest, is preserved in the cries uttered by the prophets in the context of sacral war enterprises. What is under discussion here is, for one thing, the stereotyped command to get ready for battle (cf. I Kings 20.13f.; Hos. 5.8; Isa. 13.2; Jer. 46.3f.; 49.8, 14, 3of.; 50.14f., 21, 29; 51.11, 27); for another, the commands to flee directed to people against whom there was no hostile intent, but who lived in the zone chosen for military operations (cf. I Sam. 15.6f.; Jer. 4.6f.; 6.1; 49.8, 30; 50.8; 51.6).

his own *ego* and spoke as if he were his master himself speaking to the other. Examples of this entirely secular use of the 'messenger formula' introduced by the words 'thus says so and so' are still to be found within the Old Testament itself.[5] This is the form which the prophets used more frequently than any other to deliver their messages, and the fact is important for the understanding of their own conception of their role. They saw themselves as ambassadors, as the messengers of Yahweh.

As a rule, however, the prophets prefaced this messenger formula with another form of words whose purpose was to draw the recipient's attention to the message and which, indeed, gave the first precise designation of those for whom it was intended. In the case of a divine threat, what was prefixed was a 'diatribe', in the case of a promise, an 'exhortation'. These two, the messenger formula and the prefaced clause, must both be present before we have the literary category 'prophetic oracle'. To understand the category, we must remember that down to the time of Jeremiah, with whom there is a change, the prophets always made a clear distinction between the messenger formula and the diatribe or exhortation which introduced it. The former alone was the direct word of God: the other was a human word whose purpose was to lead up to and prepare the way for God's word and give it its reference. The divine word was, of course, primary in point of time: this was what came to the prophet in a moment of inspiration, to be passed on to those whom it concerned. This the prophet did by prefixing to it a diatribe which identified the people addressed. What makes the inner connection between diatribe and threat is the characteristic 'therefore', justifying the latter and leading on to the words 'Thus hath Yahweh spoken'.[6]

But the messenger formula, frequent though it is, is still only one among many forms used by the prophets in their preaching.[7] In fact, they showed no hesitation in availing themselves of all manner of forms in which to clothe their message. None, secular and sacred alike, was safe from appropriation as a vessel for the discharge of his task by one prophet or another. What these men wanted to do, of course, was to attract attention: indeed some-

[5] E.g., Gen. 32.4ff. [3ff.], 45.9; Num. 22.16; I Kings 2.30; Isa. 37.3.
[6] Cf. for example Amos 3.11; 4.12; 5.11, 16; 6.7; 7.17; Hos. 2.8 [9]; Isa. 5.13; 10.16; Micah 2.3; 3.12; Jer. 2.9; 5.6, 14, etc.
[7] According to Köhler, it is found 14 times in Amos, 44 times in Isaiah, 157 times in Jeremiah and 125 times in Ezekiel.

times, as when, for example, they laid violent hands on some time-hallowed sacral form of expression, their express intention was to shock their audience. Thus their utterances can be couched as a priestly direction concerning sacrifice (Isa. 1.16f.; Amos 5.21ff.), as a cultic hymn, or as a pronouncement in a court of law.[8] Deutero-Isaiah took the priestly oracle of salvation and reshaped it into something more sweeping and made it *the* 'form' of his preaching. His well-known phrases, 'Fear not, I have chosen you, redeemed you, I call you by name, you are mine' (Isa. 41.10ff.; 43.1f.; 44.1f.; etc.) are modelled on the liturgical language used by the priest in the cult in response to an individual prayer of lamentation (Isa. 41.10ff.; 43.1f.; 44.1f.; etc.). In other cases the message was clothed in the form used by the teachers of wisdom (Isa. 28.23ff.; Amos 3.3ff.), or of a popular song (Isa. 5.1ff.). The best example of the changes which these literary categories underwent at the hands of the prophets, who sometimes even expanded them into really grotesque shapes, is the dirge: the later prophets actually parodied it.[9] Exegesis has therefore to be particularly careful here, because a great deal depends on correct determination of 'form', and in particular on the correct delimitation of the beginning and end of the unit under discussion. To add a verse from the unit which follows, or to omit one which properly belongs to the close of an oracle, can alter the whole meaning.[10]

The form in which a particular message is cast is also important in a still stricter sense of the word 'form', for a 'form' is never just something external, concerned with literary style alone; in the last resort, form cannot be separated from content. What determined the choice of the form was primarily the subject-matter of the message. But the content of the prophetic preaching could not possibly be housed in any traditional form – not even a specifically prophetic – for it completely transcended the whole of Israel's previous knowledge of Yahweh. The very nature of the subject-matter itself demanded nothing short of a bold method of expression – it was always, so to speak, *ad hoc* improvization – simply

[8] Isa. 1.2f., 18-20; 3.13-15; Hos. 4.1-4a; Micah 1.2-7; 6.1-8; Jer. 2.4-9; Isa. 41.1-5, 21-9; 43.8-13, 22-8; 44.6-8; 48.1-11; 50.1-2a. The cases where Yahweh speaks as the person accused, Micah 6.3-5; Jer. 2.4-13, 29f.; Isa. 50.1-2a, are particularly noteworthy.

[9] Amos 5.1; Isa. 23.1ff.; Ezek. 19.1ff., 10ff.; parodies of dirges, Ezek. 27.2ff.; 28.11ff.; 32.17ff.; Isa. 14.4ff.

[10] In this respect the Old Testament pericope series require drastic correction.

because the prophets' message thrust out at every side beyond each and all of Israel's sacral institutions, the cult, law, and the monarchy. In the same way, the very nature of prophecy also demanded the right to make use of what were entirely secular forms with exactly the same freedom as with religious ones, as if there were no difference at all between them, for ultimately prophecy moved in a direction which transcended the old distinctions: when it prophesied judgment, it also announced the end of the established sacral order, and when it foretold salvation, it spoke increasingly of a state of affairs in which all life would be ordered, determined, and sustained by Yahweh. This would, of course, result in the removal of the old distinction between sacral and secular.

3. The separate units consisting of oracles or songs were very soon gathered together into little complexes. Whether such 'divans' were arranged by the prophet himself or by his disciples, is for the most part unknown. Although our information about such possible disciples is limited, present-day criticism is certainly right in crediting them with an important part in the collection and transmission of the prophets' teaching. Thus Isaiah 5.8-24 consists of a series of oracles each beginning with the words 'Woe to', which we may be sure were no more delivered consecutively than were those in Matthew 23.13ff. – the connection is editorial. The same is true of Jeremiah's oracles against the false prophets (Jer. 23.9ff.), or the royal house (Jer. 21.11–23.8). In the complex made up of Isaiah 6.9–9.6 [7], the editor grouped on chronological grounds, for, apart from the prophet's call which stands at the beginning, the oracles and the incidents dealt with date from the time of the Syro-Ephraimitic war. Ezekiel 4–5 is a collection of the prophet's so-called symbolic actions.[11] In many cases, however, there is no recognizable principle of arrangement. This is particularly true of the formation of more elaborate complexes, that is to say, where it is a case of the collection of collections. Almost all the help we have towards insight

---

[11] Sometimes the 'principle' of catchword arrangement may also have been in operation. In Deutero-Isaiah the basis of theological concepts is of course much narrower than it is with, for example, Isaiah, Jeremiah, or Ezekiel, and in proportion it is naturally much easier to recognize a connection between the units. Nevertheless, in Isa. 1.9 and 10 the sequence may have been determined by the catchword 'Sodom', and in Isa. 8.8 and 9f. by the catchword 'Immanuel'. Similar observations have been made in the exegesis of Hosea. These instances are, however, too isolated to serve to clarify the process of redaction in general.

into how this redactional process progressed are a few headings
within the prophetic books.[12]

For all the immense range of the prophetic tradition, there are
really only three passages, two in Isaiah (8.16-18; 30.8-17) and one
in Jeremiah (36), which describe in somewhat greater detail how
the prophet's message was put into written form and handed on.
Yet, so many are the conclusions which they allow concerning the
nature of the prophets' teaching in general, and of the prophets'
own conception of that teaching, that they must be considered
here, however briefly.

'I will bind up the testimony, seal the teaching among my disciples, and will wait for Yahweh, who is hiding his face from the
house of Jacob, and I will hope in him. Behold, I and the children
whom Yahweh has given me are signs and portents from Yahweh
of hosts, who dwells on Mount Zion' (Isa. 8.16-18).

Isaiah 6.1–9.6 [7] deals with the stirring events of the Syro-
Ephraimitic war, and records the threats, warnings, and promises
which Isaiah delivered at that time. To our surprise, however, right
in the middle of these, the prophet suddenly speaks of himself, and
directs the reader's thoughts to his own person and to a group of
people gathered round him. But the particular situation revealed
in the passage at once makes the whole thing clear. The prophet
is to 'seal' and 'bind up' his 'teaching' in just the same way as we
record something in the minutes and then have the document
officially put into safe keeping. The words can therefore only mean
that at the time when Isaiah wrote them down, he thought of himself as discharged from office. The glimpse here given of his
thoughts and expectations on his withdrawal from his first public
activity makes the passage unique indeed. He has delivered the
message that was given him. The rest lies in the hands of Yahweh
who – as Isaiah is perfectly sure – will follow what his ambassador
has revealed by word with his own revelation in action. The
message tore open a deep gulf in the nation. It made it obdurate
(Isa. 6.9f.), and made Yahweh himself a snare to his people (Isa.
8.14); and yet, by a tremendous paradox, it is on this very God who
has hidden his face from the house of Israel that Isaiah sets his

[12] There may have been cases where what the prophet left behind was
handed on initially by way of oral tradition. In others the reduction to
writing had already begun in the prophet's lifetime. As early as the second
millennium, Palestine was one of the places where writing had an important
function in intellectual life and the exchange of ideas.

hope. What confidence in face of the absence of faith! But the surprise is rather that the message actually brought faith forth, even if only within a very narrow circle. Thus, even when Isaiah withdraws into the anonymity of civil life, he still remains of importance as a sign – the narrow circle of the faithful is the surety that Yahweh is still at work and that he has not abandoned his purpose in history. Significantly enough, these purposes Isaiah regarded as, in the last analysis, good: otherwise, how could he have 'placed his hope' in the coming revelation of Yahweh in person? In this connection, although the prophet's words about 'binding' and 'sealing' his message are only figurative and allusive, Isaiah presumably did in actual fact go on to make a written record of all he had said up to the time when he was relieved of office, and – also presumably – this record forms the first point of crystallization of the book of Isaiah.

'Now go and write it before them on a tablet and inscribe it in a book, that it may be for a time to come as a witness for ever, for they are a rebellious people, lying sons who will not hear the instruction of Yahweh. . . . Therefore thus says the Holy One of Israel, "Because you have despised this word, and trust in oppression and perverseness, and rely on them; therefore this iniquity shall be to you like a break in a high wall, bulging out and about to collapse, whose crash comes suddenly, in an instant." . . . For thus said the Lord Yahweh, the Holy One of Israel, "In returning and rest you shall be saved; in quietness and trust is your strength". But you would not . . .' (Isa. 30.8-15).

This passage, which comes from the latter period of Isaiah's life, makes the transition of prophecy from oral proclamation to its reduction to writing, that is to say, to the second, the literary, form of its existence, still clearer. Here the prophet is no ambassador. He is not to go out, but is to 'go into' his house, and he is not to speak, but to write 'for a time to come'. The situation is clearly the same as that in Isa. 8.16ff. The message has been delivered. Once again a phase of the prophet's work has come to an end, and once again it has resulted in failure. Isaiah had not succeeded in kindling faith; his hearers were far too preoccupied with political projects to listen. Indeed, things were even worse. They 'would not' do so, and deliberately decided against Yahweh and his pleading. And this time there are no comfortable words about a small group of disciples. The atmosphere is much more laden with rejection than it was on

the other occasion. A far deeper darkness enfolds the prophet. In
one respect the passage goes much further than Isa. 8, for it shows
the decision against Yahweh and his pleading as one which has
already been taken. This is important for the message of Isaiah, for
this is one of the very few places where the prophet himself re-
capitulates the essential content of that message in one or two
words and summarizes the ideas. His wish had been to move people
to turn to Yahweh, and to seek security in his protection, and
to find confidence and 'calm'. As it was, since they have rejected it
all, it will be their lot to lose all stability, as Isaiah so magnificently
depicts it in the picture of a wall suddenly bulging out and col-
lapsing.

Why does the prophet write down his message as a 'testament',
as it is generally called? How far is it intended for 'a time to come'?
What he thought of initially was certainly the fulfilment of his
threat. Those who came after him would be able to see in retrospect
that his prophetic word had been no empty one. It may also well
be that, as he made the record, his thoughts ranged considerably
wider than the immediate fulfilment. His own generation was written off – 'suddenly, in an instant', ruin would overtake it. Yet, even
if the fate he foretold for it actually came to pass, this was after
all only one part of his prophetic message. The promise of blessing
it contained, its invitation to seek security in the protection of
Yahweh, also remained valid. Though one generation turns a deaf
ear to it, it does not fail. Yahweh does not abandon his purposes:
the only difference is that these now reach forward to a more
distant future in the nation's history, and for this reason the
message required to be written down.

What gives the passage its great interest is that it shows how in
certain circumstances the prophet broke the connection between
his words and their original hearers and, without the slightest
alteration, carried the message over to apply to hearers and readers
of a more distant future. At the time when Isaiah wrote down his
preaching, possibly after 701, history had certainly overtaken some
of his prophecies. Looked at from the point of view of their obvious and immediate fulfilment, they had apparently failed. This
was not, however, a reason for regarding them as things of the
past, for they retained their significance for more than merely
the time to which they were addressed initially. Nor was it any
more a reason for altering their content or recasting them to suit
their new recipients. The same thing had happened with Hosea.

When it was originally delivered, his whole message was directed to the then northern kingdom. But sometime later very slight editing – the insertion of the name 'Judah' at several places – gave it a new address, to the southern kingdom. It was never presumed that the prophet's oracles were addressed to one set of people and one only, and were thereafter to be wrapped up in their rolls and deposited among the records. There must have been people who never forgot that a prophet's teaching always remained relevant for a coming day and generation, and who themselves played their part in making it appear relevant – in many cases their work can be clearly seen in the various secondary additions which they made. A clearer instance than most, showing what took place during the process of transmission, is the relationship of Trito-Isaiah to Deutero-Isaiah. The former's dependence upon the latter is so striking that it has been correctly assumed that their relationship was one of master and pupil. But the situation in which the younger man voiced the elder's words was very different from that in which they had first been coined; and, consequently, the master's sayings were radically modified. In the first phase of his activity Jeremiah, too, is a disciple – of Hosea. Again, scholars long ago marked off a large section of prose passages in his book whose diction and theological ideas approximate very closely to the tradition associated with Deuteronomy and the Deuteronomists. Obviously, we have here a characteristic reshaping by a second hand of material belonging to Jeremiah, though we do not, of course, know who was responsible for it or why he acted as he did.

Baruch's long, detailed account of how Jeremiah's preaching was set down in writing, and of the several readings of the roll, parallels the two passages from Isaiah discussed above to the extent that it describes the transition from oral preaching to written word. But it goes much further in that it tells of the strange fate which overtook the book. Like Isaiah, Jeremiah derived the order to make a written record from Yahweh's express command: what, however, is significant is the purpose of this undertaking as revealed in the account (Jer. 36). It was a final attempt to move Israel to repentance, and so to make it possible for Yahweh to forgive her. But this is only the introduction to the account of the book's fate once it had been produced. Baruch shows great artistry as he leads up to the climax. He tells how the roll was read three times. The first occasion is fairly lightly touched on. This was a public reading during a fast before Yahweh in 605. The second reading, held in

the secretary of state's office in the presence of the chief state
officials, is given a fuller description. The audience then was
alarmed at what they heard; they cross-examined Baruch, and the
roll itself was put into 'official safe-custody'. While there was
marked goodwill towards Baruch personally, the matter itself had
to be reported to the king. What a consummate artist Baruch is as
he thus prepares the way for the climax of his story! What is the
king's attitude going to be? For his decision will determine whether
the whole people – not just he himself – are to stand or fall. Now
the story gives a detailed account. The king is in the winter-house,
sitting beside the brazier, with his ministers around him. Yet in
the end it is not he who is the centre of interest, but the roll itself,
which he cuts up and throws piece by piece into the fire. Thereupon
Jeremiah dictates his preaching to Baruch anew, and makes the
second roll more comprehensive still than the first.

The story is unique in the Old Testament, since its subject is
neither a person, nor an act of Yahweh's providence or appointment, but a book. But the book's fortunes epitomize the fortunes
of the message it contained. Once more the *motif* is that of the
great failure, which Jeremiah plays with his own particular variations. We might therefore almost speak of a 'passion' undergone
by the book as well as by its author. At one point, however, the
parallel with Jeremiah's own *via dolorosa* breaks down. The scroll
is torn and burnt, but it is renewed. Yahweh's word does not allow
itself to be brought to naught.

These three passages show, of course, only the first step in the
formation of tradition, that from oral proclamation to written
record, a step sometimes taken by the prophets themselves. This
was, however, a long way from the final stage in the process of
making a permanent record of a prophet's message; instead, it
ought to be called only its beginning. As we have already seen, a
prophet's preaching was not restricted to its original audience.
As Israel journeyed through time, the message accompanied her,
even if the historical circumstances to which it had originally been
spoken had changed in the interval. The basic conviction under-
lying the process of tradition was that, once a prophet's word had
been uttered, it could never in any circumstances become void. The
time when, and the way by which, it reached fulfilment were Yahweh's concern; man's part was to see that the word was handed
on. And we must notice particularly that even the prophecies
which had plainly found their historical goal, and had thus clearly

been fulfilled, were retained as prophecies which concerned Israel and could always have fresh meaning extracted from them.

A particularly revealing instance of this centuries-long incessant process of continual reinterpretation of tradition is furnished by the so-called Nathan prophecy (II Sam. 7). Verses 11 and 16 show what is perhaps the oldest strand, a prophecy aimed directly at David himself. Compared with it, the ideas expressed in vv. 12a, 14-16 are later – the advance in point of time comes out in the interest shown in 'the son after you, who shall come forth from your body', when David 'will have lain down with his fathers'; the point is now Yahweh's relationship to David's descendants. Then, considerably later, the Deuteronomistic theology of history connected this whole prophecy with Solomon's building of the temple (v. 13), while later still Deutero-Isaiah severed the tie with the house of David and applied the saying to Israel as a whole (Isa. 55.3f.). Even after this, the old reference of the promise to the seed of David himself is not wide enough for the Chronicler: he speaks of 'the seed which shall come forth from thy sons', and thus adds a further stage in the prophecy's scope (I Chron. 17.11). In this way an oracle first spoken in the long distant past continued to have a present message considerably later than the exile.

The way in which tradition mounts and grows can be closely followed in the prophetic writings. Exegesis must be less ready than at present to look on this infusion of new blood into the prophetic tradition as 'spurious' or an unhappy distortion of the original. The process is in reality a sign of the living force with which the old message was handed on and adapted to new situations. Adaptation was in some cases effected by adding threats against foreign nations which had meantime come within the orbit of Israel's history. Thus, for example, the very old prophecy of Balaam was finally even made to refer to the Greeks (Num. 24.24). In Isaiah 23 a few later additions made an earlier oracle against Sidon refer to Tyre. To the Messianic prophecy of Isa. 11.1ff. was added in a later day v. 10, and it was applied to the Gentile world, and was taken up by Paul in this reinterpreted form (Rom. 15.12). In just the same way the Messianic prophecy in Amos passed over into the New Testament in its less restricted LXX version (Acts 15.16f.: 'Adam'; Amos 9.12: 'Edom'). In Isa. 9.11, Isaiah spoke of Aram and the Philistines; the LXX applies the saying to Syria and the Greeks.

When, however, in the course of adaptation of this kind an old oracle is converted into its opposite – when, for instance, an oracle of judgment is made into one of salvation – doubts begin to arise, at least for the modern reader. Isaiah proclaimed 'woe' to the Egyptians, 'the nation tall and smooth, feared near and far', and threatened them with destruction (Isa. 18.1-6). But as it now stands, the oracle goes on to prophesy that 'at that time' gifts will be brought to Yahweh from 'the people tall and smooth, feared near and far' (v. 7). Yet even such a conversion of an older message of judgment into one of salvation is not the plagiarism, on principle illegitimate, of a later writer who is himself devoid of inspiration. There is in the Isaiah text a genuine sense of continuity, and a genuine belief that authority has been given to reinterpret an earlier oracle, even if in opposite terms, because of the very different historical situation. The very fact that oracles are so often inverted in this way compels us to regard it as a perfectly normal and theologically legitimate procedure. For example, in the composite passage Isaiah 22.15-25 three stages of growth stand out in clear relief. In the first section, vv. 15-18, the wrath of Yahweh and of the prophet himself were poured out on Shebna, one of the chief officials of Judah. He shall not some day be laid to rest in his newly hewn tomb. Yahweh will toss his mummified corpse into a foreign land as if it were a ball. This is the end of the oracle spoken by Isaiah himself, but it continues:

'I will thrust you from your office and cast you down from your
     station.
This will come to pass on the day when I call Eliakim the son of
     Hilkiah my servant.
I will clothe him with your robe,
and bind your girdle on him, and commit your authority to his
     hand,
that he may be a father to the inhabitants of Jerusalem
and to the house of Judah.
And I will place on his shoulder the key of the house of David;
when he opens, none shall shut, and when he shuts, none shall open.
I will fasten him like a peg in a sure place,
and he will become a throne of honour to his father's house' (Isa.
22.19-23).

The very change in the style – there is a sudden transition to the first person singular – betrays that a fresh start had been made. In addition, v. 19a makes a poor transition: Shebna has already been rejected, and talk about his dismissal is out of place. The centre of interest is now Shebna's successor, Eliakim, and his installation in office (the few verses are a veritable gold-mine for information about the ceremonial language in use at the court). But there was something else to be said about Eliakim, and it was something which was quite unknown at the time of his appointment. This brings us to the third phase in the development of the Shebna texts.

'And the whole weight of his father's house will hang upon him, the offspring and the issue, every small vessel, every cup and flagon. In that day, says Yahweh of hosts, the peg fastened in a sure place will give way, it will break off and fall down, and the burden that is upon it will be destroyed, for Yahweh has said so' (Isa. 22.24-5).

This expansion hinges on the 'peg' of v. 23, but understands the metaphor in a completely different way. Eliakim is certainly to be a peg, for all his kinsmen are to hang upon him. Therefore what happens to a peg on which too many pots and pieces of kitchen-ware are hung will also happen to him. He will give way, and the whole collection will be smashed to pieces on the floor. A delightful satire on the nepotism of highly placed officials!

This way of dealing with traditions brings us up against a hermeneutic problem which can only be noticed briefly here. If a prophet's words thus accompanied Israel on her journey through history, and if they retained their character as addresses to her even long after the time of their original delivery, later ages must have felt themselves at liberty to reinterpret them freely, for the only way in which the word reaches those to whom it was later addressed was by 'adaptation' of its content. Present-day exegesis is concerned above all else to discover the content of each specific oracle as it was understood by the prophet himself. But, while not abandoning this effort, ought it not perhaps to be more aware that this is only one possible way among many of understanding an oracle? By being referred to subsequent generations and the situations confronting them, fresh possible ways of taking the prophet's oracles were opened up, and this process continued right down to the time when, in the New Testament, the prophets' preaching was for the last time reinterpreted in the light of present events. Ought we not also to remember that when a prophecy came into the hands of those who transmitted the traditions, this itself meant that the time when the prophecy could be taken in the strict sense which it had when it was originally delivered was already a thing of the past?

3 The Prophets' Call and Reception of Revelation

THE prophets themselves believed that their calling, to which we shall now turn, confronted them with a range of tasks and duties. We may, indeed, quite properly speak of the prophetic 'office' consisting on the one hand of binding commitments and on the other of liberties and powers. Of course, since this is a very general term, it will have to be more precisely defined as we proceed, for we cannot presume that each and every prophet held an identical view of it. There were very many shades of difference indeed, of which only a few can be noticed in what follows. Not only did the prophets' own conception of their office clearly change, it was also possible for a prophet even to come into conflict with his office: a further cause of conflict might be where the prophet's definition of his office differed from the ideas of others. For example, in the case of Isaiah, the idea of his office which he himself held was not at all the same as the one which forms the background of the stories told about him in chs. 36–39. The latter version is determined by the narrator's own idea of it. In principle, behind every prophetic tradition and behind even the most insignificant mention, lies a well-defined idea of what constitutes a prophet and his office. If scholarship had a still keener awareness than it has of these questions, its eyes would be much more open to the enormous variety in the idea of what a prophet was.

I. As the result of a new understanding of the cult, the question has recently been asked whether even the prophets were not much more closely connected with this institution than was once thought possible and, on the basis of what is in some degree a very original interpretation of evidence both inside and outside the Old Testament, the view has been put forward that the majority of the prophets mentioned in the Old Testament were official spokesmen of the cult, and were therefore members of the cultic personnel of the sanctuaries.

It has never been doubted that the prophets liked to pay visits to sanctuaries, both because great numbers of pilgrims resorted to them and also because the catchwords and the points to which they could link their oracles were given them in the religious excitement of the crowds, who would only be met with in such numbers at these shrines. This in itself, however, is no reason for talking about 'cult-prophets'. It may also be taken for granted that an ever-growing number of bands of prophetic 'enthusiasts' were present at the sanctuaries during festivals. These sometimes made such a nuisance of themselves to the priests that special means of supervising them had actually to be set up (Jer. 29.24ff.). But the real question is this – were the prophets members of the cultic personnel in the narrow sense of the term, that is, as its authorized spokesmen? In the case of pre-classical prophecy, it is extremely difficult to give any clear answer, for the simple reason that the material which has come down to us is so scanty. Moreover, we tend to look on this early stage of the prophetic movement as much more uniform than it was in fact. Elisha's station in life was obviously quite different from Elijah's: and both these prophets are clearly very different again from such a man as Nathan. The ecstatics mentioned in I Sam. 10.10f. came from a shrine, but it is difficult to believe that they themselves held a cultic office there. The same is true of the group which gathered round Elisha, and in an even greater degree of Elijah also. No doubt Elijah offered sacrifice on occasion (I Kings 18.30ff.), but this proves nothing, for at that time any Israelite could do the same.

The picture changes when we also recognize the fairly firmly rooted idea that at least one main function of the prophet was intercession.[1] Since, so far as we can see, this was requested on occasions of public emergency and therefore concerned 'Israel', the prophet must at that time have been regarded as in fact a duly authorized spokesman of the whole body of the people. It is also perfectly possible that such intercession by a prophet was sometimes made in the solemn context of an official act of worship. It may be, too, that on such occasions he delivered oracles against foreign nations and called down curses against particular enemies. There is also reason to believe that prophets of a certain kind had an important role assigned them in warfare – it was they who gave the command to attack (I Kings 20.13f., 22, 28; 22.6, 12, 15; II Kings 3.16f.;

[1] I Sam. 12.19, 23; 15.11. In a different way with Isaiah and Jeremiah: II Kings 19.1ff.; Jer. 7.16; 42.2.

6.9). Further, the official ultimatum issued to the neighbours of a
people against whom Israel was waging war and to the aliens resi-
dent in its midst, warning them to flee from the threatened region
(I Sam. 15.6), was a matter for the prophets. Here, too, the prophets
are seen as authorized spokesmen of the whole body of the people,
in the context of an event which was at that time still regarded
as sacral and cultic.

These and other facts show that in the ninth century the prophets were still in various ways incorporated within the official
cult. At the same time, however, it is impossible to imagine that
their function was as much subject to rules and regulations as that
of the priests. For another thing, their office was not hereditary
but charismatic, and therefore *a priori* on a different footing. Again,
is it entirely without significance that Deuteronomy gives regulations for the revenues of the priests and levites, but that nothing
of the kind occurs in connection with those of the prophets? Further, the fact that women are quite naturally spoken of as prophets
(Ex. 15.20; II Kings 22.14; Neh. 6.14), whereas the idea of women
priests was quite inconceivable, rather militates against the thesis
of cultic prophets. Nevertheless, it is clear that there were still
large numbers of such temple prophets as late as the time of Jeremiah, and, most probably, they came forward as the spokesmen
both of Yahweh and the people. However, the prophets who have
been called the 'writing prophets', Amos, Isaiah, Micah, Jeremiah,
and the rest of them, were not of their number, as their bitter
attacks on these cult prophets makes abundantly clear. They were
instead members of a radical wing which increasingly declared its
independence from the operation of the official cult.[2] Proof of
this must, of course, be drawn primarily from the content of their
preaching and their general outlook, but it can also be demon-
strated in the very forms which they used. These are characterized
by the extreme boldness of their newly-minted rhetorical devices

---

[2] 'Because we think that the freedom of the prophetic office should be
fundamentally maintained we do not deny that in certain periods many
prophets were connected with the temple . . . but we do deny that the
prophets as such were official assistants at the cult. Not only from the
character of Elijah, the remark of Amos (7.14), the figure of Huldah, the wife
of a palace official (II Kings 22.14), is it evident that there was no unbreakable
connection between prophecy and the priestly office, but from the general
tone of the prophecies of Micah, the activity of Haggai (2.12f.) and particularly from the well-known story of Eldad and Medad in Num. 11, the expectation of Joel 2.28ff., etc.' C. Vriezen, *An Outline of Old Testament Theology*,
tr. S. Neuijen (1958), pp. 261f.

and of the comparisons they employed, which they chose solely
to scandalize and startle the people who heard them, by the way
in which so often they couched their messages in completely
secular literary forms – selected *ad hoc* and subsequently abandoned – and in particular by the incredible variety of forms they
used in their preaching, ranging over the whole field of expression
then available. Such improvization was quite unknown in the cultic
sphere where all utterance, be it of God or of man, was regulated
by convention and standardization. Moreover, there was no place
in the cult for the idea that Yahweh would enter into judgment
with his own people.[3] These quick transitions which the great
prophets make from form to form are, however, merely the symp-
tom of a radical process which was at work in the very heart of
their preaching. This was a totally new understanding of God, of
Israel, and of the world, which the prophets each in turn cumula-
tively developed to a degree which went far beyond anything that
there had ever been in the past. Our main reason, however, for
thinking that the prophets were much more independent than those
who held a fixed office in the organized life of a sanctuary comes
from the accounts of their calls, and to these we must now turn.

2. The Old Testament often tells of how a prophet was called to
his office. The accounts all come from a comparatively short period
of time in Israel's history, the period of the Monarchy. This shows
both how far outside the normal range of Israel's religious experience such calls lay and that they were not characteristic of the
representatives of Yahwism from the very beginning. Moreover, in
the ancient east people did not write things down simply for the
sake of writing them down – the written record was always used
as a means to a very definite end – so that the very fact that a
call was recorded in writing shows that it was regarded at the time
it occurred as something unusual.

The prophetic call in fact gave rise to a new literary category,
the account of a call. In Israel the connection between a person's
experiences in his religious and cultic life and the way in which
he expressed himself by means of the spoken or the written word
was such a direct and living one that any innovation of importance
at once made itself apparent in the realm of form: an old form was

[3] Even the cases in which prophets were enquired of by an official deputation or requested to make intercession (II Kings 19.1ff.; Jer. 37.3), do not
show that their answers were given within the framework of the cult.
Jeremiah once had to wait ten days for God's answer, and only then could
he summon the deputation to give it them (Jer. 42.1ff.).

modified, or a new one was brought into being. Here I mean the innovation by which the accounts of prophetic calls were given in the first person singular. Of course, men of Israel had said 'I' in the presence of God even before the prophets appeared on the scene – for example in laments and thanksgivings. But this was quite a different use of 'I'. The old cultic forms made first personal singular statements about the relationships between God and man which almost anyone could have taken on his lips – indeed he should have done so. It was broadly a collective and inclusive first person. But the 'I' the prophets speak of is expressly exclusive. The men who speak to us in these accounts were men who had been expressly called upon to abandon the fixed orders of religion which the majority of the people still considered valid – a tremendous step for a man of the ancient east to take – and because of it the prophets, in their new and completely unprecedented situation, were faced with the need to justify themselves both in their own and in other people's eyes. The event of which the prophet tells burdened him with a commission, with knowledge and responsibility which placed him in complete isolation before God. It forced him to justify his exceptional status in the eyes of the majority. This makes clear that the writing down of a call was something secondary to the call itself, and that it served a different end from the latter. The call commissioned the prophet: the act of writing down an account of it was aimed at those sections of the public in whose eyes he had to justify himself. No doubt these accounts are of great importance because of the insight they give us into the experience which made a man a prophet, and they do this far more directly than does any hymn used in the cult. At the same time, however, exegesis has always to remember that these narratives are probably not simply transcripts of what was experienced at the time. They are as well accounts designed to serve certain definite ends and they no doubt to a certain extent stylize the call. There must have been many features in a call which would be of enormous interest to us, but the prophets do not mention them because in their view they were of no particular interest.[4]

Did then the writing prophets hold a regular cultic office? As I

[4] This is equally true of the question whether the reception of a revelation was preceded and prepared for by meditation, as it is also of the question of the particular psychical condition (ecstasy) in which the prophet received it. And above all we should welcome more precise knowledge of the form in which the content of each revelation appeared to the prophet, and of the way by which he ascertained its reality.

see it, the accounts of their call answer this question with a decided
'No'. If a prophet had held a definite position in the cult, would
he have laid so much stress upon his call? The importance which
the prophets attached to their call makes it quite clear that they
felt very much cut off from the religious capital on which the
majority of the people lived, and dependent instead on their own
resources.

The source material here is well known. First of all there are the
accounts in the first person singular in Amos 7–9, Isaiah 6, Jeremiah
1, Ezekiel 1–3, Isaiah 40.3-8, and Zechariah 1.7–6.8, but to these
should be added such a story as the call of Elisha (I Kings, 19.19ff.)
or that of the youth Samuel at a time when the word of Yahweh
'had become rare in the land' (I Sam. 3.1ff.), for, whatever office the
historic Samuel actually held, what the narrator wished to relate
was the way in which a young man was raised up as a prophet (v.
20). The same is true of the call of Moses in Ex. 3–4, particularly
in E's version of it; for the account of the commissioning, the
divine promise, 'I will be with your mouth' (Ex. 4.12), and Moses'
reluctance are all obviously told so as to make them agree with the
ideas about prophetic call current in the narrator's own time. It is
amazing to see such a wealth of psychological and theological
nuance in ideas which may well belong to the ninth century, and
it is equally amazing that the question of legitimation was even
then given such importance ('But if they do not believe me,' Ex.
4.1), though, of course, it is only with Jeremiah, of the writing
prophets, that the question becomes acute. There is a frank admis-
sion, also astounding at this early date, that it was possible for one
who was called to office to refuse that call (Ex. 4.10ff.). Finally, we
have also to consider I Kings 22.19-22. Micaiah ben Imlah's idea of
the way in which the call to be a prophet came about – that is, as
the result of deliberation in the privy council of heaven – can
hardly have been unique. It must have conformed to what were
fairly widely held views. These ninth-century references in themselves warn us not to underrate early prophecy, or to assume that
Amos or Isaiah imported something completely new into Israel
when they made their appearance.

The event which led to a man's call to be a prophet is described
in a considerable number of different ways, and it is also plain
that there was no conventional fashion in which it came about.
Moreover, each individual prophet was conditioned by his own
particular gifts of mind and spirit, and this led to different reactions

to the event. Yet, in spite of this, it is possible to pick out certain common features in those cases in which the prophets themselves tell us anything about their call.

The call of Elisha is admittedly somewhat different from the rest, because here it is one human being – Elijah – who presses another – Elisha – into the service of Yahweh (I Kings 19.19ff.). Elisha is called to 'follow' a man, that is, he was to be Elijah's disciple. The story of the way by which Elijah's *charisma* was transferred to Elisha is also unique (II Kings 2.15), for, strangely enough, the prophets from Amos onwards do not think of themselves as bearers of the spirit, but as preachers of the word of Yahweh. For reasons at which we can only guess, the concept of the spirit, which was obviously still constitutive in making Elisha a prophet, lapses almost completely, and, as we might think, rather abruptly, into the background. For the ninth-century prophets, however, the presence of 'the spirit of Yahweh' was absolutely constitutive. Elisha had to request Elijah for possession of it (II Kings 2.9); and only after it rested upon him is he reckoned a prophet. It is emphasized, however, that his possession of the spirit was attested by his associates, and this legitimated him in their eyes (v. 15). Delusion can only come about when the 'spirit' leads the prophets astray. This raises the question whether the spirit 'went' from one prophet to the other (I Kings 22.21f., 24). Again, the spirit could suddenly take a prophet from where he was and carry him off elsewhere (I Kings 18.22; II Kings 2.16). The almost instantaneous disappearance of this well-defined concept is not only striking: it is also important theologically, for when this objective reality, the spirit, whose presence had to be attested by a prophet's associates, ceased to operate, then the prophet of the word had to rely much more on himself and on the fact that he had received a call.[5]

As far as we can see, the prophets of the eighth and seventh centuries received their call through God's direct and quite personal address to them, and this created a totally new situation for the man concerned. The work on which he was sent was not just limited to a fixed period. The office to which he was commissioned, though perhaps not in every instance regarded as lifelong, at all events removed such a man from all his previous mode of life for at least a considerable time. Being a prophet was a condition which made deep inroads into a man's outward as well as his inner life –

[5] Perhaps the concept of the spirit was a characteristic of North Israelite prophecy (cf. Hos. 9.7).

we shall later have to remember the consequences involved in the fact that from the very beginning not only the prophets' lips but also their whole lives were conscripted for special service. The complete absence of any transitional stage between the two conditions is a special characteristic of the situation. Being a prophet is never represented as a tremendous intensification or transcendence of all previous religious experience. Neither previous faith nor any other personal endowment had the slightest part to play in preparing a man who was called to stand before Yahweh for his vocation. He might by nature be a lover of peace, yet it might be laid upon him to threaten and reprove, even if, as with Jeremiah, it broke his heart to do so. Or, if nature made him prone to severity, he might be forced, like Ezekiel, to walk the way of comforting men and saving them. So deep is the gulf which separates the prophets from their past that none of their previous social relationships are carried over into the new way of life. 'I was a herdsman, and a dresser of sycamore trees; but Yahweh took me from following the flock and said to me, "Go, prophesy against my people Israel" ' (Amos 7.14f.). This was more than a new profession : it was a totally new way of life, even at the sociological level, to the extent that a call meant relinquishing normal social life and all the social and economic securities which this offered, and changing over instead to a condition where a man had nothing to depend upon, or, as we may put it, to a condition of dependence upon Yahweh and upon that security alone. 'I do not sit blithely in the company of the merrymakers. Because thy hand is upon me, I sit alone; for thou hast filled me with indignation' (Jer. 15.17).

Flesh and blood can only be forced into such a service. At all events, the prophets themselves felt that they had been compelled by a stronger will than theirs. Admittedly, the early prophets only rarely mention these matters affecting their call. The first to break the silence is Jeremiah.

Thou didst deceive me, and I let myself be deceived;
Thou wast too strong for me, and didst prevail over me (Jer. 20.7)

What is here said in open rebellion, the avowal that he was compelled, with no possibility of refusal, was also expressed by Amos.

The lion has roared – who is not afraid
The Lord Yahweh has spoken – who does not prophesy? (Amos 3.8)

This verse has been rightly called a 'word of discussion'. That is to say, it is the answer to a query whether Amos could bring proof of his right to speak in the name of Yahweh. The prophet refuses to allow his prophecy to be called in question in this way. What he says is in no sense the product of reflection or personal resolve. It is something which bears witness to itself, and so is not unlike some unconscious reflex action which even the person concerned cannot himself explain.

3. The call to be a prophet in which, as we have said, an individual was personally addressed by God, was as a rule associated with another factor which made the future ambassador of God acquainted with the will and purpose of Yahweh in an extremely vivid way. This was a vision. Of course, in the fairly large number of visions which occur in the Old Testament there is no instance where a vision is not immediately followed by an audition and where it does not culminate in God's addressing the prophet. Nonetheless, the fact that Yahweh claimed not only the prophet's lips but also his eyes for the service of his new task is of prime importance. The purpose of the vision was not to impart knowledge of higher worlds. It was intended to open the prophet's eyes to coming events which were not only of a spiritual sort, but were also to be concrete realities in the objective world. Contrary to popular misconception, the prophets were not concerned with the being of God, but with future events which were about to occur in space and time – indeed, in Israel's own immediate surroundings. Yet even to the theologian this massive concentration upon historical events, as also the complete absence of any sort of 'speculative' inclinations even in those visions where Yahweh is seen in person, must be a source of constant wonder. For example, Amos says that he saw Yahweh holding a plumb-line to a wall. But when Yahweh asked him what he saw, his answer was 'a plumb-line' (Amos 7.7f.)! Again, in his fifth vision, where he sees Yahweh standing upon the altar, he shows an astonishing lack of interest in what Yahweh looked like (Amos 9.1). The same is also true of Isaiah's great throne vision (Isa. 6). The first prophet to attempt anything like a detailed picture of the 'glory of Yahweh', as it broke upon him from the realm of the transcendent at his call, is Ezekiel. And yet how circumspect he, too, is as he describes what he perceived above the throne and 'what was like as it were a human form' (Ezek. 1.26ff.).

The reception of revelation itself, that is to say, the more immediate circumstances in which this event in the prophet's inner self-consciousness took place, is only occasionally mentioned in the sources, and so much that we should like to know is left unanswered. On one point, however, there is universal agreement, that visions and auditions came to the prophets from outside themselves, and that they came suddenly and completely without premeditation. Only once is there mention of any technical preparation for the reception of a revelation – through a minstrel (II Kings 3.15). This, however, was exceptional. Inspiration might come to a prophet as he sat at table (I Kings 13.20). On the other hand, he might have to wait as long as ten days for an answer from Yahweh (Jer. 42.7). There is no doubt that, at the moment when the prophets received a revelation, they believed that they heard themselves addressed in words. Perhaps as a rule they first heard their name called (I Sam. 3.4ff.). The sources also allow us to make the further inference that, very frequently at least, such reception of revelation was something which caused the prophet a severe bodily shock. Be this as it may, the earlier prophets have very little to say about this aspect of their office. But when it is told of a prophet that the hand of Yahweh came upon him or fell upon him (I Kings 18.46; Ezek. 8.1), or when a prophet himself even says that the hand of Yahweh seized him (Isa. 8.11), there is every reason for believing that behind these brief notices lie experiences which not only shook his soul but caused bodily disturbances as well. Ezekiel relates how he sat on the ground awe-struck and unable to speak a word for seven days after his call (Ezek. 3.15). Daniel, too, says that all the blood drained from his face, that he fell to the ground (Dan. 10.8f.), and that after one such experience he lay sick for some days (Dan. 8.27). By the time of apocalyptic such language may have become to some extent stereotyped and conventional, but in earlier days a prophet's bodily sufferings were something very real and painful.

As whirlwinds sweeping in from the Negeb
  it comes from the desert, from a terrible land.
A stern vision is told to me:
'The plunderer plunders, the destroyer destroys.
  To the attack, O Elam, lay siege, O Media.'
Therefore my loins are filled with cramp,
  pangs have seized me, like the pangs of a woman in travail.
I am troubled, so that I cannot hear, dismayed, so that I cannot see,
  my mind reels, horror has laid hold upon me.
The twilight for which I look, it has turned for me into horror.
'They prepare the table . . .
  they eat and drink.

Up, ye princes, oil the shield!'
For thus the Lord said to me:
'Go, set the watchman,
  Let him announce what he sees. . . .'
And behold, here come chariots,
  men and teams of horses.
And he answered and said: Fallen, fallen is Babylon,
  all the images of her gods have been shattered to the ground.
O my threshed one,
  O my son of the threshing floor,
What I have heard from Yahweh of hosts,
  the God of Israel, that I announce to you.

(Isa. 21.1-10)

This passage, which comes from the second half of the sixth century and is therefore not from Isaiah himself, lets us see as no other does something of the prophet's very deeply agitated and tormented state as he received a 'stern vision'. He is greatly disturbed. Pictures thrust themselves upon his inner eye. Their outlines are scarcely fixed before they break up again. With them mingle cries complaining of the unbearable anguish and bodily pains which have overtaken him as he sees the vision (cf. Hab. 3.16). In the end all is resolved in the 'cry of deliverance' telling of the fall of the impious world-power. The prophet is now exhausted, and the last thing he summons up is a feeling of sympathy with his own threshed people, the 'son of the threshing-floor'.

How such and similar processes in the prophet's self-consciousness are to be more precisely defined psychologically is a question to which the investigations of present-day psychology are still unable to give a satisfactory answer. The idea that the prophets were 'ecstatics', once widely accepted, is now out of favour, for the concept of ecstasy has proved to be too general and imprecise. In particular, the way in which it was used suggested that while the prophet was in this state his self-consciousness disappeared, and that, ceasing to have a will of his own, he became the scene in which processes external to his own personality were played out. This, of course, put the whole thing the wrong way round; for when, in a way hitherto unknown in Israel and in the entire ancient east, the individual with his responsibility and power to make decisions came in prophecy to occupy the centre of the stage – one might almost say when the individual was discovered – it was only to be expected that it would be precisely in the event of the prophet's reception of revelation that this new factor would be apparent. And as far as we can tell with any certainty from the sources, this is absolutely the case. The literary form in which the prophets describe their visions, the first person singular, is itself evidence. Even so, this in no way excludes the possibility of a 'condition of abnormal excitation, during which the normal wakeful consciousness of the man upon whom it comes is put out of action and his relationships to ordinary life diminished to the point at which they no longer exist'.[6] In such a condition, that of direct encounter with God and with his purposes in history, might not the normal consciousness have been raised to an intensity never experienced in the ordinary way? If so, the term 'ecstasy' is much too rigid. Attempts have been made to avoid the difficulty by drawing a sharp distinction between the 'ecstasy of concentration' and the 'ecstasy of absorption'. It is quite true that none of the prophets ever in fact had any kind of experience of becoming one with the Godhead. Nevertheless, there are grave objections to a comparison of the prophets' experience with certain forms of medieval mysticism; for even in their most sublime experiences the mystics always remained within the limits of the accepted dogmas of their own day, whereas the prophets, precisely in their inaugural visions, were led out to new vistas of belief. With Amos, Isaiah, and Jeremiah the material which we could use directly in this connection is both too scanty and too obscure, but if we take the well-attested occurrences in the pre-classical prophets on the one hand and, on the other, the more numerous references in Ezekiel, impartial examination will lead to the conclusion that nearly all the prophets experienced such temporary states of consciousness in which the senses were intensified. The fact that these occur so very much more frequently in Ezekiel than in the others is no reason for regarding him as exceptional in this respect.

If, then, we have to reckon with such abnormal states of consciousness in the prophets, it is mistaken to suppose, as is sometimes done, that these have no particular importance for the theologian. Here, as everywhere else, to detach matters which belong to the central substance of Yahwism from their contingent links with history or with a person, and to regard them as no more than abstract truths, is to distort them. If Yahweh chose such a singular

[6] This definition is taken from F. Maass' article, 'Zur psychologischen Sonderung der Ekstase', in *Wissenschaftliche Zeitschrift der K. Marx Universität Leipzig, 1953/54, Gesellschafts- und sprachwissenschaftliche Reihe, Heft 2/3.*

realm as the prophet's spirit, if he chose none of the already existing institutions for his new word to Israel, and if in this psychic
realm which had been so singularly kept open he brought such a
singular thing to pass, this must stand in relationship to other
matters which theology cannot ignore. It actually means nothing
less than that in the states where the prophet saw visions and heard
himself addressed, he became in a strange way detached from himself and his own personal likes and dislikes, and was drawn into
the emotions of the deity himself. It was not only the knowledge
of God's designs in history that was communicated to him, but
also the feelings in God's heart, wrath, love, sorrow, revulsion, and
even doubt as to what to do or how to do it (Hos. 6.4; 11.8; Isa. 6.8).
Something of Yahweh's own emotion passed over into the prophet's
psyche and filled it to bursting-point. Once it is seen that the primary reference of the condition is a theological one, it becomes very
doubtful whether any special psychic preparation on the prophet's
part was required, or even whether it was at all possible. The highest degree of being absorbed into the emotions of the Godhead in
this way was reached by Jeremiah and Ezekiel, but there is
evidence that the majority of the prophets experienced it to some
degree.

A revelation received in such an unusual way can never have
been an end in itself. Least of all was it given to the prophet to let
him know that God was near to him. Its purpose was to equip him
for his office. On the other hand, when a prophet did receive such
a revelation, it was in every case something purely personal. It lifted
him right out of the common ruck. He was allowed to know God's
designs and to share in God's emotions; but he never thought of
holding his status before God up to other people as normative for
them. It is significant that no prophet ever instructed or exhorted
those to whom he spoke to reach out to a direct experience of God
such as he himself had had. Joel was the first to look forward to
the day when everyone in Israel would be like those rare beings
who are endowed with the spirit (Joel 3.1ff. [2.28ff.]). In an earlier
passage, the only one of its kind, the same wish is put into the
mouth of Moses (Num. 11.29, E).

4. In more recent study of the prophets, the question of the
psychological peculiarities of the prophet's reception of revelation
have markedly retreated into the background. A more pressing
question is that of the particular form of the account of the vision
given by the prophet and of the traditions by which he seems to

have been influenced. There is good reason for this, as the account of the vision is itself part of the proclamation.

Among the receptions of visions more elaborately described in the Old Testament, those of Micaiah ben Imlah (I Kings 22.19ff.), Isaiah (Isa. 6), and Ezekiel (Ezek. 1–3) fall into the same class, for they follow what was obviously a given basic concept, that of solemn commissioning by Yahweh as he sat enthroned in the midst of his heavenly entourage. Each of the three, however, adapts the 'schema' in its own particular way. In I Kings 22.19ff. the occasion is a regular session of the assembly of the heavenly dignitaries ('one said one thing, and another said another', v. 20), until 'the spirit' comes forward and makes the proposal to delude Ahab's prophets by means of a lying spirit, to which Yahweh agrees. The spirit is then sent out forthwith. Isaiah, too, says that he saw Yahweh in the heavenly temple, seated upon his throne. The seen element, of course, plays only a small part in the narrative. When the prophet describes what he beheld, all that he mentions is the hem of the garment which reached to Yahweh's feet. Quite obviously, he had not dared to lift up his eyes. Moreover, smoke quickly clouded the scene from him. But this enhanced what he heard. He heard the seraphim's *Trisagion*, the thunder of which made the palace shake. At this direct encounter with supreme holiness and in this atmosphere of sheer adoration, Isaiah became conscious of his own sinfulness and was appalled – indeed, the sin of his whole nation seemed to be made manifest in his own person. At his confession of sin Yahweh made a sign – Isaiah did not, of course, see this – and a rite of atonement, which now made it possible for him to raise his voice in this holy place, was performed upon his lips. On hearing Yahweh ask whom he could send (the term 'send' is used quite absolutely), Isaiah with a minimum of words and without more ado put himself at his Lord's disposal, and was forthwith given his commission, which was to make his nation stubborn and harden their hearts by the very message he was to proclaim, 'until cities are laid waste and the fields in the open country are like waste land'; a holy seed was, however, to remain. Even in the prophetic literature, where the extraordinary is not the exception but the rule, there is very, very little to compare with the grandeur of the verses in which Isaiah describes his call. Does this lie in the overwhelming splendour of its outward accompaniments, or in the mighty power of the spiritual experience? Yet even to put such a question is to tear apart the classic balance between external and internal. The description of the external embraces all the inward experience, and *vice versa*.

Ezekiel, too, sees Yahweh sitting on his throne. With him, however, the description of the vision is much more involved, since in his case the throne vision is united with what was originally an entirely different and independent idea, that of the descent of the 'glory of God', to form a single complex unit. Here, therefore, the heavens open, and Yahweh's throne, borne by four heavenly beings, comes down to earth on storm-clouds. The manner of the prophet's call to office is similar to that of Isaiah except that in this case there is a still stronger impression that he received his commission in the form of what could almost be called a state-paper. For the king on the throne hands the waiting ambassador a scroll containing his instructions. There is also another similarity between the calls of Ezekiel and Isaiah. The prophet is repeatedly reminded of the difficulty and even hopelessness of his position by the words with which Yahweh accompanies the delivery of the note: the people to whom he is sent are of a hard forehead and a stubborn heart. This whole commissioning is hedged about with words which prepare Ezekiel for the failure of what he undertakes, though the latter lays much greater stress than does Isaiah on his hearers' freedom to refuse to listen to him (Ezek. 3.7, 11).

The three visions just considered thus end by indicating a completely negative result – in no sense will the prophet's work lead to deliverance; it will only hasten on the inevitable disaster. The ideas which the three men each held about the nature of their calling must have been very much alike: there must have been some kind of common call-experience which put a stamp upon their work from the very outset. Their devastatingly negative outlook on the future of their work, and the way in which, without any illusions, they faced up to its complete failure, are again a factor which compels us to look for these prophets outside the cult. For cult always implies at least a minimum of effect; it is action which has beneficial results in one way or another.

The call of Jeremiah begins with a dialogue in which Yahweh gently but firmly breaks down the other's shrinking resistance to his commission. Then follow the two visions of the rod of almond and the seething cauldron, which indeed fall very short of the forcefulness of the other three which have just been discussed. In other respects Jeremiah was a master of expression. Here, however, his creative power is clearly less than usual. Even in the dialogue which precedes the visions Jeremiah surprises us. He says that Yahweh touched his mouth. There is no indication, however, that he saw Yahweh as well as heard him. It was not in Jeremiah's power to give a visual picture of the presence of Yahweh.

In the visions themselves he beheld two static objects – there is no motion – which in themselves are quite unremarkable. Only the words of Yahweh which follow the visions and interpret them indicate the objects' symbolic character – Yahweh is watching over his word, it is never out of his sight: and evil is to break upon Jerusalem and Judah from the north. Here, too, something of the magnificent realism which elsewhere characterizes the descriptions of the dealings between Yahweh and Jeremiah is missing. In Jeremiah's visions nothing at all is done. The rod of almond and the seething cauldron are both simply things: what the prophet sees is little more than an illustrative and symbolic picture which serves to corroborate the message given to him. The substance of Jeremiah's visions is no longer some irrevocable act which Yahweh is about to do. Compared with the visions in I Kings 22, Isa. 6, and Ezek. 1–3, those of Jeremiah display a distinct lack of action. Their content is rather the symbolic illustration of more general insights which are to dominate his preaching from now on. On the other hand, even in the account of Jeremiah's call there is still the framework of an official commissioning, an appointment to a particular service made by a superior ('I have appointed you to . . .'; 'I have set you this day over . . .'). Perhaps the outline of the external event is so markedly incomplete because the reader would himself supply what was missing?[7]

Deutero-Isaiah received his call by means of two auditions. He had no vision, nor was he directly called by Yahweh. Instead, his ear caught something of the movement that had made itself felt in the heavenly places. He heard the summons given to the angelic

---

[7] The diminution in the part played by an event in Jeremiah's reception of a call is matched by an increase in the amount of theological reflection. Even the first vision of the 'watching rod' with its very general reference to the divine word over which Yahweh watches is quite vague about the concrete details of the vision. It makes the beholder occupy himself with something which might better be called a theological truth. The same thing is true in the episode of the pots in Jer. 18. This passage is also a sign of transference into the theological, intellectual realm, for what Jeremiah sees at the potter's becomes a symbol, not of a quite unique and definite event, but of something which is always possible in principle. The instructions which Jeremiah receives remain in the realm of the theoretical.

beings to build the wondrous way over valley and mountain to
prepare for that coming of Yahweh in which he would manifest
himself to the world (Isa. 40.3-5). The first audition, therefore, only
allowed the prophet to learn something of the preparations which
were already being made in heaven for Yahweh's imminent advent
– and this before there was even the slightest indication of it upon
earth. In the second, however, he was directly addressed – evidently
by an angel – and given the theme of his preaching: amid the
transience of 'all flesh', a transience which was caused by Yahweh's
own fiery breath, Yahweh's word alone is permanent, and is the
guarantee of permanency (Isa. 40.6-8).

Little can be said about the frequency with which the various
prophets received such extraordinary revelations. The number of
visions and auditions reported in grand literary style is certainly
nothing to go on. As we saw, such subsequent elaborations had a
definite purpose to serve with visions received at a call. In other
cases there was no interest in giving an express and studied description of what the prophet had seen; then he simply confined
himself to communicating its contents. There are plenty of oracles
of this kind which quite clearly derive from genuine visionary or
auditory experiences. This can certainly be presumed in the case
of the description of the onslaught of the nations against Zion and
their miraculous repulse in Isa. 17.12ff. The same is true of the
theophany in Isa. 30.27f. or in Isa. 63.1ff., as it is also of descriptions of anguish such as Nah. 2.2ff. [1ff.], where the visual element
is particularly conspicuous. It also holds good of Jeremiah's anti-
cipations of the wars to come (Jer. 4–6): they are so shot through
with the prophet's sensory perceptions as to leave no doubt of
their visionary and auditory character.[8]

It is impossible exactly to separate out visionary experiences
which were genuinely ecstatic from other forms of the reception
of revelation. Yahweh had assuredly more ways than one of communicating with the prophets, but it is hopeless to try to gain
clear ideas about the psychical side of the processes. Isaiah says
that Yahweh revealed himself 'in his ears' (Isa. 5.9; 22.14); so, too,
Ezekiel (Ezek. 9.1, 5), and elsewhere.[9] Thus, there were also revelations which took the form of an auditory experience and nothing
more. Jeremiah makes a clear distinction between oral revelation
and revelation by means of a dream, and sets little store by the

[8] Jer. 4.23-6 is particularly characteristic in this respect.
[9] Yahweh 'uncovers' or 'wakens' the ear, I Sam. 9.15; Isa. 50.4.

latter (Jer. 23.28). The experience of receiving a word also occasionally attained a high degree of excitation; otherwise, how could Ezekiel have likened the sound of the wings of the cherubim which could be heard from afar to the resounding of the voice of Yahweh, 'when he speaks' (Ezek. 10.5)? On the other hand, we have good reason to believe that the prophets were also given inspiration in which no kind of change came over their ordinary consciousness, that is to say, in which the revelation was a mental process. This is probably so in the great majority of those cases in which the prophet speaks only of the word of Yahweh which had come to him. Nevertheless, even here the element of 'event' which the revelation had for the prophet ought not to be overlooked. It is not simply a matter of mental perception, but of the 'coming' of the word of Yahweh, and, consequently, even with this quite unsensational form of revelation the prophets never lost the feeling that there was something strange in the experience.

Oddly enough, Job's friend Eliphaz also gives an account of an experience in which he received a revelation similar to that of the prophets.

> A word stole to me,
>> my ear perceived a whisper of it,
> in disquieting thoughts, amid visions of the night,
>> when deep sleep falls on men.
> Dread seized me and trembling,
>> it made all my limbs shake;
> a spirit glided over my face,
>> the hair of my flesh stood up.
> It stood still – ; but I could not discern its appearance;
>> a form was before me, I heard a still low voice:
> 'Can a mortal man be in the right before God,
>> or a man be pure before his Maker?'
>> (Job 4.12-17)

This is easily our most comprehensive and detailed description of the outward circumstances which accompanied a revelation. It certainly cannot be dismissed by saying that Eliphaz was not of course a prophet. The clearest proof of how little a prophet he was is the 'oracle' in v. 17, which is in fact not an oracle at all, but runs counter to the whole prophetic tradition and takes the form of a rhetorical question; this means that it is a saying of the kind found in the wisdom literature. None the less, it may be assumed that when Eliphaz describes the psychical accompaniments of a revelation, he takes as his basis genuine prophetic tradition.

The time for receiving a revelation of the kind is the night. It is heralded by disquiet and feelings of fear. Then little by little the sensory organs are stimulated, first touch, then sight, and finally hearing.

The frequency with which such revelations were received is a question about which little can be said so far as each individual case is concerned, but a general survey of prophecy from the eighth to the sixth century does lead to one important result. Basically Amos had one task and one alone to do: 'Go and prophesy against my people Israel' (Amos 7.15). No doubt this embraced a considerable number of word-revelations which may have come hard on each other's heels during the time in which he was active. Yet his activity may well have been limited in duration: it was conceivably only a matter of months; then – perhaps because he was expelled by Amaziah – he went back home and his *charisma* thereafter ceased. With Isaiah it was different. His prophecy surges up in a number of separate waves, which were in each case determined by specific political situations. Yet, what we know of his activity makes perfectly clear that even he regarded the various occasions on which he came forward as of limited duration, and that, as each ended, he could consider himself released from office. With Jeremiah, however, the calling meant a lifelong office. Later on we shall have to consider in more detail the great change which came over the whole idea of the nature of prophetic service at this point – how the prophet's whole life became bound up with Yahweh's dealings with his people, and how this exhausted him. Here – at least in principle – there were no distinct phases in the exercise of his office, no several stages ending when a specified task had been duly performed. Jeremiah was a prophet because Yahweh had conscripted his whole life.[10]

As far as the reception of revelation is concerned, Jeremiah makes it clear that he sometimes had to wait a considerable time for an answer (Jer. 28.12; 42.7). When in contrast with this the Servant in Deutero-Isaiah – and his office was above all else a prophetic one – says that Yahweh 'morning by morning awakens his

[10] This change is also connected with the fact that in Jeremiah a formal separation between the words of Yahweh proper and the diatribes or other utterances of the prophet himself is much less clearly perceptible. With Jeremiah not only do the oracles in the narrower sense of this term receive the status of divine revelation; with him there is the tendency to give out his own words and compositions, too, as a word of Yahweh.

ear' (Isa. 50.4), this undoubtedly marks a decisive advance upon what Jeremiah could say about himself. Indeed, it signifies the climax of prophecy in the Old Testament. For what the Servant is trying to say is that his reception of revelation was continuous, and his converse with Yahweh unbroken.

4 The Prophets' Freedom

To speak of the prophets' call, their visions, and the other ways in which they received revelations leads on to the discussion of that mysterious compulsion which came over them often quite unexpectedly, depriving them temporarily of the free exercise of their faculties, and which they were quite unable to resist. In Jeremiah in particular, there are utterances in which the prophet very realistically – indeed almost literally – sees himself as a vessel into which wrath has been poured, wrath which he cannot suppress even if he so desires.

> But I am full of the wrath of Yahweh,
> I am powerless to hold it in.
> I pour it out upon the children in the street,
> upon the gathering of young men. . . .
>   (Jer. 6.11; cf. 15.17; 20.9)

Yet the discovery of these abnormal psychical conditions and the novelty of this aspect of the prophets' life have sometimes led to a thorough misconception of what these men were and what they did. The compulsive element in their preaching which gave them a complete lack of feeling and, indeed, made them almost lose consciousness as they functioned as God's instrument is taken to be that which gives them their peculiar character. This view, with its insistence on the element of subjugation and on the aspects which lie quite outside the normal activities and experiences of mind and spirit, was itself, of course, a reaction against the naïve picture of the prophets as national teachers and the great pioneers of an ethical and spiritual concept of religion. Nevertheless, it is misleading. To counter it, we must discuss the freedom which the prophets enjoyed – itself of supreme theological interest. This is never concretely defined, and the prophets never take it as the subject of preaching. Yet they made the fullest possible use of it in practice.

This becomes particularly clear in the case of their call. While it is true that the accounts given by Isaiah and Jeremiah are the only direct evidence of the large measure of free choice allowed to the prophet in the whole matter of his call, there is no reason to suppose that these two cases were different from the rest.[1]

It is generally believed – and rightly so – that in this respect the experience of Isaiah surpasses anything that was possible for other prophets. Isaiah was allowed to see and hear what took place in the heavenly council assembled around the throne of Yahweh. He was not, however, addressed in person, as was generally the case at a prophet's call. He only heard the question put by Yahweh to the assembly as to who might be sent. Whereupon he offered himself: 'Here am I! Send me!' (Isa. 6.8). It was a general question, but it struck home to Isaiah like a lightning flash, and even before the assembly could begin discussion of it (cf. I Kings 22.20), he at once called out and put himself at Yahweh's disposal as messenger. If this is not freedom, what is? Yet this decision was not taken once and for all. The prophet had rather to take and re-take it in face of difficulties that kept arising, for freedom also implies the possibility of refusal. Isaiah himself may at times have been in danger of refusing, for he once declares that 'the might of God's hand disciplined me not to walk in the way of this people' (Isa. 8.11).

For Jeremiah, however, this borderline between obedience and disobedience was fraught, all his life long, with even greater peril. But the situation in which he was placed was so very different from that of Isaiah that any real comparison between the two is impossible. In contrast with the latter, Yahweh's address and call to Jeremiah was a direct one. At first Jeremiah shrank back in terror. In the end, however, he did go as he was commanded. Yet this did not mean that he surrendered his freedom to God – and the best proof of this lies in the so-called 'Confessions' where, in spite of all his suffering, he continues in closest contact with Yahweh, questioning him, professing his faith in him, and complaining to him. The force used on Jeremiah was inconceivably harsher than that laid upon any other prophet. But this should not blind us to the other side of the question. We ought also to appreciate the

[1] Recall the story of the call of Moses (Ex. 4). It is clearly formed on the model of a prophet's call and gives a surprisingly large place to Moses' objections, and even opposition. Elisha was called to succeed Elijah by Elijah himself, that is to say, by a human being (I Kings 19.19ff.); this seems to presuppose a standing rule traditional in the prophetic guilds, and is therefore to be taken separately.

freedom which Jeremiah kept and used in his dealings with God. He used it to render a unique obedience, and yet it occasionally led him almost to the verge of blasphemy (Jer. 20.7, 14).

An examination of the prophetic preaching itself reveals that the case is much more complex than the widely accepted view that in most cases it was delivered under irresistible compulsion. While it is true that all the evidence suggests that at the moment when a revelation was given to a prophet he was in a state of extreme passivity, he certainly did not continue in this state. We have already discussed the extraordinary number of literary forms in which the prophets clothed their addresses as the situation demanded. Remember, however, that each instance implies a choice, and a very responsible choice at that, on the part of the prophet. For these forms into which their message had to be cast were more than just outward things. The message itself was affected by the form in which it was given – whether as a dirge, or a priestly cultic decision, or a song of the vineyard. The prophet would be very careful to find the appropriate form for each specific message. There are cases which suggest that a prophet might act in a very free and arbitrary way as he selected a form for a commission which had been given him.

Ezekiel 24.15-27 is a good example of this. Yahweh had informed the prophet that he was about to take his wife, 'the delight of his eyes', away from him, but he, the prophet, was not to weep for her nor to make mourning for the dead. Later on, however, when he was asked by the people why he acted thus, he gave the message which was really intended : the sanctuary in Jerusalem, 'the desire of your eyes', is to be profaned, and sons and daughters are to perish without mourning being made for them. There is therefore a certain gulf between the divine command (vv. 15-19) and the means by which the prophet carried it out (vv. 20-27). The prophet used great freedom in interpreting the command. He made the words 'the delight of your eyes' refer to the temple, and the command to make no mourning refer to a disaster in war.

A similar instance of independent activity on the part of the prophet is to be found in Jeremiah 27. Jeremiah is commanded to make yoke-bars and put them round his neck. The prophet proclaims the hidden meaning of this symbolic action three times, each time to a different audience : the kings of some neighbouring peoples, king Zedekiah of Judah and the priests of Jerusalem. Yahweh has handed over rule of the world to Nebuchadnezzar, king of Babylon : obey his rule and do not allow yourselves to be led astray by your interpreters of the future! That is the common theme of all the messages. There are, however, considerable differences in detail, especially between the message to the nations and that which Jeremiah directs to the priests in Jerusalem. With the nations, Jeremiah uses the argument from belief in creation (vv. 5ff.): because God has created the whole earth, he can bestow rule over it upon whom he will. To this the prophet attaches a warning against heathen divination, prophets, soothsayers and sorcerers. To the priests in Jerusalem, however, he speaks about the predictions of the false prophets (vv. 9f.), who assert that the holy vessels of the temple plundered at the time of the first deportation, will soon be returned. These prophets should intercede with Yahweh, for now the vessels still left in the temple will be taken to Babylon.

The case is rather different with the form called the messenger formula, which is particularly frequent in classical prophecy, for here the form itself required that the divine commission be reproduced exactly and without re-shaping. The prophets, however, never passed on God's words just as they were. They prefaced them – they were generally a threat – with a diatribe, which formed an introduction: in fact, it is the diatribe which connects the divine words with those to whom they applied. Only in exceptional cases were the divine words referred from the beginning to a definite person (as, for example, the king) or to a definite group. Usually their content was of a more general nature; they announced, for instance, the decimation of an army (Amos 5.3), the deportation of the upper classes (Amos 4.2f.), or that the land was to be made desolate (Isa. 5.8ff.). Addressing this message to a particular individual or group was, then, a matter for the prophet himself. This left a wide field open for the exercise of his own judgment and pastoral vigilance. Indeed, his was the most important role of all; for what is a divine oracle without a recipient? The prophet therefore addresses the threat of deportation to a luxury-loving upper class (Amos 4.1ff.; 6.1ff.), of devastation of the land to speculators in real estate, and so on. It is hardly possible to overrate the importance of the prophet's share, for without it the word the prophet receives does not reach its goal and therefore cannot be fulfilled. What makes it such a tremendous responsibility is the fact that the prophet is thus the one who puts the will of Yahweh into effect: Yahweh thereafter commits himself to stand by the decision of his ambassador.

What guided the prophets in their application of the divine message to the various groups of people? We have a certain amount of information. The prophets for their part did not simply speak

on behalf of the social interests of a particular class – not even of
their own class – nor did they speak as people who had suffered
unjustly. They regarded themselves as bound to a definite fixed
order which their announcement of punishment was designed to
restore. This raises the question of the theological relationship between the diatribe and the threat. That such a relationship does
exist is shown by the 'therefore', at once frequent and characteristic, which customarily makes the logical connection between
the two component parts, the diatribe and the divine words, and
which helps to give the reason for the threat which follows. The
prophets here show that, to a limited degree, they did have an
interest in teaching. The one against whom the threat is directed
has to be made aware of and understand what is in store for him
and why this is so. Occasionally, even, the hope is added that he
will be moved to repentance and so find safety. What he must
understand is that the punishment which is about to overtake him
is exactly commensurate with his offence, and that there is a
'retribution' in history whose author is Yahweh. In Old Testament
terms, that is to say, Yahweh causes the evil that men set in
motion to recoil on their own heads – offence and punishment
strictly correspond. For example, Elijah prophesied some time before the event that the dogs would lick up Ahab's blood in the
place where they licked up the blood of Naboth (I Kings 21.19);
'therefore' the drinkers of wine will perish with thirst (Isa. 5.13);
'therefore' those who wished to flee away on horses shall have to
flee (Isa. 30.16); 'therefore' the possessors of large estates will see
the land made desolate (Isa. 5.9; Micah 3.12) or be deprived of their
land (Micah 2.4f.) and the false prophets will sit in darkness without light (Micah 3.6f.) etc. No theological profundity is demon-
strated in this logic of events: the logic is painfully obvious. In this
department of prophetic utterance no esoteric experiences or other
supernatural forms of insight are brought into play. In principle,
what a prophet applies here is a perfectly basic piece of knowledge
which is vouchsafed not only to himself but also, in principle, to
anyone who has any experience of the world and of life, namely
knowledge of the fundamental God-given fixed orders to which
human life is subject. This is the place where prophecy makes close
and vital contact with the Wisdom literature.

Sometimes the logical connection between the diatribe and the
divine words is less strict, especially where, as in the poem on
Assyria in Isa. 10.5-19, the diatribe is elaborated to such an extent

as to take ascendancy over the threat and become a relatively independent subject in itself. Its *motif*, however, the pride that comes to a fall, is again one found in the Wisdom literature.

'I have made you an assayer among my people, that you may know and assay their ways' (Jer. 6.27).

This office of assayer, which Jeremiah believed had been entrusted to him, and which all the prophets from Amos to Malachi each in his own way regarded as theirs also, demanded sustained vigilance in passing judgment upon men and circumstances. Here abnormal states of psychical excitement and the rule of thumb application of legal norms were equally valueless. This called, rather, for men of extreme intellectual versatility, whose judgment was incorruptible, who possessed a profound knowledge of human nature, and who, above all, were very familiar with the religious traditions, both those of the saving history and those found in the hymns used in worship (Deutero-Isaiah). The frequent quotations which the prophets wove into their utterances and used to characterize their audience and its way of thinking and to hammer home its collective guilt, were one of the fruits of their acute observation of mankind. How attentively they must have looked around them and observed people before they could have made these succinct characterizations! We must not, of course, imagine that the prophets were concerned to give an objective and faithful reproduction of what they saw. In many instances they generalized, or even caricatured, the behaviour or the utterances of those whom they attacked, in order to demonstrate the end of the evil road which they saw their audience treading.[2]

Finally, we have to consider the literary category of 'discussions', which have already been mentioned. If these were analysed, they would open up quite a number of other standpoints from which to view this aspect of the prophet's task in which everything depended on the cogency of the theological proofs he adduced; for here the prophet was initially on the defensive. In the tense moments when an argument flared up out of the blue, the factors which determined whether or not a prophet would succeed in passing over to the offensive were not only his superior intellectual and theological equipment, but also his quickness in repartee. Of course, the prophet was not always successful. In one such argument of Jeremiah's, to which a large audience doubtless listened

---

[2] Examples of such harsh representations of opponents' words and actions are to be found in Isa. 5.20; 28.15; Jer. 2.20, 25, 27; Amos 2.12; Zeph. 1.12.

with keen interest, the prophet came off second best. He could do nothing to counter Hananiah's oracle of weal played by the latter as his trump card, and had simply to quit the field (Jer. 28.1-11).

All that has been said, and a great deal more that has been left undiscussed, may help to give some idea of how a prophet, though under orders, yet at the same time enjoyed a unique freedom, that is to say, a freedom which left it open to him, to take decisions of the utmost moment.

While it is important that this aspect of the prophets' words and actions should be more clearly recognized – it is often underestimated – the question nevertheless arises whether the previous discussion does in fact indicate anything more than the outward manifestations of a freedom whose roots are considerably deeper, and which is itself only a pointer to some ultimate and fundamental experience of the prophet when he encountered Yahweh and was commissioned by him. It is, of course, difficult to put this in proper theological terms, and perhaps we can do no more than grope our way, because, as everyone knows, the prophets themselves never reflected on these matters or spoke of them. We have already discussed the way in which the claim which the prophet's office made upon him became more and more all-absorbing, until, as for example with Jeremiah, it took his whole being into itself to the extent of abolishing any distinction between the vocation assigned to the prophets and their, as we might say, extra-official and private lives, a distinction which still has to be reckoned with in the case of a prophet like Amos. Yet, wherever a man's prophetic office and his private life became conjoined – and this was at least partially the case even with some of the earlier prophets – the very violence of this meeting inevitably set its stamp upon them and made them what they were. This means that the prophets were a very special type of men displaying characteristic traces of the exceptional.

Yet it is possible to say, with all due caution, that a definite pattern here and there emerges. The picture we see is of a man appointed to hear the word of God. As the result of this divine call he surrenders much of his freedom – occasionally he is completely overwhelmed by an external compulsion: but paradoxically, just because he has received this call he is able to enjoy an entirely new kind of freedom. Drawn into ever closer and closer conversation with God, he is privy to the divine purposes and is thereby given the authority to enter into a unique kind of converse with men. The man reflected here is not, of course, an integrated personality. He is divided and sorely troubled as God hides himself from him more and more. Yet, as the martyrdom of Jeremiah testifies, he is in some mysterious way free to choose suffering and so to stand up to God's test. We have already seen further how their office intensified all the prophets' mental capacities to the highest possible degree, so that even their treatment of poetic forms becomes quite daring. To put it in the language of the present day – and it is not inappropriate – we may say this: we are shown men who have become persons because God has addressed them and they have had to make a decision in his presence. This was something new in Israel. And these men were subject to the word of Yahweh in a far more intense form than ever before in Israel. We must guard against looking at this whole subject in contemporary terms: the people of the ancient world used the pronoun 'I' in a sense quite different from ours. The 'I' of which the prophets became conscious because Yahweh spoke to them differed both from the 'I' used by the oriental rulers of the period and, to an even greater degree, from the 'I' used by present-day Western man, the meaning of which has been so influenced by idealist philosophy and the romantic movement.

A remarkable facet of this attainment of personality by the prophets was that their messages were issued under their own names. It is very surprising that ancient writings whose author was already dead should have been issued under his name; indeed, in view of the accepted usage of the ancient east, including Israel, it is something quite exceptional. In the editing of legal and cultic traditions we expect current practice to be followed. Again, the intellectual achievement – often considerable – of the men we rather feebly term 'redactors' is anonymous in principle. And in the case of works like the Succession Narrative or J, where the intellectual stamp is so distinctive that we feel these writings bear the marks of individual genius, the anonymity is still more surprising. Yet this is the rule throughout in the Old Testament. When, therefore, the rule is broken in the prophetic writings, the only possible explanation is that in the case of the prophets a message was uniquely bound up with the name of a single person, and he alone could be regarded as responsible for it. The same cannot, however, be said of the Yahwist or of the author of the Succession Narrative, because in spite of all the individual genius at work there also, and in spite of these men's great power to make their story speak to their contemporaries, they did not go in principle beyond the religious heritage which Israel already possessed. But the prophets, particularly the pre-exilic prophets, were able to do this. Here, with an exclusiveness that had never before been known in Israel, God turned to an individual and made him the instrument of a revelation that was given once and once only. One man could not take the place of another, nor was the word entrusted to him to be heard on any other lips. He was the only one who knew it, and was responsible for the conscientious delivery of the message. The logical end of the process which began here was martyrdom for the prophet, if Yahweh so willed it.

Now that we have tried to understand the prophetic office in its unique freedom, logic demands that we next consider the possibility of a prophet's refusal or disobedience, a possibility which must in fact have been a danger at every step he took and every decision he made. Is all the prophecy which survives today the prophecy of obedience? If not, on what side were the prophets particularly vulnerable? When on one occasion Jeremiah complained about the sufferings and hostility which were wearing him away, and lamented that God sent him no help, Yahweh answered him thus:

> If you return, you may serve me again.
> If pure thoughts you utter, and not base,
>   then you may again be my mouth.
>
> (Jer. 15.19)

The complaint which prompted this answer was, then, 'base'. The particular reference is to an outbreak of despair, when the prophet even went the length of reproaching Yahweh with leaving him in the lurch. This leads us to a further question: did such a refusal affect only the prophet's personal relationship with God? Did it have no effect at all on what he said in public? Here the modern reader of the Bible will perhaps think of certain passages in the post-exilic prophets where enemies of Jerusalem are forewarned that their flesh will rot fearfully away (Zech. 14.12), but where Israel is shown the prospect of her enemies serving her as servants and handmaidens (Isa. 49.22), and even of herself treading down the wicked (Mal. 3.21 [4.3]) and of wading in the blood of her enemies and becoming drunk with it (Zech. 9.15). Can these be called cases where a prophet's darkness was so deep as to allow human instincts and passions to gain the upper hand over the message from God, so that they perhaps testify to human hatred rather

than to God's will for the future? Such a judgment, however, presupposes a knowledge which we do not have of the circumstances
in which such messages were delivered, to say nothing of the
inherent element of risk involved in making use of such psychological interpretations, based as they must be on conjecture about
the prophet's spiritual state. What we must take as our starting
point is the objective content of such prophecies, and we must try
to understand them in the light of the whole teaching of the prophet concerned, and if need be compare this with that of the other
prophets. As far as the last of these is concerned, the fact that
Amos, Hosea, and Isaiah do not strike this note may give us pause.
But is there only one explanation of the difference? In dealing with
such passages, exegesis has above all else to be clear about the
criteria it proposes to apply. It ought to be perfectly obvious that,
since these passages to some extent already verge on the bizarre
conventions found in the literature of Apocalyptic, our modern
Christian humanitarian ideal completely fails as a standard. of
judgment. But if such critical questions are left open – though there
is no reason why they should be – it is, theologically, a bad sign
that, as usually happens, they are asked only of aspects of the
prophetic message which seem to us immoral or inhumane. The
'base thing' which Yahweh rebuked in Jeremiah was certainly not
his implacable feelings towards his persecutors: it was his disobedience to God and his angry rebellion against his office. Did the
prophets, and in particular those whom we usually and perhaps too
carelessly think of as later and feebler members of the succession,
have, each in his own day, a true estimate of their office, or did
they fall short of the task to which they were called? And yet,
what knowledge have we of their task? Nevertheless, now that
examination of tradition has revealed the extremely close link
between the prophets' preaching and the perfectly well-defined
traditions upon which they depended, we can make a cautious
judgment about the way in which a prophet adapted his material,
what he chose to include and what he relegated to the background.
We know, for example, that they felt themselves free to modify
the traditions they employed to suit their own day and age, and
they did this more by pointing up detail than by making changes
in their actual content.

5 The Prophets' Conception of the Word of God

W E must turn to a subject which is equally central for all the prophets, namely, the 'word of Yahweh'. Yet, although the word of Yahweh is both a necessary precondition of prophetic preaching, and also forms its subject matter – though, indeed, it is the fundamental basis of the prophets' existence – they only occasionally made it the subject of theological reflection. Their relationship to it was so personal and direct, that is to say, the word was so exclusively bound up with the specific time at which it came to them and with the specific message which it gave them, that for the most part they found it simply impossible to think of the word of Yahweh in objective terms and as something having very specific properties of its own. It is only exceptionally that they furnish us with direct information about its nature; in general, it is only indirectly that we can reconstruct the prophets' concept of the word of Yahweh – that is, by drawing conclusions from their preaching. A critical account of the prophetic concept is needed all the more urgently today in that we simply cannot assume that our conception of 'the word of God' or of the function of words in general is identical with that held by the prophets.

In modern languages, or at least in modern European languages, the almost exclusive function of the word as an aggregate of sounds is to convey meaning. It is a phonetic entity which enables men to communicate with one another, and is therefore a vehicle used for purposes of intellectual self-expression. This noetic function of the word, the conception of it as bearing and conveying an intellectual idea, is, however, far from covering the meaning which language had for ancient peoples. Indeed, our conception of the word, as that which conveys an intellectual meaning, seems to be the complete opposite of the conception which we must suppose existed in the cultural state represented by the myth. There, a word is much more than something which indicates and designates a certain object; it is quite the reverse of a label attached to an object at a later stage. At the early mythical level of thought, man's apperception of the world about him is of it as a unified entity. He makes no distinction between spiritual and material – the two are intertwined in the closest possible way; and in consequence he is also unable properly to differentiate between word and object, idea and actuality. Such thought is thus characterized by an inherent absence of differentiation between the ideal and the real, or between word and object; these coalesce as if both stood on one plane of being. In a way which defies precise rational clarification, every word contains something of the object itself. Thus, in a very realistic sense, what happens in language is that the world is given material expression. Objects are only given form and differentiation in the word that names them. This idea of the word's power of mastery was very familiar in the ancient world. Even in J's story of the Garden of Eden, the word of the man is noticeably given precedence over the world of objects. It was only when man gave the animals their names that they existed for him and were available for his use (Gen. 2.19f.).[1] Myth is more than merely early man's way of expressing his comprehension of the world; it is also what brings the world into being – the myth has to be recited, because this is the only means of countering the perils which everywhere beset the fixed orders of creation, and of guaranteeing their continued existence. From this it is only a step to what we term 'magic', though for early man, use of magic was one of the basic ways in which he gained control over the world. A curse was effective upon an enemy in virtue of the power inherent in its form; and at a hunt, magical rites, or even a drawing of the hunted animal, could be used to bring it into the power of the man who had bewitched it, whether by word, rite, or representation. These and countless other examples to be found in comparative religion rest on a conception of language which we can call dynamistic, since here a word (or a symbol or symbolic action) is thought to possess a power which extends beyond the realm of the mind and may be effective in the spatial and material world also.

But early civilizations did not for long remain in the stage in which the world was conceived in terms of magic and dynamism:

[1] 'Just because the creation of the word is itself a kind of conjuration, in which being itself comes to light, man at all times has the obscure feeling of touching on existence with [it].' W. F. Otto, *Die Musen und der göttliche Ursprung des Singens und Sagens*, 1956, p. 80.

indeed, if we follow the *schema* usually adopted for the great phases in the history of culture, this stage was soon almost entirely left behind. The *schema* does not fully exhaust itself on the issue of language and of the many functions which devolve on it within the various cultures and religions. If we try to explain this in terms of evolution, by saying that on occasion the dynamistic possibilities of language remained alive for a much longer time, and, even in advanced cultures, could automatically come to the surface again, this would hardly be a true description of what actually happened; we should then be measuring the development of language against a preconceived picture of the history of human culture, and giving the impression that, wherever language is 'still' thought of as possessing power, this always indicates that initial stages or relatively unchallenged remainders are being carried over from a cultural level already in principle left behind, and are forcing their way into another level to which they are quite foreign. This, of course, does happen : but one could equally well ask whether language has become impoverished because it has lost functions which at an earlier cultural level had once belonged to it. It would be an unhappy state of affairs if we had to try to make excuses for the language of the prophets because 'traces of a magical use' of the word are still to be found in it. We may notice in passing that this is in no way something peculiar to Israel. It is well known that in many old and sometimes highly developed cultures language was not restricted simply to the description of objects; in out-of-the-ordinary situations, because of a mysterious power of creation, language could produce either something new, or an intensified form of something already in existence : that is to say, language itself became creative; and this is a possibility which language has never lost, even to this day.

There are a number of different departments in the cultures of the ancient east where we meet the word of power, the chief of them being, of course, the more restricted realm of the cult, and the rituals connected with exorcism and with blessing and cursing : it is also to be found in specific theological traditions. The idea of a god's word of power played an important part in Old Babylonia and Old Egypt – these cultures go even to the length of conceiving it as a physical and cosmic force. Even in everyday life, however, certain words were thought of as having power inherent in them, as for example people's names. A man's name was not looked on as something additional to his personality, something which could

be changed at will; on the contrary, it contained an essential part
of his nature and was at times actually looked on as his double;
he was therefore particularly exposed to the baleful influence of
magic by its use. An ill-starred name could threaten its bearer's
life. Jacob valiantly rescued one of his children from the dark fate
which was beginning to descend upon him because of the ill-starred
name Ben Oni ('son of sorrow'), by giving him instead a name of
happy omen (Gen. 35.18).

While we are taking random examples like this, we may also
consider a linguistic usage, the background to which is often mis-
interpreted – that of aetiologiés which depend on etymology and
the play on words. In Israel, as elsewhere, such aetiologies were
not treated as a literary or rhetorical pastime, but were taken very
seriously as a means of reaching certain important pieces of knowledge. Present-day taste dislikes the absence of a recognizable connection, either in logic or in meaning, between the words thus co-
ordinated – indeed, to our way of thinking, the choice may seem
perfectly arbitrary. Are we, however, only to keep the immediately
understood meaning which attaches to a word? In such 'plays on
words' the word has a different and much more primitive way of
acting: on solemn occasions it can release meanings and establish
mental affinities which lie at the deeper level of its magical matrix
and which apparently have little or nothing to do with its obvious
and everyday meaning. What happens in such etymologies is
rather peculiar. On the one hand, the word in question loses a
certain amount of its meaning, and apparently acts as a series of
sounds rather than as a way of conveying meaning; but this series
of sounds, which is the word reduced to its original value, is at the
same time given a greatly intensified meaning, in that it is now, in
respect of its form, surrounded by new associations and new meanings. The play upon *qayiṣ—qēṣ* in Amos's vision has meaning for
us too; but only because we also can with fair ease make the mental
jump from 'harvest' to the idea of 'end' (Amos 8.2). Again, in what
is said in Jeremiah about the almond tree ('watching rod') and about
Yahweh 'watching over' (*šāqēd—šōqēd*; Jer. 1.11f.) his word, it is
only the conceptual connection that meets our eye. It is different
with the improvized word-plays in Micah 1.10-15 and Isa. 10.29-31,
for here the names of the places suggest associations, and give hints
at the fate in store for them, which are still only linked to them
by the 'outward' sound of the words. This kind of thing is done all
the more easily in Hebrew in that the Hebrew speaker, even when

he is using language noetically, is in general far less concerned
with linguistic precision and the avoidance of ambiguity than we
often assume. If in prophetic diction a phrase or a word could
have several possible references, so much the better, for the saying
was thereby enriched.[2]

What has here been said about the Hebrew language regarded as
a phenomenon composed of sounds which almost possesses a creative power of its own to conjure things up also holds true, in a
different way, in Greek. Here, in addition to conveying meaning, its
melodiousness and rhythm affect men even in their physical nature,
of. T. Georgiades, *Musik und Rhythmus bei den Griechen*, 1958, pp.
42ff. In Greek, too, the gap between the word and the objective
thing it denotes can be so narrowed as to give even the modern
reader the impression that the objects in all their material solidity
have been taken up into the word.
'The characteristic of classical Greek is that the word operates as
a rhythmic and musical force and at the same time as language, as
a phonetic formation, as that which conveys ideas and emotions.
The word serves not only a phonetic purpose: it is at the same time
something more, it is a rational art-material which is shaped for
its own sake. Undoubtedly it is "language" like our own, inasmuch
as it serves to establish semantic connections. It has also, however,
a quality which we today can hardly understand, that of appealing
directly to the senses as music does. It is rhythm which, independently of the word's linguistically conditioned sound properties,
grants it a strength which is actually based in another sphere.'
'What impression may the Greeks have had of their own language?
They must have had the feeling that it was mightier than they' (p.
43). A Greek word 'is like a solid body that the hands can grasp.
The words of a verse in Greek as it were stone one' (p. 45). This can
also be said with equal truth of many of the utterances of the Old
Testament prophets.

Israel, too, was thus aware that her language possessed possibilities other than those demanded by everyday personal conversation.
She was aware of a use of language in which the primary requisite
was in no sense a partner in conversation, but *simply* that the words

[2] In this content, mention should also be made of the names of ominous
import in Hos. 1.4ff. and the renaming in Hos. 2.25 [23] or Jer. 20.3. The
reality of the name must correspond with the reality of the happening.
Finally, paronomasia should also be mentioned here; for with its juxtaposition of words with a similar sound, this figure is also primarily based on
the sound of words. Linguistic assonance is not, however, an outward thing;
a peculiar power issues from the linguistic body of the expression. The precision of the paronomastic expression is diminished in favour of its greater
breadth of meaning.

should *just* be spoken, that they should simply be brought on the scene as an objective reality endowed with mysterious power. This was, of course, only one possibility among others, but Israel never abandoned it, not even at the time when she learned the use of very polished and rhetorical utterance, as for example in political and diplomatic conversations or in the exchange of ideas with wise men of other nationalities. As is only to be expected, she also employed this new skill in the realm in which her intellectual activity was at its strongest, the realm of religion and theology. Both in her most ordinary and in her sublimest statements, in magic, and in the deepest insights of theology or prophecy alike, Israel took as her starting point her conviction that the word possessed creative power.

Israel's theologians and prophets were, of course, certain that, for all the mysterious possibilities inherent in every word of man, the word of Yahweh towered incomparably high above them. Moses, as we see him in Deuteronomy, is most insistent in warning his people that they should not think of Yahweh's word as 'empty' (Deut. 32.47), and this obviously embraces the belief that the word of man is to be regarded as, in greater or lesser degree, 'empty' in comparison with the word of God. Deutero-Isaiah also says that the word of God is not 'empty', but effective (Isa. 55.11). The part which the concept of the creative word of Yahweh played in the priestly cosmological traditions, particularly in the Priestly Document's account of creation, is matched by corresponding concept in a cultic hymn.

> By his word the heavens were made,
>   and all their host by the breath of his mouth.
> For he spoke, and it came to pass;
>   he commanded, and it stood forth.
>
> (Ps. 33.6, 9)

Another of the Psalms says that 'Yahweh calls the stars by name' (Ps. 147.4), and this idea is taken up by Deutero-Isaiah who, as is well known, made the creation of the world by Yahweh, and creation by the word, a theme of his preaching (Isa. 40.26; 48.13; 50.2). The mention of this creative word of Yahweh in Ps. 147.15-18, a Wisdom poem whose aim is instruction, is of particular interest, since here the word of Yahweh and its 'going forth' are connected with the snow, the frost, the ice, and the wind, which also come from heaven. It has long been known that in this respect Israel shares in many ways in ideas found at various points in the religions of the ancient east. But this must not blind us to the fact that her ideas of the power of God's word went entirely their own way, and that in this very respect she evolved a magnificent and quite unique theological achievement. We need hardly say that to make generalizations based on the theory of evolution, and to say that here is an example of a primitive or magical view of language, only hinders the proper understanding of such an exceptional phenomenon, since this reduces it to a common denominator of cultural development which does not apply here. There were archaic survivals in all religions, and Israel was certainly not exempt from them. The striking fact remains, however, that the way by which she came to make her most important statements about the properties of the divine word was not that of remaining uncritically bound to these primitive elements, but that of exercising her most concentrated reflection; and that what is said, for example in the prophets, about the 'magical' power of the divine word occurs in the context of and in closest association with a very advanced and even positively revolutionary view of the spiritual world. The reason for this, to put it briefly, is not to be looked for among the general phenomena of religion, but in the unique character of the subject itself expressed here.

The prophets' statements about the word Yahweh are relatively independent of those made by the priestly theology. With the former we encounter what is obviously a self-contained set of ideas and traditions. The term, 'the word of Yahweh', occurs 241 times in the Old Testament writings; of these no less than 221 (92 per cent) relate to a prophetic oracle. There can, therefore, be no doubt but that this collocation was used as a technical term for an oral prophetic revelation. The phrase, 'the word of Yahweh came to so and so' (123 times), is particularly characteristic, because it represents the apperception of the divine word as event, a unique happening in history, which a man is looking for or which takes him by surprise, and which therefore in either case sets the person concerned in a new historical situation. It is very significant that the phrase always appears with the definite article, '*the* word of Yahweh', and never in the indefinite form, '*a* word of Yahweh', as a superficial glance at the extremely large number of such 'word-events' might have led one to expect. The latter would, however, have shown a radical misunderstanding of the process, for however brief and concise the word might be, it was intended as *the* word of Yahweh for the man who received it and for his situation. The word that came on each occasion is not to be set alongside the rest of the words of Yahweh, so that it is only in the synthesis that it yields something like the message the prophet has to announce; on the contrary, for the person concerned it is the complete word of God, and has no need of tacit supplementation by the other words which the prophet had already spoken on other occasions. At different times and to different people the prophet takes different ways of saying the same thing. Paradoxical as it may seem, in principle the prophet says the same thing to everyone; he plays variations upon it only to meet differences in the conditions of his audience. This is the main reason why it is so difficult to set out a prophet's teaching. We are bound to make the attempt, but at the same time there is no possibility of achieving the result by taking, as it were, the average of his ideas from the sum total of his prophetic *logia*.[3]

But we shall be disappointed if we imagine that, in all the really abundant and varied material available, the prophets give a complete account of the phenomenology of the word of Yahweh. Indeed, we may even come to think that the prophets are the last people to provide an answer to this question, because their attitude to the word they receive is so far from neutral – the word presses in upon them, they make it their own, and allow it to absorb all their emotions. In his word Yahweh meets his prophet in the most personal way possible; how could a man then talk of it as if it were a neutral thing? Thus it would be better to apply for information not to the prophets but to their audience, who were less directly involved in the word of God : but, to do this we would have still to be able to discover what impression the prophetic word made upon them!

It may be noticed in passing that this difficulty lends added importance to the verdict passed by Amaziah the high priest on the

[3] We find exactly the same state of affairs, which is of course very important for exposition, in the synoptic gospels. 'The Gospels tell the story of Jesus in "pericopae". These story-scenes give his history not only when pieced together, but each one in itself contains the person and history of Jesus in their entirety. None requires explanation in terms of previous happenings. None is directed at later events for the unfolding of what has gone before. We are always being held in the beam of this scene and this scene only. . . . This way of telling his story has its exact counterpart in the transmission of his words. Here again each word stands by itself, exhaustive in itself, not dependent on context for its meaning or requiring a commentary on it from some other word.' G. Bornkamm, *Jesus of Nazareth*, 1960, p. 25.

message of Amos. It is well known that he reported Amos's appearance at Bethel to the king, and, like a true official, added a note
giving his own comment on the matter: 'the land is not able to
bear all his words' (Amos 7.10). The verb 'bear' is ordinarily used
of the cubic capacity of vessels; the words therefore imply that the
land – note that he speaks of the land and not of Israel – had a
certain limited capacity. This was certainly no dull-witted official
report: the man who wrote it was a keen-eyed observer with real
insight into the force of Amos's words. Paradoxically enough, therefore, we have to allow that Amaziah had a certain understanding of
the prophet's message – he saw it as a real danger to the Israel of
the day and to its religious and economic life to that date.

   As has been said, with the earlier prophets in particular, reflection on the nature and properties of the word which they spoke is
not *a priori* to be expected. Their feelings are intensified, and they
deliver it almost as if it were a ritual, and are perfectly sure of the
effects which it accomplishes. One of the oldest utterances of the
prophets is that attributed to Elijah, that there should be neither
dew nor rain in Israel 'except by my word' (I Kings 17.1). To
whom, however, is he to speak this word which is to break the
drought? When the proper time comes, does he mean to speak it
to Yahweh, or to the heavens and the clouds? This last is not
beyond the realm of possibility. What is, however, more likely is
that he expected Yahweh to commission him to command the rain.
The reader who has studied comparative religion may here feel
reminded of the self-understanding of the 'bearer of power' among
primitive peoples and of the magical force latent in his word. Yet,
to discover, as we think, such phenomena still 'lingering on' in
Elijah does not take us very much further forward. On the evidence
available, it could equally be argued that we see in Elijah the beginning of a concept of the prophetic word which can be traced down
from his own time almost to the moment when prophecy finally
disappeared. We may even go further: it is easy to show how
the old concept became of more and more theological importance, to reach its fullest development in Jeremiah and Deutero-
Isaiah.

   The verse which stands at the head of Amos' oracles (in a position which suggests that it is intended to serve as a statement of
policy for the whole collection) states that Yahweh 'roars' (Amos
1.2). This is a term which goes far beyond the limits of the normal
language of worship or of any other department of religion. Oddly
enough, it says nothing about the subject-matter of the roaring:

there is no definite verbal utterance on the part of Yahweh, just as there is no mention of any human hearers to whom the oracle refers. The only thing spoken of is a sound, and all that is said of it is that it echoes. Nevertheless, the effect of this sound is tremendous, for when it goes forth from Zion it makes the pastures of the shepherds desolate and withers even the summit of distant Carmel.[4] Amos' near contemporary, Isaiah, also on occasion uses strange language about the word of Yahweh, and speaks of it as if it were a material thing, achieving its effect simply in virtue of its physical weight:

> The Lord has sent a word against Jacob,
> and it has lit upon Israel.
>
> (Isa. 9.7 [8])

The prophet's way of speaking of the 'word' here is very absolute, as if it were something known to everyone. What is even more remarkable is that the people are given no explanation of the subject matter of this word; there is no mention of the prophet who spoke it or of any audience to whom it was spoken. Since this word was directed against the Northern Kingdom, and the event referred to possibly lay now in the past, it is not even certain that it was spoken by Isaiah himself. Yet the prophet, whoever he was, speaks of the word's coming down to earth and its historical effect as if they were objective realities. In some respects the poem presents difficulties for exegesis, but one thing is quite clear: it speaks throughout of reapted sendings-forth of this word which, as it makes its way through history, is not quickly spent:

> For all this his anger is not turned away,
> and his hand is still stretched out.[5]

While such expressions are rare in the eighth-century prophets and only serve to show that in certain circumstances these men see the word of Yahweh operating in a way which is quite different from the normal one, with Jeremiah they occur frequently, and

---

[4] The saying Amos 1.2 must be taken entirely by itself; it has no connection either with what precedes it or follows it. The words of threat which Seraiah was to read aloud in Babylon also required no one to hear them; they were simply to be proclaimed aloud; the sheet was then to be cast into the Euphrates (Jer. 51.59ff.).

[5] Isa. 9.11, 16, 20 [12, 17, 21]; 10.4.

suggest that here some change has come over the prophet's basic conception of the word.[6] Even in the call itself, through which Jeremiah is summoned to prophesy 'against nations and kingdoms', everything is made to depend upon the power of the prophet's word. How is it possible for one solitary individual like Jeremiah 'to pluck up and to break down, to build and to plant' in respect of whole nations (Jer. 1.9f.)? Clearly only by means of the word of Yahweh which Yahweh injects into history; for this word is very different from that of his degenerate professional fellow-prophets – it is like a fire, like a hammer which breaks the rocks in pieces (Jer. 5.14; 23.29). At the very same moment that Ezekiel was voicing the words he had been inspired to speak against Pelatiah, the latter fell down dead (Ezek. 11.13). Thus, the reason why these men were hated and feared was this power inherent in the word. Their power to bring about disaster, and the possibility that they might do so, were not contested. If the 'wrath of Yahweh' which filled Jeremiah was to be poured out, this meant catastrophe and death (Jer. 6.11f.). For the prophets themselves, however, the word held more than simply terror. Jeremiah tells us something of its effect on him: he says in one place that the word became a joy to him, and that he ate it like a starving man. We cannot assume that he made any exception, in principle, of the oracles portending calamity (Jer. 15.16). When he speaks of eating the divine words, we should not take this in too spiritual a way, and regard it as metaphor and hyperbole: it is perfectly possible that a prophet even felt physically dependent on the word and so, in a sense, was kept alive by it. The idea of eating the word of Yahweh reappears in Ezekiel in a very radical form; at his call he was ordered to eat the scroll which was offered to him (Ezek. 2.8–3.3). Later on we shall have to consider how the entry of the message into their physical life brought about an important change in the self-understanding of these later prophets. (We may ask whether this entry of the word into a prophet's bodily life is not meant to approximate to what the writer of the Fourth Gospel says about the word becoming flesh.) Earlier, of course, Amos had spoken of a famine of the

[6] The widespread use of the very characteristic phrase, 'the word of Yahweh came to . . .' also occasions thought. It is found – in each case, of course, only in a very small number of instances – in practically all the older prophets. In contrast, however, there is a sudden increase in Jeremiah (30 times) and Ezekiel (50 times). This must link up with the new emphasis now laid on the word of Yahweh as event, and indeed with a 'theology of the word' which is now appearing in these prophets.

word of God which was to press so hardly upon men that they would stagger hither and thither in exhaustion seeking the word, and would faint (Amos 8.11ff.). This looks very much as if the prophets regarded Israel's whole life as in some special way dependent upon the word of Yahweh, and thought of her as directed towards it right down to the most elemental levels of her life. When Deuteronomy makes Moses exclaim, 'this word is your life' (Deut. 32.47), and when it draws from the miracle of the manna the lesson that man does not live by bread alone, but 'by everything that proceeds out of the mouth of Yahweh' (Deut. 8.3), there can be no doubt that it was making use of ideas generally current among the prophets. Yet, while this idea of man's total dependence upon the word of God originates with the prophets, it apparently only came to the surface, at least in so emphatic a form, in the seventh century; and the prophets themselves were certainly the first people to realize that their own lives were totally dependent on Yahweh.

In the case of Deutero-Isaiah, the tradition gives no information about the prophet's own relationship to the word. This is, however, offset by the great place which he gives to commenting on the efficacy of the word in history. At his call a voice from heaven sharply contrasts men's whole being ('all flesh') with the word of Yahweh. The former – the prophet is thinking first and last of man as he behaved in history in the great empires – is utterly transient; the breath of Yahweh will blow upon him in wrath and destroy him completely. As for the latter, however, 'the word of our God stands for ever' (Isa. 40.8). The phrase is extremely terse, but it is perfectly clear that by 'the word of our God' the prophet means to point to that other power which confronts the first one, the power of man as displayed in the historical empires. He is not, therefore, thinking of the word which will endure because it calls forth an echo in the inner realm of the heart, but of the word which Yahweh speaks into history and which works creatively on that plane: it will 'arise'. Nor will anything endure except what this word brings about; for the bewildered exiles in Babylon it is the one solid ground under their feet. The book ends as it began on this same note:

'Verily, as the rain and the snow come down from heaven and return not thither without watering the earth, making it bring forth and sprout, giving seed to the sower and bread to the eater, so it is with my word that goes forth from my mouth. It does not return

to me empty without accomplishing that which I purposed or ful-
filling that for which I sent it' (Isa. 55.10-11).

This is prophecy's most comprehensive statement about the word
of Yahweh and its effects. At the beginning of the prophecy the
word was contrasted with 'all flesh'; here it comes down from
heaven, down from the lips of Yahweh on to earth, in order there
to 'give effect to' its task and 'bring it to a successful conclusion',
and then at the end to return to Yahweh.[7] When the word of Yahweh is likened to rain and snow, what comes into a modern
reader's mind are simply the laws of nature; ancient Israel, however, regarded both of these, the sending of the rain and the sending of the word, as contingent events which took their origin from
Yahweh alone (Ps. 147.15ff.). Deutero-Isaiah thus sets the word of
Yahweh in the grandest of perspectives. The most important part
of its universal activity is admittedly its action in history, yet this
is only one part. There is absolutely no saving event not foretold
(Isa. 42.9; 46.10; 48.5). If, however, Yahweh sends this word which
heralds what is to come and allows his chosen people knowledge
of it, this is only a concession to Israel's lack of faith :

> Because I knew that you were obstinate,
>   and your neck is an iron band
>   and your forehead brass,
> I declared it to you from of old;
>   before it came to pass, I announced it to you.
>   (Isa. 48.4f.)

If we ask what it is that this word of Yahweh effects in history,
we must turn to the content of the message – Deutero-Isaiah thinks
above all of the return of the community of Israel, the second
Exodus with all its wonders. That the prologue and epilogue of the
book, the frame of our prophet's total preaching, deal so radically
with the word of God, is a statement of policy of great importance.

The passages quoted here suggest that there was a strong element of theological reflection in Deutero-Isaiah – something which
Jeremiah and Ezekiel had foreshadowed. This 'theology of the
word' was intended to give a systematic explanation of the phenomenon of the word of Yahweh, and this explanation, in its turn,

---

[7] The idea that the word in the end returns to Yahweh as in a circle is
odd, and is not found elsewhere. It is to be assumed that the figure of the
rain which begets like chthonic force (v. 10) has an old mythological idea
as its basis; but it is very unlikely that the prophet was aware of this.

was to serve as a basis for the huge project of surveying the phenomenon of prophecy itself. In such words as those contained in
Isa. 55.10f., prophecy thus also to a large extent presents the results
of reflection on its own nature; for through this view of the word
of God, prophecy gave itself the central place in the whole inter-
action of God and the world.

In this theoretic attempt to come to a proper understanding of
the nature and effects of the word of Yahweh, another work should
be placed beside that of Deutero-Isaiah; and this, though the two
must have been roughly contemporary, is of a very different kind.
It is the Deuteronomic history. As we have already seen, it pictured
Israel's history as a history of Yahweh's effective word; it postu-
lated a number of predictions as the real causes of events, and at
the appropriate places drew special attention to the way in which
each particular one was fulfilled ('this came about in order that the
word spoken by the prophet . . . might be fulfilled'[8]). The Deuteronomist here applies these ideas to the past in order to show it as a
scheme of history shaped by Yahweh: but they are undoubtedly
prophetic in origin. At the same time, within the larger framework
of the Old Testament, it is he who gave the word of God in its
form as the dynamic of history its broadest theological basis, for he
saw the word of Yahweh, whether in salvation or in judgment, as
the real motive-force and creator of Israel's history. The word is
extremely active, 'it runs swiftly' (Ps. 147.15); 'it [even] hastens' to
its fulfilment, and people must be able to wait for it (Hab. 2.3); for
God's thoughts and designs began their historical fulfilment at the
point at which they became words on the lips of the prophet.

In the Wisdom of Solomon the divine word is the subject of some
verses of great poetic merit, and in one respect these have close
affinities with the prophetic utterances mentioned above. The subject is the night in which Yahweh smote the first-born of Egypt:
'While deep silence enveloped all things, and night in its course
was now half gone, thy all-powerful word leaped from heaven,
from the royal throne, a stern warrior into the midst of the land
that was doomed. Carrying as a sharp sword thy unalterable com-

---

[8] The Deuteronomist had an established set of theological terms at hand
to show how this word functioned in history: the prophetic word 'does not
fail': Josh. 21.45; 23.14; I Kings 8.56; II Kings 10.10; 'it will be established':
I Sam. 1.23; 15.11, 13; II Sam. 7.25; I Kings 2.4; 6.12; 'it comes to pass': Josh.
25.15; 'it is fulfilled': I Kings 2.27; 8.15, 24; cf. also Ezek. 12.25, 28: 'Thus
has the Lord Yahweh spoken: None of my words will be delayed any longer;
the word which I speak is performed, says the Lord, Yahweh.'

mand, it came and filled all things with death. It touched heaven as it strode about on earth' (Wisdom 18.14ff.). This obviously departs from the prophets' line of thought, for they never spoke of the word of Yahweh as an independent entity to this extent, as if it were a being with an existence of its own. For them the word was mobile to the highest degree, and they could never have tied it to places in such a way, or described it like this. Here faith has fallen silent and given place to speculative thought.

The articulate word was not, however, the only means used by the prophets to express the future. They also performed all kinds of symbolic actions, some of which were extremely odd. Ahijah the Shilonite tore his garment into twelve pieces and gave them to Jeroboam (I Kings 11.29ff.); Isaiah drew up a tablet with a name written on it (Isa. 8.1-4) and went about 'naked', that is, in modern language, in the dress of a deportee (Isa. 20.1ff.); Jeremiah broke a flask (Jer. 19.1ff.), wore a yoke of wood (Jer. 27.2ff.), and bought a field (Jer. 32.6ff.); and Ezekiel in particular is credited with a whole series of extremely curious 'symbolic actions' (Ezek. 4–5). It took scholars a long time to recognize the special significance of these prophetic signs – indeed, they did not do so until they realized that such signs are not to be regarded simply as symbols intended to bring out the meaning of oral preaching. While in some cases the prophet's purpose was to reinforce in visual ways what he had said, or was about to say, it is clear that this idea does not give the full picture. For antiquity, the sign, like the solemn word we have already discussed, could not only signify a datum but actually embody it as well; this means that it could act creatively, and in early cultures it probably had an even greater power to do so than the word. For us today, this way of looking at a sign is difficult to understand, whereas we can still perfectly easily experience the creative properties of the word; there are situations where it matters very much whether a word is spoken or not – even when it is in everyone's minds. But in primitive cultic practice especially, solemn word and solemn sign lie in the closest possible co-ordination, and this is not just in the sense that the sign is the servant of the word and so merely an additional accompaniment of it; on the contrary, in the form of a sacred rite, for example, the sign can be taken as completely independent from the word.

Like other ancient peoples, Israel was aware of the efficacy of sacred signs, and this not merely in the restricted sphere of the cult but also in the realm of the law (in legal symbolism and symbolic actions in connection with oaths), in sacral medicine, and even in the language of gesture in the dance. Thus, symbolic actions were by no means simply the prerogative of the prophets. Their contemporaries were not surprised that the prophets performed such actions: what shocked them was the meanings which the prophets expressed in this way. Yahweh himself acts in the symbol, through the instrument of his prophet. The symbol was a creative prefiguration of the future which would be speedily and inevitably realized. When the prophet, by means of a symbolic act, projects a detail of the future into the present, this begins the process of realization, and on that account the prophetic symbolic act is simply an intensified form of prophetic speech. The only difference is that in the case of the sign, it was less important that its full implications should be understood by those who saw it performed. Do not symbolic actions sometimes seem to conceal more than they reveal? In both of Isaiah's symbolic acts, the command to perform them anticipates the full disclosure of their meaning by some years (Isa. 8.1ff.; 20.1ff.)! Even if we do not adopt the extreme position that the prophet himself was, to begin with, ignorant of the significance of what he was ordered to do (though in both cases this is what the text apparently suggests), it is quite certain that for a long time the people did not understand his behaviour; and this completely rules out the idea that the function of symbolic actions was to teach and illustrate. For to do this they would have had to be visual illustrations chosen by the prophet to produce a better understanding of his message.

This way of regarding symbolic actions, which was only opened up by the study of comparative religion, is therefore basic for exegesis. Exegesis will, of course, discover that this idea of the power of the symbol which acts creatively in history is by no means present in its pure form in every case. Examination of the way in which the symbolic act is related to the spoken word reveals a variety of concepts of the former's function, with the result that exegesis has in each specific case to ask what the action was intended to signify.

Prophetic symbolic actions were originally directed towards a future event (II Kings 13.14ff.); but the classical prophets also applied the sign to their own times, and it thus became a little ambivalent. The idea that the sign had power to create history is clearly still present: but it now contains a proclamation as well. Because greater emphasis is now put upon its appeal to the mind, it turns to the people of its own day, in order to prepare them for the future. Thus, Isaiah's going about naked becomes a 'sign' for the nation once Yahweh discloses its meaning; it becomes the portent of a deportation which still lies in the future (Isa. 20.3). In just the same way Ezekiel, in making no mourning at the death of his wife, becomes a 'sign' for his people, a pointer to a calamity in which no one will make ritual mourning for his relatives (Ezek. 24.15ff.). These symbolic actions come much closer to being actual prefigurations of the events to which they refer; unlike Ahijah's torn garment, they do not merely foretell the bare fact, but also actually portray what it will entail (prisoners going naked, no proper rites at funerals), and to this extent they can be the better understood by those who witness them.

In the story of Jeremiah's wearing of a yoke the concept underwent an even more radical change, for Jeremiah used the yoke as a warning – only the nations who submit to Nebuchadnezzar will escape deportation (Jer. 27.1ff.). Here the form the future will assume is still completely open, and the symbolic action lays upon the witnesses themselves the decision whether it will be weal or woe. Here the sacramental significance of the symbolic action has completely disappeared. It is, of course, possible that the responsibility for the way in which the symbol loses its earlier meaning lies at the door of the narrator of the incident, for elsewhere in the book of Jeremiah there are symbolic actions quite identical with the older understanding of them (particularly Jer. 19.1-2a, 10-11a, 14-15, and Jer. 32.1ff.).

6 The Origins of Hebrew Thought about History

T H E question of the specific way in which Hebrew thought understood time and history brings us into an area of great importance for the correct understanding of the prophets. Earlier exposition was quite unaware that there was a problem here, and uncritically assumed that its own Western and Christian concept of time also held good for Israel. Today, however, we are beginning to realize that her experience of what we call 'time' was different. Yet this in itself does not bring us very much further forward, for we find it extremely difficult to move beyond the terms of our concept, which we naïvely believe to be the only possible one, and to understand the specific details of another in such a way as to be able to make much of reconstructing it. The idea of time accepted more or less naïvely by Western man is linear; time is seen as an infinitely long straight line on which the individual can mark such past and future events as he can ascertain. This time-span has a mid-point, which is our own present day. From it the past stretches back and the future forwards. But today one of the few things of which we can be quite sure is that this concept of absolute time, independent of events, and, like the blanks on a questionnaire, only needing to be filled up with data which will give it content, was unknown to Israel. It is true that in the Deuteronomic history the notices which synchronize the concurrent reigns of the kings in Judah and Israel presuppose a high degree of intellectual and scholarly activity (as is well known, they have their parallel in, and are perhaps modelled on, the synchronistic lists of the kings of Babylon and Assyria). Yet, these chroniclers failed to go on to what we should expect to be the next logical step – they did not take these two chronological series together in order to enter them on one single time-line. Each of the two lists of kings keeps its own time. Are we to say that what prevented this simple logical conclusion was certain intellectual limitations of the age? What is much more likely to have made the step absolutely impossible is the ancient world's concept of time. If exegesis regards this way of viewing time as merely a stage of cultural infancy, it bars the way to understanding. It should rather be ready to accept that Israel's perception of time was taken from a different angle from ours.

In addition to being without any idea of absolute and unlinear time, it also seems evident that Israel was not capable of thinking of time in the abstract, time divorced from specific events. She found the idea of a time without a particular event quite inconceivable; all that she knew was time as containing events. Hebrew completely lacks a word for our modern concept of 'time'. Leaving aside the Hebrew word for 'eternity', which means the distant past or future, the most important term which comes under discussion here is the word which means 'time' in the sense of 'a point in time' or 'a period of time'. There is a time of giving birth (Micah 5.2 [3]), a time for animals to be gathered together (Gen. 29.7), a time when kings go forth to battle (II Sam. 11.1). When something out of the ordinary was projected, such as the rebuilding of the temple (Hag. 1.4), there could be debate whether this was the time to undertake it. The tree yields its fruit 'in its time' (Ps. 1.3), and God gives his creatures food 'in due time' (Ps. 104.27); that is to say, every event has its definite place in the time-order; the event is inconceivable without its time, and vice versa. This is, of course, self-evident in the case of processes determined by the cycle of the natural year. As antiquity understood it, however, this temporal ordering holds good for all the concerns of mankind – even for the emotions – because every matter under heaven has its own time: a time to be born, to die, to plant, to pluck up, to weep, to laugh, to mourn, to dance, to seek, to lose, to rend, to sew, to keep silence, to speak, to love, to hate (Eccles. 3.1ff.). This profound insight is not, of course, simply that of Ecclesiastes alone; it was one of the basic insights of the people of the age in general, and the utmost degree of wisdom was necessary not to miss the times appointed for things and their discharge, and to recognize their mysterious kairos. Finally, on the basis of these leading ideas it is not surprising to find that Israel could also speak of 'times'. This plural form had a realistic significance for her. When a man at prayer says: 'my times are in thy hands' (Ps. 31.16 [15]), we must remember that he had no idea at all of time as such; in his eyes human life is made up of a series of many times.[1]

[1] Further references for this use of the plural, Ezek. 12.27; Job 24.1.

The statement just made, that our concept of time is linear, requires to be supplemented by saying that to a large extent it is actually eschatological. For a thousand years in our Western world it was eschatological in the strict Christian sense of that term; and even when our way of looking at the world and history became a secular one, time itself was still in a certain sense thought of eschatologically – mankind, or a particular nation, was thought of as moving towards some ultimate fulfilment. Even the nihilist is today conscious of being in a time-stream; indeed, his precise trouble is that he cannot master its onrush. What puts such a question-mark to man in his now secular existence is simply the fact that while other Christian concepts have crumbled away, an eviscerated eschatological concept of time still lives on. Old Testament exegesis must, therefore, completely exclude this concept. It is, in any case, not even Greek; in this abstract sense it is not ancient at all.[2]

In more than one respect the comfortable words which form the close of J's account of the Flood, 'while the earth remains, seedtime and harvest, cold and heat, summer and winter, day and night, shall not cease' (Gen. 8.22), are characteristic of the concept of time held in Israel in the early period. In the first place they are in the highest degree non-eschatological, in that what they expect from the future is precisely the absence of the abnormal : the future (though the term is not really appropriate) is the extension of the present. The words 'while the earth remains' are a solemn assurance, equivalent to 'for all time', and they certainly do not imply any consciousness of a limit, meaning that the sentence was to be interpreted in the sense of 'only' while the earth remains. Next, it is typical that the only way of conveying the idea that the earth will remain in being for ever is to construct a series of times having various contents. Thirdly, the words show that this series follows a definite rhythm : it is not arbitrary, but is subject to a fixed order. This we should call a natural order, since it is determined by the rhythm of earth and of the heavenly bodies.

Any description of the concept of time in the ancient world in general and in Israel in particular would, however, be perfectly inadequate unless something was said of the significance of the festivals, for these were not merely the highlights of people's lives : rather, in fact, the rhythm of festal and non-festal times gave their

[2] Cf. here the important observations on Greek thought about time as distinct from biblical and Christian thought made by K. Lowith, *Meaning in History*, 1949, pp. 6ff.

own lives their rhythm in time. Indeed, one might even go a stage
further and describe the time of cultic festival as the one and only
'time' in the full sense of the word, for it alone was time furnished
with content in the truest sense of the term; for the observance of
these cultic festivals did not rest upon any human arrangement
and, besides, earlier on there were no ecclesiastical and civil years
running parallel.[3] We must make an effort to realize how much
sacral festivals must have meant to people who completely lacked
any concept of absolute and linear time to which these festivals
had then to be related. The festivals, not time, were the absolute
data, and were data whose holiness was absolute. There were days
of which it could be said that Yahweh 'has made' them (Ps. 118.24).
The sabbath was an objectively hallowed day, that is to say, a day
set apart for Yahweh, on which the community shared in the
divine rest and, in so doing, was conscious that this rest upon
which it entered was as it were an ontological reality. The Feast
of Tabernacles was a time of joy, whose appointment by Yahweh
was absolute. It was holy time absolutely, and even the most
wretched must have been filled with delight as they entered upon
it. Beside these, there were times of mourning and fasting, which,
from the sacral point of view, were negative in character. Failure
to observe a time of fasting was not the infringement of a mere
human arrangement but of a divinely appointed fixed order. There
might occasionally be uncertainty; it might be asked whether the
community was misunderstanding a divine order and misconceiv-
ing the nature of a time – whether it was, for example, observing
a time of mourning where God had already ordained a time of
blessing (Zech. 7.1ff.). Such questions were not just ritual niceties,
but affected the very basis of these men's faith, and in dealing with
them exegesis has no right to withdraw into its own supposedly
superior philosophical understanding of time.

For this supreme importance of the cultic festivals one may compare what W. F. Otto says on the festivals in ancient Greece (*Die
Gestalt und das Sein*, 1955, p. 255): 'The festival always means the
recurrence of a great hour in the world when what is most venerable, august and splendid is once again present; a return of the

[3] The introduction of the 'Spring calendar', i.e., the transference of the
beginning of the year to the spring, which took place under Assyrian influence in the later monarchical period, did not in fact affect the cycle
of the cultic festivals, but nevertheless it must have been regarded as a sign
that the old sacral understanding of time was breaking down.

golden age, when the forefathers associated so intimately with the gods and spiritual beings. This is the reason for the festal sublimity which, when there are real festivals, is different from any other kind of solemnity and any other kind of joy. Hence the awe-inspiring forms, striving towards magnificence, of genuine worship, whose style cannot possibly belong to the realm of practical purposes. It testifies to a holy plenitude, to an enraptured geniality of the soul which appropriates the extraordinary, the primeval and eternal, the divine. Men have entered into the heights; the return of the great hour has exalted them.'

The rhythm of Israel's great festivals was originally determined by nature's ordering of the Palestinian year. The festal calendar is, of course, Canaanite in origin, and as such is the expression of a farmer's religion which looks on the processes of sowing and reaping as direct sacral events. Obviously, however, in Israel, very soon after the settlement, and in spite of the fact that she herself had become a completely farming people, the content of these festivals underwent a change. At Unleavened Bread, the festival which falls at the beginning of the barley harvest, the Exodus from Egypt was commemorated (Ex. 23.15), and at the great harvest and vintage festivals the sojourn in the wilderness and the dwelling in booths (Lev. 23.42f.). Before this the festivals had been purely agrarian, but Israel 'historicized' them. We can scarcely overestimate the importance of such changes, brought about as they were by a unique understanding of the world and of human existence. Israel's belief that she was not bound primarily to the periodic cycle of nature but to definite historical events, was the expression of a faith that was probably at the time still completely unaware both of its absolute difference in kind from the Canaanite religion, and of its own vigour. While, therefore, it is perfectly correct to say that Yahwism is founded in history, this does not, of course, involve any thought of the modern concept of history which, as we know, lays great stress on the idea of relativity and of the transitoriness of all events. The historical acts by which Yahweh founded the community of Israel were absolute. They did not share the fate of all other events, which inevitably slip back into the past. They were actual for each subsequent generation; and this not just in the sense of furnishing the imagination with a vivid present picture of past events – no, it was only the community assembled for a festival that by recitation and ritual brought Israel in the full sense of the word into being: in her own person she really and truly entered into the historic situation to which the festival in question was related. When Israel ate the Passover, clad as for a journey, staff in hand, sandals on her feet, and in the haste of departure (Ex. 12.11), she was manifestly doing more than merely remembering the Exodus: she was entering into the saving event of the Exodus itself and participating in it in a quite 'actual' way. The same is true of Tabernacles, or of the festival of the renewal of the covenant at Shechem, when she celebrated the giving of the commandments and the making of the covenant respectively.[4]

This transformation of what were once agrarian festivals, itself the result of the character of Yahwism as a historically determined religion, was, however, only one stage of development, Israel's first step, as we might call it, towards the understanding of her historical existence. For she did not stop short at basing her existence on a single historical event: she went on to specify a whole series of them, and it was this series of events as a whole which called the people of Israel into being. The Exodus from Egypt was prefaced by the patriarchal age, and rounded off by the events connected with the entry into Canaan, and from the aggregate of a whole series of saving acts developed a span of historical time. Israel's faith began to take as its basis not just one single event alone, not even one as momentous as the Exodus commemorated at Passover, nor again a number of disconnected events, but she began to think of a series of consecutive data, or, to put it in another way, she began to realize that her present was based on an earlier series of

---

[4] This cultic experience, which is so hard for us today to understand, becomes rather more comprehensible when it is remembered that in olden days the worshipper regarded himself as an individual to a much less extent than we do. He knew himself entirely as a member of a collective body, and in religious matters he could only be moved and filled by the experience of the totality of the worshipping community.

Psalm 114 gives us a good idea of what this actualization of saving events looked like in the cult. The Exodus event and the choice of Zion are almost brought together in point of time (vv. 1f.). The crossing of the Red Sea (Ex. 14f.) and that of Jordan (Josh. 3f.) – separated, according to the Pentateuch's reckoning, by forty years – are mentioned in the same breath (v. 3), as if it were a matter of one event and not of two. And all this is so contemporaneous for the psalm, which is of course centuries later, that, as this saving event is enacted, it can address it and ask it questions (v. 5)! On the other hand, this contemporaneousness is not so exclusive as to prevent mention of an event of the wilderness days, the miracle of the water from the rock (Num. 20.11), which in point of time lay after the crossing of the Red Sea and before that of Jordan. This kind of thing cannot be explained as 'poetic freedom', but only on the basis of the thought-world of the cult.

creative events, a somewhat involved historical development. How was Israel led to this way of conceiving her history? All that can be said is that there must have been a time when each of the individual historical events was cultically celebrated in isolation and, indeed, at entirely different places. Bethel kept alive a tradition about Jacob, Shechem was the scene of the festival of the renewal of the covenant, it seems likely that at Gilgal there was a commemoration of the conquest which in many respects overlapped the Passover-Exodus festival, and so on. Later, however, these traditions were amalgamated to form a sequence of events from which no single component part could be omitted. At the same time, each of them was to be understood only as a part of the whole which was itself very much more than simply the sum total of all its various parts. The oldest known results of this certainly revolutionary procedure of assembling the various saving acts commemorated in the cult into a historical sequence are concise summaries of the saving history (Deut. 26.5ff. and Josh. 24.2ff.). Israel had in this way broken through to the concept of a linear historical span, and she achieved this break-through not by means of philosophy or mythology, but by gradually building up the time-span through the summation of the various divine saving acts as they were remembered in various places. Or, more properly, Israel came to realize that Yahweh had a definite plan for her, and that her ancestors had made a long journey with him during which Israel gradually obtained her identity. This realization – that Israel was not founded upon one single event, but that there was a long road, that is to say, a history, which led up to her formation – is an epoch-making step. What we see here is not what we are accustomed to understand as history: the idea of history which Israel worked out was constructed exclusively on the basis of a sequence of acts which God laid down for her salvation. Thus, Israel's history existed only in so far as God accompanied her, and it is only this time-span which can properly be described as her history. It was God who established the continuity between the various separate events and who ordained their direction as they followed one another in time.

This very distinctive view of Israel's history was laid down in principle as early as the period of the Judges. She became able to make it more comprehensive and, with it as the theological basis, to see and describe her history from many different angles. But the fundamental thought that history can only exist as the times in which God performed his acts and gave his guidance never altered. Israel was constantly at work in extending the period of time included in the old canonical picture of her history. Reaching from the patriarchal age to the conquest, E still keeps to the original limits. J and P, however, begin with creation and end at the conquest. The Deuteronomic history begins with Moses, but it reaches beyond the others to include the period of the Monarchy, and it ends with the disaster of 587. Chronicles, which stretches from Adam to the post-exilic period, takes in the longest time-span. There was thus a growing desire to survey a linear time-span and to come to a theological understanding of it; the periods considered become wider and wider, though, of course, this does not mean that the process of increasingly consistent expansion of the length of time surveyed finally links up with our present-day concept of history; for not even in her large historical surveys did Israel abandon her own peculiar view of her history as a history with God, a road on which she travelled under God's guidance. It is particularly important to realize that this did not as yet open a door to understanding universal history also as history. Israel only succeeded in doing this in the book of Daniel, in which for the first time apocalyptic drew up an eschatological picture of world-history taken as a whole.[5] The idea that history has a beginning was established by implication in Gen. 1, for, as we have already shown, the creation story with its subtle ordering of the time-divisions sees in creation the beginning of Israel's history with God.

This idea of history which Israel developed theologically in various directions over a period of centuries is one of this people's greatest achievements. (It is well known that the only other people in the ancient world who also wrote history, though of course in an entirely different way, were the Greeks.) We have still, however, to consider the question of the interrelation of this linear and chronological idea of history to which Israel gave birth and the actualizing of the saving history at the great festivals which was discussed above. Was not an actualization of the saving history, as this took place within the framework of the cult, excluded in principle by this chronological concept of history? The idea of contemporaneousness – at least in the strict sense of the term –

---

[5] But even apocalyptic pictured the new aeon as a time range of 'countless weeks in eternity', Enoch 91.17. And, when the prophets made statements like Amos 9.13; Isa. 60.19f.; Zech. 14.7, were they not perhaps intending to point to something beyond time, at all events to a cessation of the present rhythm of time?

in virtue of which worshippers at a festival were enabled to enter into the saving occurrence in a real and actual way (that is, into *the* saving occurrence, and not into a long sequence of successive events), was certainly shattered; for the cult in the ancient world was essentially 'anti-historical'. Were there, then, two ways open for Israel by which history could be actualized, one cultic and the other chronological? As a matter of fact, one can only assume that, for some time at least, both of these persisted side by side. It is extremely unlikely that worshippers at one of the pilgrimage festivals at Bethel or Beersheba had any idea that scholars in Jerusalem were producing more and more comprehensive versions of Israel's history. And in Jerusalem itself people did not stop celebrating Passover in the traditional way after the chronological view of the saving history had been established.

Nevertheless, the case was hardly as simple as the peaceful co-existence of these two ideas, which we can here only sketch. Even once the saving events were dissociated from the sphere of the cult and made available for the construction of a linear period of history, the old form, cultic actualization, could certainly have persisted for some considerable time alongside the other. Yet, out of this concept of the saving event as a historical series composed of more than one divine act, an attitude of mind developed, so sweeping in its consequences that it was bound, in the long run, to affect the cultic form of actualization. It was now no longer really possible to regard history as turning back on itself, to say nothing of the fact that this new view of history was bound to develop beyond its original conception. The exodus from the sacral sphere made it possible for rational understanding to contribute to the construction of a picture of the history; a critical way of thinking sprang up which learned how to select, combine, and even reject, data from the wealth of the tradition, and which was also able to use its own insight to draw attention to particular high-points in the long chain of events, as, for example, by ordering the course of history under various covenants. It is, of course, difficult to decide whether from the very beginning this advance into the dimension of history was assisted by a certain exhaustion, that is to say, an eclipse of the naïvety of cultic actualization, or whether the advance itself was the cause of such weakening. However this may be, there is evidence pointing to a crisis in the cultic actualization of Yahweh's saving acts. In Deuteronomy, the preacher makes it apparent that the generation which he addresses is well aware

of the distance which separates it from the one with which the
Sinai covenant was originally made. In these circumstances, the
covenant, contemporaneous for earlier generations, now requires
to be put on a new basis in order to be valid:

'Yahweh, our God, made a covenant with us in Horeb; not with
our fathers did Yahweh make this covenant, but with us, the living,
with all of us who are here today' (Deut. 5.2-3).

In a later passage, where the method of argument takes a different line, the preacher's endeavour is the same:

'You stand this day all of you before Yahweh . . . that you
may enter into the covenant with Yahweh, your God. . . . But it
is not with you only that I make this covenant and this oath, but
also with those who stand with us this day before Yahweh, our
God, as well as with those who are not here with us today' (Deut.
29.9-14 [10-15]).

Here, too, the speaker is trying to establish the present-day
validity of the old covenant at Sinai. The theology which voices
such ideas is obviously determined not to allow the saving events
to belong simply to the past. Here Israel is still within the sphere
of the cult. The scene described in Neh. 8 shows us how, after
Ezra's reading of the law, the Levites addressed the solemn assembly
and explained the situation to them, but this is no longer in the
old style of cultic celebration – rational considerations and arguments have now to be adduced in order to keep the actuality of
the saving events. It is also this which gives its tone to the constant
'today' which the admonitions in Deuteronomy drum into their
hearers' ears. Furthermore, we should also remember the remarkable way in which the Deuteronomic history makes the transition
from the age of Joshua, that is to say, from the end of the canonical
saving history, to the period of the Judges. It makes a clean break
after Joshua (Josh. 21.43-5), and then brings on the scene a generation which knew nothing either of Yahweh 'or the work which
he had done for Israel' (Judg. 2.10). The clarity with which it was
recognized that a thoroughgoing historical understanding of the
saving events could create definite problems for faith is simply
amazing.

Looked at from the point of view of comparative religion, this
idea of history made a radical division between Israel and her
environment. While it is possible to recognize in her cultic cele-

bration of the saving acts, which followed the rhythm of the year, certain continuing lines of connection with ideas which belonged to neighbouring religions of the ancient east, with her idea of saving history she completely parted company with these religions. Not one of them understood the dimension of history in the way that Israel did! The most that can be said of their concept of time is that there is a 'primeval time', which is not, however, one era amongst others, but a beginning which remains determinative for all further periods. The various conditions of creation were given their divine orders at that time, and the task assigned to cult and ritual was that of giving continuing effect to these primordial orders; for from the cult issue the creative forces which keep safe and stable a cosmos which is always exposed to danger. The religions of the ancient east did not, however, regard this divine process by which the world was sustained as historical, but as cyclical. The ancient east's view of the world bears to a greater or lesser degree the clear impress of cyclical thinking in terms of myth, that is to say, of a way of thinking which understood the cultic event on the basis of the rhythm of the fixed orders of nature. This comprehensive range of concepts originated in the contemplation of the heavenly bodies and of the rhythm of nature on earth dependent on them. In myth, early man reflected upon natural powers with which he met as he lived his life – and fixed orders, too, are powers. These he sees as the basis of the world and of the rhythmic event which sustains it, and he looks on them as divine. It was always this basically cyclical order of nature on which the ancient peoples of the east conferred the dignity of divinity and which they regarded as a divine event, both in the myths which deal with theogonies and in those which have as their subject the dying of gods. This sacral understanding of the world is essentially non-historical; at least, it leaves absolutely no place for the very thing which Israel regarded as the constitutive element in her faith, the once-for-all quality of divine saving acts within her history. The Babylonian sanctuary at Uruk, the Erech of the Old Testament (Gen. 10.10), was a well-known cultic centre as early as the third millennium; but the finds in the latest strata, from the Seleucid period, show the worship of the same gods, Ea, Shamash, Marduk, and Ishtar, still going on just as in the earliest times.

We are thus confronted with an intensely interesting fact of comparative religion. The view of the world current throughout the ancient east, which originated in and stemmed from the age-old cults of Mesopotamia, and to which even the nations within the orbit of Syria freely submitted, is confronted with an entirely different understanding of the divine saving action, and that by a tiny people. This is not, of course, to say that Israel forthwith declared war on it, or that by gigantic efforts she extricated herself from its embrace. Rather, what we see is that it was in the earliest period of her life that, with great and unconscious assurance, she rested in her own peculiar religious ideas, and grew stronger and stronger in them. Struggle and temptation came only much later.

7 History Related to Eschatology in the Prophets

W H E N we turn to the prophets, we find many other examples of this same understanding of history. Indeed, the prophets paid serious attention to the theory that Yahweh accompanied Israel along her road through history, and they were particularly concerned with the obligations which this involved, in a way which was markedly different from their contemporaries who were, apparently, no longer very greatly aware of these things. In addition, however, the prophets also show something else that is quite new – a keen and unprecedented awareness of the great historical movements and changes of their own day and generation. Their whole preaching is characterized by an unrivalled ability to adjust itself to new historical phenomena, and by a power of adapting itself to these phenomena which, on occasion, leads them to the point of self-contradiction and makes it very difficult to give any coherent explanation of the prophetic message. The relationship between that message and the events of world-history is so close that it has to be accepted as one of cause and effect: Amos and Isaiah work in the shadow of the threat from Assyria, Jeremiah sees disaster coming from the north, from the neo-Babylonians, Deutero-Isaiah is full of the emergence of the Persian Cyrus, and Haggai and Zechariah take account of convulsions which shook the Persian Empire in 521. This correlation between the prophets and world-history is the real key to understanding them correctly, for they placed the new historical acts of God which they saw around them in exactly the same category as the old basic events of the canonical history – indeed, they gradually came to realize that this new historical action was to surpass and therefore, to a certain extent, to supersede the old. They were in fact called forth by their conviction that Yahweh was bringing about a new era for his people. It would be entirely wrong to suppose that this glance into the future was no more than a kind of prognosis of the likely course of historical events based on evaluation of some of the leading political characters of the day. What makes the difference between the prophetic outlook on the future and any sort of political calculation is their unshakable conviction that in the coming events God was to deal with Israel in the most direct way: in other words, from the theological point of view the meaning of what was about to happen was absolutely clear. Political calculation depends on seeing analogies within history: the prophets looked forward to historical events planned by the sovereign freedom of the will of Yahweh. As will presently be shown, however, they too understood this new action of Yahweh in history in terms of an analogy.

Theology was surprisingly slow to abandon the idea that it was enough to say that the prophets were the embodiment of their nation's conscience, and to recognize what is the prime characteristic of the wide range of their preaching. If the prophets were more than particularly characteristic representatives of Yahwism, the sole reason for this lies in their turning towards the future. The new element which in a certain respect differentiates them from all previous spokesmen of Yahwism is – to use the controversial but unavoidable term – the eschatological element.[1] This is now almost universally accepted, for all that there is no agreement on the minute definition of the term.

Of course, it would be wrong to understand eschatology as a great, consistent body of ideas, made up of complex cosmic and mythological expectations about the future, from which the prophets drew what they wanted. It was a long time before research was delivered from this erroneous view. The proper definition of 'eschatological' is still anything but settled even today. Not a few scholars fight shy of the term: they want an exact use of terms, but this one, they say, obscures rather than clarifies. They are only prepared to let it stand when it is used in connection with the end of this world's time – that is to say, when it refers to a consummation of the historical process in events which lie beyond the scope of the world's history. This would mean that it can only be used of the very latest of the prophetic writings – indeed, it can only be properly applied to apocalyptic literature, and even there not with absolute precision, for apocalyptic envisages the continua-

---

[1] We deal here with prophecy from the time of Amos and Hosea. Whether the prophecy of Elijah or Elisha can be described as eschatological is open to question. That of a Nathan (II Sam. 7) or a Gad (II Sam. 24.11ff.) was certainly not.

tion of time and history after the historical consummation. But to define 'eschatological' so narrowly would mean that the term has no place at all in the Old Testament and can only properly be applied to Christian doctrines. In this view, every application of the term in the Old Testament is more or less *ab extra* and has nothing there to which it exactly corresponds. We can, therefore, understand the uneasiness of scholars when the term is used to interpret predictions of the prophets. There should be a different definition of the term, in the light of prophetic prediction.

The characteristic feature of the prophet's message is its actuality, its expectation of something soon to happen. This should be the touchstone of the use of the term 'eschatological'. It is also the point on which criticism of the admissibility of the term is based, for the fact that these expectations exist is made the ground for disputing that the prophetic predictions embrace the idea of an absolute end of time and history. To do this, however, is tantamount to applying a concept of time to the prophets' teaching of which they themselves were quite unaware. If, as I have already suggested, this concept of time simply did not exist for the prophets, it is perfectly possible to say that the event which they foretell is a final one even if we, with our different presuppositions, would describe it as still 'within history'. Of course, the idea of 'something final' does not itself describe what is specific in the prophetic teaching; there is also the contribution made by what has been called the 'dualistic conception of history', the idea of the two 'aeons', including the break which is preceded by Yahweh's great act of demolition, and followed by the new state of things which he brings about. The relevant passages do not, in my view, call for a distinction to be drawn between Yahweh's action within history and his action at the end of it, and there is consequently no need to confine the term 'eschatological' to the latter. To my mind, it is far more important to realize that there is this break which goes so deep that the new state beyond it cannot be understood as the continuation of what went before. It is as if Israel and all her religious assets are thrown back to a point of vacuum, a vacuum which the prophets must first create by preaching judgment and sweeping away all false security, and then fill with their message of the new thing. Here, it is important that history has recently been brought in again to provide a definition of eschatology, and the prophetic vision has been described as 'the renewing act of the historical drama'.

With this as starting-point, we soon arrive at a proper understanding of the eschatological message of the prophets. Briefly,
within the horizons of eschatology as elsewhere, Israel's ideas about
saving history must be given back their proper place and their due
weight.[2] It is impossible to understand the eschatological message
of the prophets in the light of any kind of mythological or specifically cultic complexes of ideas, or in that of disappointed hopes.
It can only be understood from the point of view of the distinctive
character of Israel's thought about history, a subject in which the
prophets engaged with the utmost intensity and to which they in
fact gave a new dimension by drawing attention to an entirely new
action in history on the part of Yahweh.[3] Like the writers of the
canonical history, the prophets regard certain election traditions
as normative, that is to say, they hold a view of history in which
Israel was given legitimation as she was called and founded by
Yahweh. Indeed, the preaching of some of them can actually be
regarded as a great continuing dialogue with the election tradition
which they inherited. This tradition is not, of course, the same for
each and every prophet. While Hosea stands within the Exodus
tradition, Isaiah only knows of the saving institutions connected
with the David-Zion tradition. The Exodus tradition is also prominent again in Jeremiah and Ezekiel, and especially so in Deutero-
Isaiah. One point, however, is very remarkable. On the one hand,
we see with what force and ardour the prophets catch up these
election traditions in their preaching; on the other, their relationship to them is a broken one, for they regard the coming judgment
as sealing the end of Israel's present existence: the security given
her by these election traditions is cancelled out because of her
guilt. The only thing she can hold on to is a new historical act on
the part of Yahweh, the outlines of which the prophets already see,

[2] It is not surprising that in their pictures of the new the prophets introduce here and there ideas which were not current in earlier periods, but
which had in the interval come into Yahwism from other religions. In any
case, this process is of no importance for the determination of the phenomenon of the eschatological.

[3] The psychological explanation of the phenomenon of eschatology is not
a sufficient one, though disillusionment may well have been one of the
contributory factors in the 'rise' of eschatology; only, the object by which
the disillusionment was called forth ought to have been given more exact
theological definition, and also the experience of disillusionment should
have been assigned its due place within the total phenomenon. If we hold
by what the prophets say, it will not do to put the 'experience of disillusionment' at the head as the evocative factor proper.

and to which they point with passion. The prophetic message differs from all previous Israelite theology, which was based on the past saving history, in that the prophets looked for the decisive factor in Israel's whole existence – her life or her death – in some future event. Even so, the specific form of the new thing which they herald is not chosen at random; the new is to be effected in a way which is more or less analogous to God's former saving work. Thus Hosea foretells a new entry into the land, Isaiah a new David and a new Zion, Jeremiah a new covenant, and Deutero-Isaiah a new Exodus. There are, of course, differences in the prophets' ideas of the completeness of the break between the old and the new situations, there are even considerable theological differences. For Isaiah the old saving acts and institutions are still valid enough to allow Yahweh to link his coming to them. This is true both of the new Zion (Isa. 1.26), and of the new David (Isa. 11.1). On the other hand, for Jeremiah and Deutero-Isaiah the break is so complete that Yahweh has to re-enact his former deeds – the covenant is to be made anew (Jer. 31.31ff.), and there is to be a new Exodus (Isa. 43.16ff.). This was never Isaiah's way of putting it; he never said that Yahweh would choose Zion, and make the covenant with David, afresh. In contrast, Deutero-Isaiah's vision could lead him to demand that the former saving history should be remembered no more (Isa. 43.16ff.). This again could not have been said by Isaiah of Jerusalem. However, such differences are only relative; for even Isaiah had no doubt that Israel's sole ground of salvation lay in the new actions in history.

On this view of the matter, the message of the prophets has to be termed 'eschatological' wherever it regards the old historical bases of salvation as null and void. But we ought then to go on and limit the term. It should not be applied to cases where Israel gave a general expression of her faith in her future, or, as does happen, in the future of one of her sacred institutions. The prophetic teaching is only eschatological when the prophets expelled Israel from the safety of the old saving actions and suddenly shifted the basis of salvation to a future action of God.

This view of the eschatological message differs from the earlier one in that it does not presuppose either a whole 'complex' of eschatological expectations on which the prophetic preaching could draw or an already made eschatological *schema*. The eschatological phenomenon is simplified once more; it is reduced to the extremely revolutionary fact that the prophets saw Yahweh approaching

Israel with a new action which made the old saving institutions increasingly invalid, since from then on life or death for Israel was determined by this future event. The reason for this change in outlook is to be found primarily in history, which had begun to move again in a quite unprecedented way: but it is also to be found in the realization that Israel under the Kings had become quite detached from the old relationship to Yahweh. How little the prophets drew on any predetermined 'complex of ideas' (whose origin would still have to be discovered) is made plain by the fact that they expected the new saving action to take exactly the forms of the old one, and that therefore, even in expounding the new, they had recourse to Yahweh's saving appointments of the past. We can thus see how close was the attachment of even the prophets to the saving history; it was in fact the norm for their representation of the most distant last things. To be sure, their hearers must have felt that this call to prepare themselves for a coming act of God and to seek their salvation in it made very strong demands on their religious faith. They are bound to have thought that they were being led to a realm which lay beyond the ken of their religious knowledge and experience. They had no way of conceiving a dimension outside the saving area of Yahweh's canonical saving acts: in their eyes this could only have appeared to be strange in the highest degree.

8 The Day of Yahweh

SPECIAL consideration needs still to be given to the expectation of the Day of Yahweh, which has often been regarded as the very heart of the prophetic eschatology. Do we not have here, at any rate, attaching to this day a relatively well-defined complex of eschatological expectations? There is, in fact, something peculiar about the expectation of the Day of Yahweh, for wherever it occurs in prophecy, the statements culminate in an allusion to Yahweh's coming in person. It has often been asked how this concept originated, and rightly so; for, could we find the answer, we would come much nearer to an understanding of the thing itself.

There are not very many passages which refer to the Day of Yahweh in so many words.[1] Of the sixteen, Amos 5.18-20, which has always been regarded as a key passage, offers little towards clarification of the term; also, the long poem in Isa. 2.9ff., with its repeated refrain, deals much more with the general results and effects which the coming of Yahweh is to have than with the thing itself and its concrete accompaniments, though we do read of people fleeing, and throwing away their now worthless idols in the process.

We start with the poem on Babylon in Isa. 13, which is generally taken as an anonymous prophecy of the sixth century. It begins with a call to the fighting men to muster for Yahweh's host; signals are to be raised. Yahweh himself summons his 'consecrated ones', his mighty men, and they come in such numbers that there is an uproar of nations. Then Yahweh musters the host in person.

> Wail, for the day of Yahweh is near;
>   as mighty power from the Mighty One it comes.
> Therefore all hands are feeble . . . every man's heart melts. . . .
>   they look aghast at one another.
>
> (Isa. 13.6-8)

[1] Isa. 2.12; 13.6, 9; 22.5; 34.8; Jer. 46.10; Ezek. 7.10; 13.5; 30.3; Joel 1.15; 2.1, 11; 3.4 [2.31]; 4. 14 [3.14]; Amos 5.18-20; Obad. 15; Zeph. 1.7, 8, 14-18; Zech. 14.1.

Yahweh comes in person to the battle, the stars are to withhold their light, the earth quakes, the carnage is terrible. The poem ends with an allusion to the complete desolation of the empire. Its concepts are all of the same kind; it tells of a war which begins with the muster of the fighting men and ends with a description of the devastated and depopulated land. The war is made to take on gigantic dimensions; not single warriors but whole nations stream to the muster. At the same time, the events described have their parallels in real warfare.

The oracle against Edom in Isa. 34, which again is not the prophet's own, is constructed in just the same way as Isa. 13, and even if it does not contain the actual term 'day of Yahweh' but speaks instead of 'the day of recompense for Yahweh' (v. 8), it should be mentioned here. It begins with the announcement of Yahweh's furious wrath against Edom, then goes on to a description of the destruction of Edom by the sword of Yahweh, and ends, like Isa. 13, with a picture of the land completely desolate and inhabited only by wild creatures. Here again the concept of the holy war of Yahweh is prominent. This is expressed in the words that Yahweh has 'put his foes to the ban' (v. 2). Here also terrible changes appear in the heavens in connection with the war; 'the skies roll up like a scroll, and all their host shrivels' (v. 4). The comparison made between this war and the slaughter of animals for sacrifice (v. 6) will be taken up later.

Ezekiel's oracle against Egypt (Ezek. 30.1ff.) is also an elaborate poem, though it is a single unit. It begins with a call to lamentation because of the Day of Yahweh: 'a day for Yahweh is near'. It is a day of clouds; the sword shall come upon Egypt, the Egyptians and their allies shall fall, and afterwards the land and its cities shall lie waste. Though shorter, Ezek. 30.1-9 also obviously parallels the course of the prophecies in Isa. 13 and 34. This raises the question whether all three are not dependent on an already existing prophetic *schema*.

The same is also true of the great picture given in Ezek. 7. Here again, in view of the exclamations, 'the day is near' (v. 7), 'behold, the day' (v. 10), and 'the day has come' (v. 12), the fact that the full term, 'the day of Yahweh', is not used makes no difference. Practically every verse makes plain that the prophecy deals with the Day of Yahweh. Here again it is only the basic concepts in which we are interested: the end is coming, and this upon the whole earth, though of course upon Israel in particular. In contrast with the previous examples, the opening cry is here developed to an unusual length. The description of the war itself does not begin till v. 14. The enemy is said to have made ready, 'but none takes the field' (v. 14); sword and famine ravish. 'All hands are feeble' (v. 17); the city's riches are to fall into the hands of foreigners, and it itself is to be profaned. These verses describe practically the same final state as was signified in the other poems by the word 'depopulation'. Jer. 46.3-12, with its description of 'that day', 'the day of vengeance' on Egypt, also fits exactly into this group. There are important occurrences in Joel which confirm the picture just arrived at. Joel 1.15 is of decisive importance for the understanding of the whole chapter: 'The day of the Lord is near.' All the signs indicate that it is Yahweh himself who is setting out on a fearful campaign (cf. Zech. 14.1, 3). In the case of Joel 2.1-11, it is today generally agreed that a real plague of locusts is envisaged. However, the prophet's conception of this event and, in particular, the means which he uses to describe it, are interesting. Joel is clearly dependent on traditional and, to a greater or lesser degree, conventional, prophetic concepts for the vivid way in which he illustrates the distress; that is to say, on concepts which he only secondarily relates to the distress itself. He equates the locusts with the armies of the Day of Yahweh marching into battle, and is thus able to draw on the whole range of war concepts connected with the Day of Yahweh.

Blow the trumpet in Zion, sound the alarm on my holy mountain; all the inhabitants of the land shall tremble, for the day of Yahweh is coming.
Verily, it is near, a day of darkness and gloom, a day of clouds and thick darkness.

(Joel 2.1-2)

An army advances, mightier than has ever been hitherto seen. 'Before it people shudder, all faces glow' (v. 6). Before it the earth quakes; the heavens tremble. Sun and moon are darkened, and the stars lose their brightness (v. 10). 'Great is the day of Yahweh, and terrible; who will endure it!' (v. 11). At this point the poem passes into a call to repentance and the demand to gather together for a fast; for Joel 2.1-11 is in fact only a part of a great liturgical composition. It is, therefore, all the more striking to realize how very little influence the actual starting-point, the locust plague itself, was able to exert on the traditional picture of the sequence of events once the catchword, 'the day of Yahweh', had been introduced. The traditional sequence of summons to war, dismay, earthquakes, darkness, and the voice of Yahweh, has certainly not very much in common with the advance of a locust plague.

Zephaniah's prophecy concerning the Day of Yahweh is certainly one of the most important sources of material at our disposal for the various concepts connected with this subject (Zeph. 1.7-18). The form of this passage is difficult, but it is a single unit in itself. What we have here is a description of the day of Yahweh into which various sayings have been inserted in certain places. For our pur-

poses, only the first of these two component parts is important
(vv. 7, 10-11, 13-18). The description apparently begins with the
cry that the day of Yahweh is near. This day is designated as a
sacrificial feast which Yahweh prepares for the guests whom he
invites. This is a metaphor which we have already met in Isa. 34.6.
Its clearest expression occurs in Jer. 46.10: at the great festivals
the blood of the victims flows in streams – Yahweh's war against
his foes will be equally bloody. What follows also shows that the
event is war: crying and wailing are to be heard in all the quarters
of Jerusalem (vv. 10-11). This day is a day of distress, of darkness
and gloom, a day of trumpet-blast and battle-cry against fortified
cities. Men will be overcome with fear; the panic which is to break
out shows itself in the fact that they 'go about like blind men'
(v. 17); they will be unable to save themselves, for the earth is
to be consumed with the fire of Yahweh's zealous wrath. This
closes the description, the main outlines of which correspond with
those given in Isa. 13; 34; Ezek. 7; and Joel 2.

   The first result of this survey is to show that the prophets expect
the day of Yahweh to bring war in its train. Now, the widespread
employment of this concept in the prophets suggests that we are
dealing with a well-established component part of eschatological
tradition. But this runs counter to the fact that the expression 'the
day of Yahweh' could occasionally be used in connection with past
events (Ezek. 13.5; 34.12; cf. Lam. 1.12; 2.22). In view of this somewhat ambivalent reference, the proper procedure for investigation
is first to rule out all possible interpretations based on a rather
far-fetched mythology, and then to ask whether Israel herself did
not have, in her own old traditions, some knowledge of the concept of Yahweh's coming specifically to wage a war, with its
accompaniment of miraculous phenomena. This is, of course, the
case. In itself, the almost stereotyped connection of the day of
Yahweh with intervention in war reminds one of the holy wars
and all the phenomena which traditionally accompanied them.
In this concept of Yahweh's coming in an act of war we have at
least one concept clearly stamped with Israel's own tradition, and
we should establish its relationship with the prophetic utterances
about the day of Yahweh before we try any other methods of
interpretation. This becomes even more obvious when we consider
that a prophet himself twice connects the eschatological event of
war quite directly with one of the holy wars of the past (Isa. 9.4 [5]
=Judg. 7; Isa. 28.21=II Sam. 5.20, 25). People recounted all manner
of miracles which accompanied these wars once waged by Yahweh (thunder, I Sam. 7.10; stones falling from heaven, Josh. 10.11;
darkness, Ex. 14.20; Josh. 24.7; clouds dripping water, Judg.
5.4f.). A particularly important part is played by the terror
caused by God himself, a panic confusion and demoralization of
the enemy, whose effect was to paralyse their confidence in their

fighting powers and so lead them to compass their own destruction.[2]

In view of all this, there can be no doubt that the same principle is at work both in the old stories of the theophanies in bygone wars and in the prophets' descriptions of the future Day of Yahweh. The various constitutive elements and conventional stock subjects of the former reappear one after another in the prophets' predictions. To refer just once more to the sacral panic, we read in Jeremiah:

> What do I see? They are dismayed, they turn back!
> Their warriors are scattered, fleeing hither and thither. . . .
> The swift cannot flee away, nor the warrior deliver himself.
>   (Jer. 46.5f.)

The concepts connected with the Day of Yahweh are, therefore, in no way eschatological *per se*, but were familiar to the prophets in all their details from the old Yahwistic tradition. The prophets, however, also believed that Yahweh's final uprising against his foes would take the same form as it had done in the days of old. It is beyond question that the prophetic vision of the concept of Yahweh's intervention in war became greatly intensified; for the war was now to affect all nations, even the fixed orders of creation, and even Israel herself. The event has been expanded into a phenomenon of cosmic significance. Thus, under the influence of this traditional element, the prophetic concept of the *eschaton* was also to some extent systematized, that is to say, predictions connected with the expectation of the Day of Yahweh which began from different traditions were to some extent blended. One can well imagine that Amos's contemporaries cherished the expectation of such an uprising to war and victory on the part of Yahweh. Amos, however, asks them if they never think that this day is to bring a darkness that might also be fraught with danger for them. It is most improbable that Amos's contemporaries already possessed a fully developed 'popular eschatology'. In this connection far too much weight has been given to Amos 5.18.

---

[2] Ex. 15.14f.; 23.27f.; Josh. 2.9, 24; 5.1; 7.5; 24.12. The term 'Day of Yahweh' first occurs in Amos; there, however, it is, as has often been insisted, something already well-known. Since the cry, 'the Day of Yahweh is near', has particularly deep roots in the whole cycle of tradition (cf. Isa. 13.6; Ezek. 30.4; Obad. 15; Joel 1.15; 2.1; 4.14 [3.14]; Zeph. 1.7, 14), we may ask whether this was not the stereotyped cry by which men were summoned for military service in earlier times, or a cry with which men once went into battle with Yahweh.

9 'The Message' of the Prophets

AFTER these more general theological considerations on prophecy and the way in which it was proclaimed, we must now try to describe the message of the various prophets individually. Here, it is all important not to read this message as if it consisted of timeless ideas, but to understand it as the particular word relevant to a particular hour in history, which therefore cannot be replaced by any other word. The prophetic word – far more than any of the other forms of speech used by Yahwism – has its origin in an impassioned dialogue; yet the dialogue never tries to climb into the realm of general religious truth, but instead uses even the most suspect means to tie the listening partner down to his particular time and place in order to make him understand his own situation before God. In order to reach this partner in the specific situation in which he has to make a decision and which, as stated above, cannot be replaced by any other, the prophets use every possible rhetorical device – they are not afraid to use extremely radical forms of expression or even caricature. With certain exceptions, their concern is not the objective proof of what was generally believed, but rather to be highly critical of Israel's religious traditions. Yet this, too, could be a misleading statement, for nothing was further from the prophets' minds than a theoretical solicitude about teaching for teaching's sake. Their concern was not the faith, not even the 'message': it was to deliver a specific message from Yahweh to particular men and women who, without themselves being aware of it, stood in a special situation before God. But since the prophet's partner in the dialogue (it is not simply 'the nation') is constantly changing, this allows us to admire the unexampled inner versatility and power of adaptation of the prophetic address, which, though it has in fact a minimum of 'basic thoughts' upon which it rests, yet functions as if it had a splendid abundance upon which to draw. By the same token, however, any confidence that we might have of being able to think of the message as an interconnected whole necessarily disappears. It would, nevertheless, be a mistake simply to sit back in face of this; it is, on the contrary, wise to realize from the very start that what we are in the habit of calling a prophet's 'message' is a very problematic entity. We do not gain understanding of the prophet's 'message' either by reducing the sum total of his sayings to general basic religious concepts, or by co-ordinating the separate sayings to make a synthetic whole. As was stated above, each saying was, for those to whom it was addressed, *the* word of Yahweh. There is therefore, strictly speaking, no such thing as a 'message' to which each single word was subordinate and from which each single announcement was derived; all that we have are the various individual words in which, on each specific occasion, *the* word of Yahweh was proclaimed in a different guise.[1]

Nevertheless, however bewildering the ease with which the prophets pass from one form of address to another, there are two constant factors which never fail to find a place with them all. The one is Yahweh's new word for Israel which he allowed the prophet to read off from the horizon of world-history. The other is the election tradition, within which the prophet and his hearers alike stand. The comfortable words of the tradition are, however, both called in question by the prophet's message of judgment and reconverted by him into an anti-typical new form of prediction. Thus, tensions created by three factors bring the prophet's *kerygma* into being. These are: the new eschatological word with which Yahweh addresses Israel, the old election tradition, and the personal situation, be it one which incurred penalty or one which needed comfort, of the people addressed by the prophet. It is obvious that these three factors do not all appear in the same way in each prophet; we shall, instead, find a great difference in treatment. With Amos, for example, projection of the election tradition into the realm of eschatology is almost completely absent.

[1] This is different in apocalyptic; for at every point there the total course of the great apocalyptic drama, of which the specific detail is a part, has more or less to be kept in view.

10 Amos

W E must not imagine that Amos' home, Tekoa, which lies about two hours' walk south of Bethlehem, was a remote country place, for from the time of Rehoboam onwards it had been a garrisoned fortress.[1] Amos himself was also, so far as we can judge, a man of some reputation and substance. The only reason why a man of solid peasant stock came to join the ranks of the prophets was a very remarkable call from Yahweh. The words which have given rise to so much debate, to the effect that he was no prophet ('I am, or I was, no prophet') and did not belong to any prophetic guild (Amos 7.14), are not meant as disparagement of the prophets as a class, but only to explain the strange fact that he suddenly began to speak by inspiration (Amos 7.15), though as a peasant he was not entitled so to do.[2] When, therefore, Yahweh was forced to fall back on a man from the peasantry, he did so as an emergency measure.

The prophetic call itself is a fact which needs no further discussion. The peasant Amos' call is almost certainly to be connected with the reception of the five visions (Amos 7.1-9; 8.1-3; 9.1-4). Surprisingly enough, none of these contains any explicit instruction to proclaim what he had seen. They are reports of communications made by Yahweh to Amos and to him alone; and their sequence shows the various steps he had to take before he finally realized the inevitable end. These visions record a drama between Yahweh and Amos played out in the deepest solitude. Initially, since he did not understand, Amos cast himself on Yahweh's mercy, and twice – on the occasion of the vision of the locusts and on that of the judgment by fire – he even succeeded in averting the disaster. But when it came to the burden of Israel's piled up guilt, he ceased to intercede. In the third vision, that of the plumb-line, Yahweh

[1] II Chron. 11.6.
[2] It is debated whether Amos meant to say : 'I was not a prophet, but now I am one', or whether he wished to repudiate all connection with the prophetic profession.

anticipates the prophet in a word which he speaks concerning it, and from then on Amos begins to yield. The vision of the basket of fruit brings the word: 'the end has come upon my people', and to this Amos listens in silence; while the final vision, the most circumstantial, makes known that Yahweh is to let no one, not one single person, escape from the coming calamity, which is perhaps to take the form of an earthquake.

This series of visions is virtually isolated in prophetic literature. Unlike Isaiah or Ezekiel, Amos seems to have no older tradition on which he depends for the contents of his visions. There is also a remarkable absence of any very close connection between these and his message; for the final catastrophe of Israel's exile which he spoke of again and again and in unmistakable terms in the prophecies is not even hinted at here. Obviously, all that was initially communicated to the prophet was the bare fact of the end and judgment; certainty as to its manner only came under special conditions, and clearly not without reflection and observation on his own part. Still less do the words which describe Yahweh as roaring from Zion, his voice penetrating far and wide throughout the land and causing disturbances in the world of nature (Amos 1.2), speak to any human ear which had to note a particular communication and pass it on; rather, all that we are told of is the sound of a voice of divine wrath which has yet to be clearly articulated. The greater part of Amos's message must, then, be ascribed to his own pondering on the situation which he saw before him. He had first to put his own stamp on everything he had learned from Yahweh, for it constantly needed interpretation *ad hominem*. Such knowledge, as we have already observed, must have given the man to whom it was entrusted a unique status far above any human grade of honour, and placed him in a position where all social and sacral distinctions of rank became irrelevant. What is even more important, however, is that intensive intellectual process which must have followed such a revelation. Amos went about amongst a people who had been condemned to death; and as a result his environment at once assumed a different appearance and he became acutely aware of the abuses around him. Thus we see Amos particularly engaged in the task of giving convincing reasons for the coming disaster and, as he goes about his business, we see the man's vitality and intellectual acumen brilliantly at work. No doubt fresh oracles kept coming to him and inspiring him, but the contribution made by his own alert mind must not be underrated.

Since Amos was a Judean, we must assume that he took his stand
on the election traditions of the South, those attaching to David
and Zion. Unfortunately, there are no real clues to help us to
determine his own personal attitude to the Exodus tradition which
was the most cherished one in the Kingdom of Israel. Was it so
alien to him that he could only regard it as positively heretical and
illegitimate? When he spoke to the North Israelites about their
traditions, did he do so only as an outsider? In view of the urgency,
the ardour even, of the historical retrospect in Amos 2.9-11, this
is far from likely. In particular, the insistency with which he pins
his hearers down to these traditions, and the conclusions which he
draws from their indifference to them, suggest that he, as well as
they themselves, took these saving data very seriously. Israel's
election is in fact the very reason given for Yahweh's imminent
act of judgment (Amos 3.2). We have no understanding of Amos'
preaching at all unless we note the way in which he, over and over
again, comes to grips with the election concept, and how it was
the nerve of a great part of his message.

Amos was also concerned with the changes and tensions in
Israel's political world. David's empire did not endure. The Philistines regained their independence, as did the Edomites and Moabites;
and the secession of Aram-Damascus had particularly momentous
consequences. Certainly, under Jeroboam II (786–746) the Kingdom
of Israel was enjoying another time of peace, and had in fact increased its power to some extent, but the Assyrians had appeared
on the fringe of the Palestinian scene long before this, and the year
after Jeroboam's death saw the accession of the great Tiglath
Pileser, whose campaigns ushered in the beginning of the end for
Israel. Even the few references to political matters which Amos
does make are enough to leave us amazed at the clearsightedness of
his observation of history. How accurate he was when he connected the so-called 'Aramaean migration' with the entirely different movement of the 'sea-peoples' (Amos 2.7)! Both thrusts occurred
at nearly the same time (i.e., c 1200), and political conditions in
Palestine were fundamentally affected by them for long afterwards.
The long poem comprising Amos 1.3ff. supplies us with acute
comments on what was going on within the Palestinian national
group. The prophet has his own opinion of the value of minor
successes against Damascus, such as the capture of Lo-Debar and
Karnaim (Amos 6.13). His gaze ranged wider, too. He spoke of what
befell the north Syrian cities of Calneh and Hamath; and when he

cryptically announced exile 'beyond Damascus', of course he had the Assyrians in mind (Amos 6.2; 5.27). In his keen interest in political matters, Amos must have been head and shoulders above his contemporaries.

It would be a complete misunderstanding, however, if the modern reader were to consider the prophet as a detached observer who foresaw the inevitable march of events in the realm of world politics. Certainly, Amos's actual prophecy of the future can be reduced to the simple statement that Israel is to suffer a calamitous military defeat and to be taken into exile.[3] Just as certainly, concrete observation of the way in which Assyria was accustomed to treat her subject peoples contributed to this picture. Yet Assyria was of little importance. It is no accident that the name never appears in the text as we have it today.[4] The culminating point of Amos' message is that Israel now has to deal direct with Yahweh; not the Yahweh of the sanctuaries and pilgrimages, but an unknown Yahweh who was coming to perform new deeds upon Israel. It must have been this closeness to Yahweh, the 'I, Yahweh' of the coming events, that most surprised and upset Amos' audience. 'I smite the winter house' (Amos 3.15), 'I take you into exile' (Amos 5.27), 'I pass through the midst of you' (Amos 5.17), 'I rise against the house of Jeroboam with the sword' (Amos 7.9), 'I destroy it from the surface of the ground' (Amos 9.8)! Any hope that Yahweh would leave a remnant was regally discounted in a discussion (Amos 3.12); the scraps of the torn animal are the proof that it is dead, cf. Ex. 22.12 [13]). Amos hardly ever spoke in such a way as to suggest that Yahweh had not as yet pronounced his final sentence on Israel: but there must have been occasions when, in the company of a few chosen men, even he indulged in a fainthearted 'perhaps' (Amos 5.15, 6).

All that Amos learned in his visions was that Yahweh would no longer forgive his people. But Israel's actual offences were not named by Yahweh – they were left to the prophet to interpret. Almost without exception, the reasons for the coming judgment are to be found in the diatribes – that is, in terms of form-criticism, in the section which the prophet himself prefixes to his threat and which he uses in every case to direct the oracle to those whom it particularly concerns. The reader, therefore, inevitably feels an unevenness in Amos' preaching. While the subject-matter of the

---

[3] Military disasters: Amos 2.13ff.; 3.11; 5.3; 6,9f., 14; 7.9; 8.3; 9.10.
[4] In Amos 3.9 'Assyria' is generally read instead of 'Ashdod'.

threats tends to be rather monotonous, the diatribes reveal a really rich variety of observation, of striking snapshots, and of examples of normal or abnormal human behaviour. Each one of these glimpses of the full life of humanity is intensely alive, and is yet at the same time ominous and foreboding. Little is gained by attempting to order and inter-relate them, for each unit really stands on its own. Nevertheless, it is not an inadmissible simplification to say that the charges point in two directions, contempt of God's law and religious complacency.

1. The poem against foreign nations revealed the strength of Amos' reaction to breaches of the unwritten law of international relations – and not simply to those breaches which brought suffering to Israel. In this respect, the stanza against Gaza is of particular interest, since its subject is injuries done by the Philistines to the Edomites, that is to say, injuries which did not affect Israel at all (Amos 1.6-8). Amos' Yahweh watches over the established orders of international law not only in Israel but also among the other nations, and whenever they are broken he imposes a historical punishment upon the culprits. Israel's breaches are, of course, immeasurably more serious, since she was the nation with whom above all others he had made himself intimate (Amos 3.2). Actually, Amos shows us a society whose social life is cleft in two – a property-owning and therefore economically self-sufficient upper class lived at the expense of the 'little people' (Amos 5.11; 8.6), and the wrongs done were particularly apparent in the administration of justice, since only full citizens could sit and speak in the law courts; at the same time, however, as owners of property, these men were interested parties and, often enough, judges in their own cases; slaves, foreigners, orphans, and widows had no one to uphold their just claims. Bribery was the order of the day (Amos 5.7ff., 12), and there was also dishonesty in business (Amos 8.5b). At the same time, however, great zeal was shown in religious matters. People went on pilgrimages (Amos. 4.4f., 5.4), and took part in noisy festivals (Amos 5.21ff.). In Amos' eyes, however, these were provocations of Yahweh. Sacrifices offered by people who scorned his will as expressed in law could have no value in Yahweh's sight.

Amos says absolutely nothing about the way in which Yahweh's will as expressed in law became known to Israel. Yet the way in which he raises God's claims suggests that his audience would at once acknowledge their validity. He never appeals to any tradition, written or oral, to support their authority. Nevertheless, it is highly unlikely that he based himself on no other authority than 'the ethical element'. Rather, as recent research has made clear, these fixed orders are to be found point by point in the older tradition of sacral law, especially in the Book of the Covenant (Ex. 20.22–23.19). Now, comparison of the charges brought by Amos with the older legal tradition makes it plain that Amos ties his contemporaries down to the simple, obvious, literal sense of these commandments. It cannot properly be said that he made them more radical, and that on his lips their content is intensified, given a keener edge. Yet, in spite of this, the whole thing feels different. There is a new factor, the element of threat, which questions the continued existence of the whole people of Israel. The old commandments were regarded as possible to fulfil, the apodeictic formulae stood almost as acts of confession; at all events, in the earlier period, reflection on whether the commandments could or could not be fulfilled had not become widespread. There must always have been individuals who broke the commandments; these the law dealt with. Now, however, at one fell swoop not individuals but the whole of Israel – or at least her leading men – were sharply accused of flagrant breaches of the law. This was something entirely new.[5] We cannot reconstruct the history of popular understanding of the commandments, so we do not know whether Amos' attitude was an entirely new departure or whether there had been considerable preparation for his ideas. Whatever the case may be, we do see how with him the commandments which Israel had once received from Yahweh's hands with love and praise, because the people saw in them evidence of his faithfulness towards her, now turned against her. Even Israel's right to profess her loyalty to these commandments (as in the ritual of the liturgies at the gate) was called in question by the prophet's charges.

2. Since the prophet's polemic, and especially that of Amos himself, is couched in very radical terms, it is difficult to reconstruct the spiritual and religious climate of the time on the basis of this source, and yet we have no other. Amos gives us a picture of a thoughtless upper class complacent in its material prosperity. As we listen to him upbraiding it for its luxury, we have to remember that all asceticism and any kind of suspicion of material good was really quite alien to Yahwism as such. Eating and drinking, taking one's enjoyment, in a word, every material blessing that enhanced the

---

[5] Elijah probably only attacked the royal house and its protegés, the cult officials.

quality of life, were accepted in simple thankfulness from Yahweh's hand. It can only have been extreme indulgence which necessitated the raising of such complaints about the enjoyment of material things. Amos reproaches those who are 'secure on the mountain of Samaria' with not 'being sick' because of the 'ruin of Joseph' (Amos 6.6). Like so many others of his pregnant enunciations, this matchless statement is not more closely defined. It is probably the havoc in social life which is particularly in the prophet's mind. At all events, it is a quality of heart and mind that he finds lacking in the upper classes; the breach of particular commandments is certainly not in question, for there was no commandment which forbade reclining on ornate beds or anointing oneself with choicest oil, any more than there was one which obliged people to be grieved at the 'ruin of Joseph'. What Amos refers to, therefore, is a general attitude, the way men should live together, and jointly and severally be fellow-sufferers in the experiences of God's people. Indeed, did not Amos here unconsciously use himself and his own suffering and injuries as the criterion? His contemporaries were all in the grip of a cruel delusion. They looked for a 'Day of Yahweh', when Yahweh would rise up to vanquish their enemies, and did not fear the night which Yahweh's coming was to bring.[6] They knew of Israel's election by Yahweh, and no doubt they took comfort in the fact of it, as guaranteeing them salvation, but they never thought that this very thing would bring them so much the closer into the light of the divine holiness (Amos 3.2). For men who had become so complacent, even the great event of the Exodus had to be reduced to the rank of a part of God's general guidance of history; the saving aspect of that divine redemptive act had to be extinguished for them (Amos 9.7). But they had no inkling of their true position *vis-à-vis* Yahweh! Time and time again, with one calamity after another, famine, drought, failure of the harvest, failure in war, and epidemics, Yahweh kept knocking at their door, but they paid no heed (Amos 4.6ff.). Now, however, this time of indirect warning is over. Israel must now hold herself in readiness to meet her God in person – Amos was no doubt thinking of the judgment at which the 'I, Yahweh' mentioned above would himself appear on the scene.

At the end of the book of Amos comes the prophecy of the future raising up of the 'booth' of David that is fallen (Amos 9.11f.). Grave

[6] The new thing is not that Amos spoke of darkness at the Day of Yahweh, but that he believed that the darkness would also threaten Israel.

doubts are raised as to its genuineness, and this was, of course, inevitable as long as Amos' prophecy was regarded as the deposit of some kind of 'prophetic religion', the outcome of spiritual struggle and personal conviction. If Amos' prophecy had been of this nature, then we might have expected it to be free of major contradictions. Things wear a different look, however, once we see the prophets as men who addressed themselves to definite sacral traditions as these still survived in the nation, and once we regard their whole preaching as a unique discussion of these ancient inherited traditions, a discussion which submitted them to criticism and made them relevant for the prophets' own day and generation. Now, Amos was a Judean. Would it not surprise us if there had been absolutely no mention of the traditions in which he was most at home? This Messianic oracle is distinctly restrained in the matter of its content. There is no hint of any sensational upheaval in world events as a result of which the heavens and the earth are shaken (cf. Hag. 2.20ff.). The sole thing mentioned is the rebuilding of the fallen house, the restoration of an edifice whose foundations were laid long ago. And what will thereafter follow is an integration of the old Davidic empire, which in the interval has suffered severe damage. Yahweh is not to blot out what he once 'built'; in particular, he is not to surrender his claim upon the nations 'who had been called by his name'.

11 Hosea

I T was at one time generally believed that we knew more about Hosea's personal circumstances than about those of the other prophets – except, of course, for Jeremiah. But this idea collapses once we interpret the much-discussed pericope containing the symbolic representation of his marriage (Hos. 1–3) as an account of a prophetic symbolic action, that is to say, as a part of his preaching; for this limits any attempt to interpret it biographically. In actual fact, the book of Hosea has extremely little help to give us about the prophet himself. Practically the only thing certain is that he lived and worked during the calamitous last years of the Northern Kingdom up to about the time of the capture of Samaria by the Assyrians (721). We know as little about his home as we do of the place where he made his appearance, or of any conflicts in which he may have been engaged, or of other personal circumstances. It has been assumed, with some probability, that he was closely connected with the Levitical movement in the Northern Kingdom, which, like the prophetic one, had been pushed aside in the general Canaanization; both reforming groups fostered and preserved the old traditions of Yahwism.

As to the general tenor of Hosea's message, the first impression it makes upon expositors is the extraordinary difference between it and that of, say, Amos or Isaiah; and this difference they try to pin-point. But its really disturbing feature is the unique factor in it. Hosea is the only 'writing prophet' of the Northern Kingdom. This means that there is no one with whom we can compare him, and that we cannot separate what is his own in his message from those matters of style, subject-matter, and prophetic tradition which he may have inherited. For his writings allow us to gather that the situation in the Northern Kingdom was, even for a prophet, very different from that in, say, the Jerusalem of Isaiah, and that, to a very great extent, it had its own peculiar problems. Only two basic data specific to the north need be mentioned; the disintegration of patriarchal Yahwism in the Canaanite fertility cult, and the pecu-

liar political and governmental system which existed there, which
meant that even a prophet's intervention in public affairs and their
problems took on an essentially different aspect from that in the
Southern Kingdom. These are also the two factors which give us
a clear picture of Hosea.

There is a further difficulty. Hosea's message is different from
that of his contemporaries Isaiah, Micah, or Amos in respect of
form. Instead of short, clearly-contoured units easily detachable
from one another, what are most prominent in Hosea are larger
entities with a relatively uniform subject-matter. The messenger
formula is certainly still found, but with Hosea the process of com-
bining short sayings into larger units seems to have gone on side by
side with the permanent establishment (perhaps in writing) of the
component parts of the tradition.[1] On the other hand, the borrowing from non-religious literary categories which is so marked a
feature of Amos or Isaiah is almost completely absent in Hosea.
The result of these factors is to give Hosea's way of speaking, taken
as a whole, a much greater uniformity. Using his diction to draw
conclusions about his person, we are given the impression that
Hosea was a man of extremely strong feelings. His preaching, more
than that of any other prophet, is governed by personal emotions,
by love, anger, disappointment, and even by the ambivalence between two opposite sentiments. Since the prophet lends this emotional ardour to the words of God himself – or, to put it better,
since Yahweh catches the prophet up into his emotions ¬ in Hosea
the divine word receives a glow and a fervour the intensity of
which is characteristic of the message of this prophet alone.

Hosea's whole preaching is rooted in the saving history. It might
almost be said that he only feels safe when he can base his arguments in history.[2] Yahweh is Israel's God 'from the land of Egypt'
(Hos. 12.10 [9]; 13.4); by the prophet Moses, Yahweh brought Israel
up from Egypt (Hos. 12.14 [13]). This early history of Israel was
the time when Yahweh was able to give her his entire love (Hos.
11.4). What an appalling contrast the present shows! Israel has forsaken Yahweh like a faithless wife who runs after her lovers. Hosea
depicted this completely subverted relationship of Israel to Yah-

---

[1] The thrice repeated 'therefore' within the large unit of Hos. 2.4ff. (vv. 8,
11, 16 [2ff. (vv. 6, 9, 14)]) allows us to conclude that originally smaller units
have here been deliberately shaped into a large composition. The original
units, which must be presupposed in Hosea's case also, can consequently be
much less clearly separated off.
[2] Hos. 1.4; 2.10; 6.7; 9.9, 10; 10.1, 9, 11f.; 11.1-4; 12.4f., 10, 13f.; 13.4-6.

weh under the image of his own marriage, and used the symbolic names of the children born of it to announce the message of Yahweh's wrath and his turning away from his people.

The passages in question raise a considerable number of exegetical problems. The existence of one account in the third person (Hos. 1) and another in the first (Hos. 3) is itself remarkable, and the explanation is certainly not that both of them are reports of the same incident. Since the second story bears quite another hallmark – its subject is the wife's re-education – we must assume two successive events. In this case, the same woman is the subject of both accounts. It is now generally accepted that the stories represent an actual happening, and are not merely an allegory as was formerly believed – on the grounds that God could never have ordered so objectionable an action! Incidentally, the Hebrew word for adulteress does not signify a woman of particularly depraved moral character, but a woman who took part in the Canaanite fertility rites. In fact the woman is not exceptional, but serves as a typical representation of Israel. There is less agreement on the question as to how far the texts afford a glimpse of the prophet's own personal relationships and experience. The view has often been put forward that bitter experience in his married life, particularly his unhappy love for his faithless wife, taught the prophet understanding of God's love for his people, and in retrospect made him aware that this marriage was divinely predestined. In my own view, the two chapters provide far too few data to allow of such a psychological and rationalizing interpretation. The primary thing was not an intimate personal experience, but Yahweh's command to perform a symbolic action. On this the text gives sufficiently clear information; but it has practically nothing to tell us about what lies beyond this 'vocational' task and its execution – something which might possibly give us some biographical information. More particularly, Hosea had absolutely no need to look to his own private life to find a symbol for the relationship between Yahweh and Israel. The idea of marriage between a deity and an earthly partner had long been familiar to him and his contemporaries through the rites of the Canaanite nature religion (the marriage of Baal to the earth is an example).

This symbolic action, Hosea's marriage, is only one part of what the prophet proclaimed; yet, especially when it is taken along with its closely related context (Hos. 2.4-25 [2-23]), it gives the keynote for practically all the topics characteristic of Hosea – his passionate indignation at Israel's disloyalty, her approaching punishment, and also what lay beyond these, and about which it was difficult to be precise – the hint of a fresh saving activity, and indeed of an entirely fresh start with Israel, to which God's love impels him. Hosea was the first to describe Israel's submersion in the Canaanite nature religion as 'harlotry', 'leaving Yahweh in order to play the harlot'; the term expresses both the idea of the indissolubility of Yahweh's covenant and abhorrence of the fertility rites and sacred prostitution of the cult of Baal.[3] Yet, while Yahwism's reaction to this sexual aspect of the nature religion was particularly sensitive, this was not the only reason which brought the prophet on the scene: he was also prompted by Israel's general breach of faith, her violation of the first and also the second commandments (Hos. 4.12, 17; 8.4-6; 13.2). The trouble was that Israel's husbandry was prospering, but she believed that it was the Baals whom she had to thank for these blessings. Israel 'does not know that it was I who gave [her] the grain, the wine, and the oil, and lavished upon her silver and gold' (Hos. 2.10 [8]). These amazing words represent Yahweh as the bestower of all the precious gifts of the soil. Israel, however, misunderstood both the giver and the gifts; she failed to see that she had been brought into a *status confessionis* before Yahweh because of these gifts; rather, she fell victim to a mythic divinization of husbandry and of its numinous, chthonic origins. The Rechabites followed a different and much simpler course when they were faced with just such a hopeless perversion of the blessings of the soil. They embarked on a programme of radical separation, and roundly denied that use of the products of the land was compatible with obedience to Yahweh.

Hosea clearly grades the charges which he brings against the parties responsible. Because of his interest in cultic matters, he inevitably laid a particular measure of failure at the door of the priesthood (Hos. 4.6, 9; 5.1; 6.9). They – though this is also true of the whole nation – lack the proper 'knowledge of God'. Unfortunately, this term, so characteristic of Hosea, is not easy to translate. 'Knowledge of God' really points too much in the direction of what is theoretical in the problem of religious and philosophical epistemology. On the evidence of its occurrences, however, the term must also mean something much more specific than simply a general inner disposition towards God; in fact, it seems actually to convey the essence of the priestly service, for in Hos. 4.6 it is parallel to *torah* It must, therefore, describe a particular form of knowledge of God which, to her hurt, Israel had lost; the term will therefore have to be related in particular to familiarity with the historical acts

[3] Hos. 1.2; 2.7 [5]; 3.3; 4.10, 12, 13, 14, 15, 18; 5.3; 9.1.

of Yahweh. It could also be put in this way – Israel had lost her profession of loyalty to Yahweh.[4]

The apparent split between religion and politics in Hosea is a modern distinction. For Hosea himself, living more fully than any other prophet in the old sacral thinking which saw life as a whole, Israel's political experience was in no way on a different plane. We must again remind ourselves that the charismatic structure of monarchy in the Kingdom of Israel was actually dependent on the active co-operation of the prophets. Thus, in his keen participation in political affairs, particularly in the revolutions at the court of Samaria, Hosea acted the part of a genuine prophet of the Northern Kingdom, and continued the line of action already illustrated by Elisha. Of course, a radical change had come over the situation as compared with the time of Elisha and Jehu inasmuch as Yahweh wants to have nothing more to do with the ever more frequent palace revolutions and coronations which took place in these last years before the fall of Samaria. 'They made kings, but not through me' (Hos. 8.4). While the people still believed that in these coronations in Samaria they could see Yahweh in action as the protector of his people, Hosea recognized precisely in these political events that Yahweh's judgment upon Israel was already in full sweep. 'I give you a king in my anger and take him away in my wrath' (Hos. 13.11). This is, in fact, quite one of the most essential elements in Hosea's view – while his fellows eagerly strive to repair the ravages in the state, and to guard themselves against threats by taking political measures, Hosea sees that the root of the trouble goes much deeper. It is God himself who has turned against them: the nation is suffering from God, who is seated like an ulcer in its belly.

> But as for me, I am as pus to Ephraim
> and as worm grub to the house of Judah.
> But when Ephraim saw his sickness,
> and Judah his ulcer,
> then Ephraim went to Assyria and sent to the great king.
> But he is not able to cure you,
> or rid you of your ulcer.
>
> (Hos. 5.12f.)

When he speaks of the judgment itself, which Israel cannot possibly

[4] Cf. here particularly Hos. 13.4: 'I, Yahweh, am your God from the land of Egypt; you have no knowledge of God except by me.'

avoid, he gives only brief general hints. The political and historical side of the process is seldom outlined very clearly. Once or twice the prophet speaks of disaster at the hands of enemies (Hos. 8.3; 10.14f.; 11.6; 13.15), and sometimes of the prospect of deportation. In this connection, the thought of Assyria is paralleled, surprisingly enough, by that of a 'return' to Egypt (Hos. 9.3, 6; 8.13; 11.5). On the one hand, Hosea follows a very old line of thought in representing this judgment as brought upon Israel by herself, that is to say, by her evil deeds. She is so firmly entangled in the despotic power of the evil which she herself unleashed that she can no longer extricate herself from it (Hos. 5.4f.). 'Their deeds encompass them'; they are so completely blockaded by the evil they have brought about that no real freedom of movement is left them (Hos. 7.2). This concept of the 'sphere of action which creates fate' does not, however, in the least imply that it is simply an impersonal law which is working out on Israel. On the contrary, it is Yahweh, who now remembers her deeds (Hos. 7.2; 8.13; 9.9) – they are 'before his face' (Hos. 7.2). Indeed, it is the fact that the whole force of the prophet's utterance is channelled into showing that Yahweh himself is now rising up against his people that makes his descriptions of the concrete accompaniments of the judgments rather blurred. Yahweh is to chastize his people (Hos. 5.2); he will be a lion to them (Hos. 5.14); he captures them like a hunter (Hos. 5.2, 12; 7.12). Compared with this 'I' who is to engross and determine the whole compass of history from then on – 'I, even I, rend' (Hos. 5.14b) – the actual way in which the judgment will take historical form almost loses all interest.

In view of prophecies foretelling such a merciless darkness, the accompaniment of Israel's judgment, one hesitates to go on to discuss Hosea's prophecies of salvation; for this gives the impression that the almost intolerable gloom to which he continually alludes is not after all the final word, with the result that the darkness is lightened. Can we be sure, however, that the men to whom he announced the judgment and those to whom he spoke of the coming salvation are the same in both cases? It is enough to say that – no matter to whom or for whom – Hosea quite undoubtedly also spoke of a coming salvation. More than this, he was himself aware of the paradox; he saw how the struggle between wrath and love came to be resolved in God's own heart. This led him to an utterance whose daring is unparalleled in the whole of prophecy:

How could I give you up, Ephraim, abandon you, Israel?
My heart recoils within me; all my compassion is set on fire;
I will not execute my fierce anger, I will not again destroy Ephraim,
For I am God, not man, a Holy One in your midst. . . .

(Hos. 11.8f.)

Hosea gives us further assistance in understanding his juxtaposition of judgment and salvation: it is his idea of training, which plays a greater role with him than with any other of the prophets.[5] In Hosea, Yahweh's dealings with Israel seem at times to be something like an educative plan aimed primarily at setting the erring ones on the right path by depriving them of certain things and circumscribing their actions. This leads – at least in one or two passages – to the achievement of something like a rational balance between God's action in judgment and his action in salvation.

Many days shall the Israelites remain
without king, without officials, without sacrifice,
without ephod and without teraphim;
then the Israelites will return
and seek their God.

(Hos. 3.4f.)

The things of which Yahweh is to deprive his people are so numerous, and so important for Israel's life, that it is impossible to say what kind of existence Hosea envisaged for them in this interim period; they are not only to be without the fixed orders of civil life, but even without those of the cult! To elucidate the matter we may bring in the passage from the great poem on Israel's re-education in which Yahweh's plan for her is disclosed in terms so intimate as to be almost overwhelming. After blocking his people's way to the Baals, he purposes to 'allure' them, he intends to 'speak tenderly' to them, and to bring them again into the wilderness (Hos. 2.16 [14]). This means nothing less than that God is going to take them back to the place where he originally began with them, back, as it were, to the beginning of the whole road. There, in the wilderness, no gods of fertility can come between Yahweh and his people; there Israel will be thrown back completely upon Yahweh; Yahweh will have her all to himself, in order that from the desert he can once more grant her the land. Hosea thus sees the new saving event as typologically prefigured in the old one, though, of course, everything that marred the first saving event and all its imperfections, which the older saving history did not conceal, are to be cancelled

[5] Hos. 2.11ff. [9ff]; 3.3-5; 11.1ff.

out by the marvels of the final one. The valley of Achor – the place of sacrilege and of the stoning of Achan – is to become 'the door of hope' (Hos. 2.17 [15]; cf. Josh. 7), and Yahweh is to be betrothed anew to Israel. A final oracle has a form which suggests that of an incantation, inasmuch as it depicts the free circulation of the powers of blessing which emanate from God; there is no break in the tightly closed circle (God – heaven – earth – the blessings of the soil – Israel) for the possible entry of Baal and his functions (Hos. 2.23ff. [21ff.]).

The word of promise at the end of the book, which is couched in very antiquated, almost mythological, metaphors, also speaks wholly in terms of the natural world. Yahweh will love Israel, he will be a green cypress, and dew from Israel, and Israel will blossom and strike root, and her fragrance will be like that of Lebanon (Hos. 14.5-8 [4-7]). It is a remarkable fact that the same prophet who thinks so emphatically in terms of saving history can at the same time move Yahweh's relationship to Israel over into the horizons of an almost plant-like natural growth and blossoming, where all the drama of the saving history ebbs out as if in a profound quiet.

12 Isaiah and Micah

THE preaching of Isaiah represents the theological high-water mark of the whole Old Testament. Such at least must be the judgment of all who regard the theological range encompassed by one single man as more impressive than any body of anonymous tradition, however vast. Not one of the other prophets approaches Isaiah in intellectual vigour or, more particularly, in the magnificent sweep of his ideas. Even the ideas which he took over from tradition were usually remodelled in the most daring way. Isaiah's versatility is only fully apparent when we remember that as a man of the ancient world his whole intellectual apparatus was very much more bound by tradition than ours is. So great is the supple power of his message to adapt itself to every change in the political situation that it can show us the specific historical situation simply in the clear-cut contours of the items of the messages themselves, just as in a photographer's negative. Apart from one or two quite meagre biographical references, we only have his style from which to form some idea of him as a man. Yet, what a wealth is here disclosed! Its compass ranges from the incisive diatribe to texts which express depth of feeling with a stately amplitude, from the curt conciseness of an oracle to the sonorous hymn that revels in words.[1] The chief characteristic of everything Isaiah says is, however, moderation; and it is this restraint, preserved even in moments of deep passion, which gives us such a strong impression of nobility in the man. Though we have no exact statement of this, the most obvious assumption is that Isaiah belonged to Jerusalem, and was therefore a townsman. We would expect to find him among the higher ranks of society there. Only such a station as this could account for his freedom of intercourse with the king or with high officials. He was married, and had children to whom he gave symbolic names (Isa. 7.3; 8.3). We know nothing more of his personal circumstances; there is no evidence that he held formal office in connection with

[1] Isaiah's similies, with their striking points of comparison, form a distinctive side of his rhetoric: Isa. 1.8; 7.4; 18.4; 29.8, 11f.; 30.13, 17; 31.4.

the temple – indeed, there are weighty arguments against this
theory.

Whereas in the ninth century the Kingdom of Israel was in constant conflict with enemies who sometimes represented a serious
danger to her, and had to defend herself against the Syrians, the
Philistines, the Moabites, and even the Assyrians (Ahab fought
against an Assyrian army in Karkar in 853), the Kingdom of Judah
was spared such serious threats. This trend continued in the eighth
century and only changed with the end of the reign of Uzziah,
which approximately coincided with the accession of the great
Tiglath Pileser (745–727)[2]. Significantly enough, Isaiah's call came at
this turning point (Isa. 6.1). In a very short time the Assyrians were
to appear on the immediate horizons of Judah : in 734 Tiglath
Pileser advanced along the coastal plain of Palestine as far as the
frontiers of Egypt. In the following year Judah was to be compelled
by main force to join an anti-Assyrian coalition. In the ensuing
Syro-Ephraimitic war Jerusalem, of course, suffered nothing worse
than siege; for the Judeans appealed to the Assyrians themselves
for help (II Kings 15.37, 16.5ff.). Tiglath Pileser did in fact then turn
his attention to the Kingdom of Israel and took away a considerable part of its territory (II Kings 15.29). Then in 732 came the end
of Syria-Damascus as an independent power, and in 721, after the
capture of Samaria, Israel was incorporated into the Assyrian provincial system. This made Assyria Judah's nearest neighbour : the
imperial boundary ran only a few miles to the north of Jerusalem!
From this time onwards there could be no more peace for the still
independent nations of Palestine. Three events stand out in the pro-
longed effort to maintain independence from Assyria by means of
coalitions and, particularly, of Egyptian help. The first was the
rebellion of Hamath and of King Hanun of Gaza, who was in
alliance with Egypt, c 720. The Assyrian victory at Rapihu ended
that hope. The movement towards revolt in the years 713–711,
whose moving spirit was Ashdod, involved the Kingdom of Judah
much more closely; for in this case, under Hezekiah, she broke off
her allegiance to Assyria, whose vassal she had been since 732, and
joined a movement in which Edom and Moab also took part. This
rebellion, too, Assyria stamped out by sending Tartan against it
(Isa. 20.1). Judah was once again successful in escaping with im-
punity, but unfortunately we do not know how. In contrast to
these, however, the third movement of rebellion, which broke out
in Askelon at the time of a change on the throne of Nineveh (705)
and in connection with which Judah was again a partner, was destined to lead to a great calamity for her and for Jerusalem. Admittedly, it was not till 701 that Sennacherib appeared in Palestine, and

[2] The year of king Uzziah's death is not certain; it may have been 735.

even then, to begin with, he confined his attention to the coastal plain, and to reducing the Philistines; but after his defeat of the Egyptians also near Altaku, the coalition's power was broken, and there followed the well-known capitulation of Hezekiah, which cost him the greater part of his kingdom (II Kings 18.13-16).

As we have already said, historical events are very exactly reflected in Isaiah's prophecy. The last on which he commented was the fall of Jerusalem in 701 (Isa. 22.1ff.; 1.7-9). Of course, Isaiah saw the history of his own time in colours entirely different from the modern historian. Perhaps his prophetic view of it would come out more clearly if we did what we actually can do and presented his preaching not in its chronological sequence, but according to its roots in tradition. It can be shown, of course, that, wide-ranging and comprehensive as his message is, it rests on a quite small number of religious concepts, all of them furnished to him by tradition, and in particular by the Jerusalem tradition.

Like Amos, Isaiah watches inexorably over the divine law of which he is spokesman. He carries forward Amos's indictments of every form of miscarriage of justice and of exploitation of the weak on so broad a front and with such passion that we may fairly assume that the eighth-century prophets must already have fallen heir to a certain tradition, a heritage which furnished them with the subjects on which prophets spoke. Isaiah's concern for the divine law cannot be stressed too strongly.[3] It is society's attitude to this law which determines whether its relationship to God is in good order. For Isaiah, the administration of justice displays most clearly man's attitude to God; and this explains why his predictions are full of references to a Jerusalem with irreproachable judges and an anointed one who is a guarantor of justice (Isa. 1.26; 11.3ff.). In his eyes, the divine law is the greatest saving blessing. In this connection, the modern reader has to remember that in Isaiah's time legal decisions lay in the hands of the general body of citizens, and were not the concern of professional law-officers.

What we have so far seen – and we should also remember the cry, 'Obedience, not sacrifice' (Isa. 1.10-17) – strongly reminds us

---

[3] This is already apparent in the use of the terms 'righteousness' and 'justice', which have a central function in Isaiah's preaching: 'righteousness': Isa. 1.21, 26, 27; 5.7, 16, 23; 9.6 [7]; 10.22; 28.17; 'justice': Isa. 1.17, 21, 27; 4.4; 5.7, 16; 9.6 [7]; 10.2; 16.5; 28.6, 17.

of Amos, and also of Micah.[4] Nevertheless, Isaiah's concern for law has one or two features that are absent in Amos. The passages cited above, which deal with the restored city of God and the rule of his anointed, in themselves show clearly that in Isaiah's eyes the real significance of the divine law does not lie in this law in itself: it only becomes significant in wider, i.e., political, contexts. Quite a number of Isaiah's utterances reveal a remarkable concentration of thought about questions concerning the national life, that is to say, a concern for the forms of government appropriate to a society whose founder is Yahweh, and also for the necessary offices.[5] In this connection, he never once thinks in terms of the amphictyony; first and foremost, he thinks of the chosen people as a city state. At the *eschaton* Jerusalem is to be restored as a city state, complete with all its officials (Isa. 1.26), and in the city state the delivered are to find refuge (Isa. 14.32). As will presently be shown more clearly, all that Isaiah has to say about Israel's deliverance and renewal rests on this city state concept. As token of this keen interest in the problems of state affairs, we need only refer to Isa. 3.1-5, where Isaiah conjures up something almost like a vision of the complete dissolution of the civil order. With the disappearance of the duly appointed officials, the judges, the officers in the army, and the elders, anarchy breaks in. Youngsters and political failures rise up from the dregs of the populace to become officers of state; 'the youth is insolent to the man grey-haired with age and the scoundrel to the honourable', and people seek a man to 'rule over this heap of ruin'. These wider contexts of the life of the city state are the place where Isaiah's charges concerning the violation of the divine law are at home.

There is, however, one striking feature peculiarly Isaiah's own, namely the fact that these charges are not only, as in Amos, directed *ad hoc* against the specific transgressors, but are sometimes set in a wider context, that of the saving history. Thus, in Isa. 1.2f. Yah-

---

[4] Isaiah and Micah are particularly close in their opposition to the *latifundia* economy of the ruling classes in Jerusalem, in whose hands the hereditary land of many impoverished peasants was joined together (Isa. 5.8; Micah 2.1-5). Micah, of course, differs from Isaiah in that he envisages the complete blotting out of Jerusalem from the pages of history (Micah 1.5; 3.12), and, as a Judean who lived in the country, looks for the 'assembly of Yahweh' to restore the patriarchal arrangements for land tenure.

[5] A study of the administration and offices of the Jerusalem of the time would derive important material from Isaiah: 'judge' Isa. 1.26; 3.2; 'leader' Isa. 1.10; 3.6f.; 22.3; 'governors' Isa. 3.12; 'major domo' Isa. 22.15; 'steward' Isa. 22.15; 'prince' Isa. 1.23; 3.3, 14; 'patron' Isa. 9.5 [6]; 22.21.

weh complains that his people have renounced their obedience to
him. This oracle, however, is given the form of a charge made by
a father who, in terms of Deut. 21.18ff., has recourse to the last
desperate expedient of handing over a rebellious son to the jurisdiction of the civil court. Here, a long road in history – Yahweh
shows what trouble he has had in bringing up his child – has come
to a completely negative end. In Isa. 1.21-26 the road runs in an
opposite direction, from woe to weal; yet here, too, the violation
of the commandments has its place in a comprehensive divine design for history. This historical perspective, within which the divine
disappointment at the demoralization in law is set, is shown with
particular clarity in Isa. 5.1-7 – again in allegorical form. The poem
is short: but consider the detailed description of the man's pains-
taking work in his vineyard – work which proved completely
fruitless.

Yet God erected a terrible barrier against Isaiah and his preaching: he hardened Israel's heart. Isaiah was told as early as the time
of his call that it was his task to make the heart of this people 'fat',
and their ears dull, and to 'plaster over' their eyes, that they 'might
hear with their own ears and yet understand nothing, and see with
their own eyes and yet perceive nothing' (Isa. 6.9f.). It may perhaps
be that these words were given their present extreme form some
time after Isaiah had received his call, when he was able to make
some estimate of the results of his work. On the other hand, there
are striking similarities between Isa. 6 and I Kings 22.21, and both
have been described as typical stories of a prophet's commissioning.
If this is so, then it was the prophetic tradition which furnished
Isaiah with this very motif of hardening of the heart. However
this may be, the motif holds so prominent a position in Isaiah that
we must take the trouble to assign to it its proper place within the
wider context of Yahwism.

Many commentators have found no great difficulty in this. They
appealed to the undisputed fact that when the word of God is
continually rejected, the capacity to hear and understand it dies
away. 'Deliberate neglect of God's truth and habitual deafness to
God's warnings inevitably bring indifference to God's working in
their train.'[6] 'Will not' is punished by 'cannot'. But this interpretation of the hardening of the heart is open to an objection. It depends entirely on the conditional clause, and so becomes a general
truth of religion which can be constantly confirmed in the broad

[6] Cf. W. Eichrodt, Theology of the Old Testament, Vol. II, 1967, pp. 38off.

realm of religious experience. This means that the process would be a rational one which could be explained in psychological terms; and the most that could be said for the prophet would be that he fulfils 'a necessary moral ordinance'.[7]

This interpretation of the condemnation to obduracy as only a particular form of the *lex talionis* is not, however, consistent with statements made about it in the Old Testament; for there, hardening of the heart is always represented as an act of God and not as the result of a law of human nature. Each time that God addresses man he finds him in a state of alienation, and this is true even of his contact with his chosen people. But this raises the real question : how is it that Yahweh sometimes elects his chosen and sometimes hardens their hearts? How is it that in Isaiah's message Yahweh suddenly withdraws into an obscurity such as Israel had never before experienced? If Israel's alienation from God was due to a psychological process, then it could surely have been brought to its conclusion without waiting for a message from Isaiah. Any attempt to come to terms with what Isaiah says about hardening of the heart by the way of understanding the words indirectly, that is to say, by taking them as the secondary result of theological reflection, and therefore as the way out from a theological dilemma or an account of a general law of the psychology of religion, is, from the point of view of hermeneutics, *a priori* to import a standpoint from outside the text itself. But exegesis can do this only when every attempt at understanding the subject in its direct sense has failed. In the particular case of Isa. 6.9f., however, this has, generally speaking, never been attempted.

There is no tolerably uniform, consistent pre-history of the con-

[7] F. Hesse understands the idea of the hardening of the heart as the result of an intellectual difficulty. On the one hand, it was observed that persistence in sin often makes men blind to the 'reality of God'. Since, however, it was impossible for Yahwism to derive such baffling phenomena from the sphere of demonic powers, 'the only way out was to make a connection between Yahweh and even such things as could properly have had nothing to do with him, his nature being what it was' (*Das Verstockungsproblem im Alten Testament*, BZAW 74 (1955), pp. 41-3). That, 'his nature being what it was', Yahweh had nothing to do with the idea of the hardening of the heart, is precisely what is open to question. In addition, for the explanation of the idea of hardening the heart as due to difficulty in the solution of a theological problem, there are no exegetical indications whatever which would give us the right to interpret the statements in question in reverse, in the sense that Israel made Yahweh the one who hardened, and not Yahweh Israel the one who was hardened.

cept of hardening the heart. Nevertheless, it is certain that from the
very first Israel believed the act of deluding or hardening the heart
to be prompted by Yahweh, and this is in one way or another the
background to Isaiah's saying. The 'evil spirit' which brought about
an upheaval in the Shechem of Abimelech's day (Judg. 9.23), the
evil spirit which came over Saul (I Sam. 16.14; 18.10; 19.9), the
deception practised on Absalom's council of war whose result was
the rejection of the wise advice given by Ahithophel (II Sam. 17.14),
and last, Rehoboam's decision which, foolish as it was, was nevertheless ordained by Yahweh (I Kings 12.15), are all precursors of
this saying of Isaiah. They offer no escape from the theological
dilemma; indeed, in a sense they enhance it, for they show that
Yahwism had little difficulty in accepting even such obscure acts
from the hand of Yahweh. We must also consider another factor:
infatuation, a form of political madness whose inevitable end was
self-destruction, meant much more to the whole of the ancient east,
as to the Greeks, than it does to us, and they found it impossible
to regard the causes of something so atrocious, such a plunge into
madness and ruin at one's own hands, as lying simply on the human
and immanent level: in the last analysis they could only be the
inscrutable working of the deity. The case of the hardening of
Pharaoh's heart is, of course, somewhat different; for the sources
regard it as the first event in a comprehensive historical design.[8]
Yet this rather isolated cycle of tradition can itself prove all the
more important for the understanding of the concept of hardening
of the heart in Isaiah. For some kind of logical reason for Yahweh's
attitude is given here, and, of course, it was there from the beginning. The hardening took place, Pharaoh is told, 'to show you my
power, and that my name may be declared throughout all the earth'
(Ex. 9.16, J?).[9]

It is not my purpose to abstract a general concept of hardening
the heart from the various references to it. Our task is to understand Isaiah; and to do so we have to realize two things. On the one
hand, as far as this concept was concerned, he inherited an outlook
which was unchallenged in Israel and, indeed, in the whole of the
ancient world. But, on the other hand, he voiced something entirely
new and unprecedented. This was his radical opinion that Yahweh
himself was to bring about Israel's downfall, his conception of the
creative word of Yahweh (Isa. 9.7 [8]), and, finally, his concept of
Yahweh's 'work', the far-reaching nature of God's designs in history. It is this range of theological concepts which forms the framework for what Isaiah has to say about the hardening of Israel's

[8] Ex. 4.21 (J); 9.12 (P); 10.1 (J), 20 (E), 27 (E).
[9] Cf. also Ex. 7.5 (P); 11.9 (P); 14.4 (J), 17 (P).

heart. The declaration of a hardening of the heart to be brought about by the prophet himself is not to be understood apart from the concept of the creative word of Yahweh, which was treated in fuller detail above; indeed, it would appear that this ancient concept was given its ultimate and sharpest theological determination in Isaiah's saying. No doubt the idea that the prophetic word was able to effect acts of judgment and calamity by its own power alone had on occasion been very forcibly expressed before Isaiah's time; now, however, with him it is suddenly seen that this word effects judgment not only in the external world of history, but in human beings, in the most hidden recesses of their own hearts, namely, their refusal of the appeal by which Yahweh would save them.

The saying about hardening of the heart in Isa. 6 sounds as if it shut the door on everyone, and it was intended to be understood in this way. This cheerless background makes it all the more amazing that Isaiah's message was nevertheless accepted by a little group. A few years later the prophet was to sum up the net result of his earliest efforts in the words, Yahweh 'has hidden his face from the house of Jacob' (Isa. 8.17), and he returns to the same point in his last statement of accounts – Judah and Jerusalem were resistant, which means that in this context the obduracy is expressly shown as blameworthy (Isa. 30.8ff.). Because of this, Isa. 6.8f. ought not to be called a 'peripheral saying'; for the enigma of obduracy to Yahweh's offer runs through the whole of Isaiah's activity; it is nothing less than the foil which sets off Yahweh's reiterated invitation.

> Stupefy yourselves and be in a stupor! Blind yourselves and be
>   blind!
> Be drunk, but not with wine, stagger, but not with strong drink;
> for Yahweh has poured out upon you a spirit of deep sleep
> and has closed your eyes and covered your heads. . . .
> . . . Therefore I again do a marvellous thing with this people,
> wonderful and marvellous, so that the wisdom of the wise men
>   perishes,
> and the discernment of their discerning men is hid.
>   (Isa. 29.9-14)

'Therefore I act on this people,' says Yahweh; thus for Isaiah the hardening of Israel's heart is a particular mode of Yahweh's historical dealings with her. One of our chief tasks in what follows will be to demonstrate that what Isaiah speaks of is always an action, the 'work' of his God. The first thing he has to say in this connection is his utterance about hardening of the heart; it is not to be the last.

This means, however, that we must learn to read the saying about hardening of the heart with reference to the saving history. Any psychological or devotional explanation, or any understanding of it merely as punishment, means understanding it as the end, the final stage of a process which operates in a greater or lesser degree according to fixed laws. This is not consistent with the plain evidence found in Isaiah; for, paradoxical as it may be, its position there is emphatically at the beginning of a movement in the saving history. It was at the beginning, at his call, that Isaiah was given this word, and in Isa. 8.17 he says paradoxically that his hope is founded precisely in this God who hardens the heart; here, too, hardening of the heart is an event, from which the prophet looks out into the future; and in Isa. 30.8ff. the position is no different. As we have already seen, the fact that a prophet's word is not heard is far from meaning that this is the end of it. The message against which Jerusalem hardened its heart is to be written down for a generation to come. At that time – such is Isaiah's meaning – all that had fallen on completely deaf ears in his own day and generation will be fulfilled. Absolutely everything in Isaiah points out into the future – even the saying about the hardening of Israel's heart which is the action of Yahweh himself.

I. ZION

We spoke a moment ago of God's invitation without defining it in any way: we must now briefly attempt to give a more precise account of it as we find it in Isaiah.

In giving an account of Isaiah's message, we must keep in mind from the outset the question of the sacral tradition on which, as a native of Jerusalem, the prophet could have taken his stand, and we have also to remember the special conditions which obtained in that city: because of its relatively late incorporation into the cultic sphere of Yahwism, it lived a life of its own in respect of tradition. To this question the prophet's message in fact gives a perfectly definite answer. During the course of his long years of activity, Isaiah certainly clothed his preaching in different garbs to suit the hour and the audience whom he was addressing; yet there is one form – indeed it is almost a *schema* – for which he had such a preference that, if we wish to understand him, it is wise to take it as our starting point. It is only Isaiah's amazing ability to vary and diversify the different component parts in his discourse which blinds the reader to its schematic construction. The way in which these units are built up can be seen with almost model clearness in Isa. 17.12-14. A thunderous throng of nations dashes against Zion; Yahweh rebukes them : thereupon they flee far away. 'At evening time, behold, terror! Even before morning, they are no more.' Oddly enough, the nations here spoken of are not historically determinable; they appear rather as a formless, surging mass completely without political configuration, an idea which was made necessary by the inclusion of *motifs* from the myth of the struggle with the chaos dragon. Neither is their defeat a military one; it is achieved by a miracle, and takes place unobserved between nightfall and dawn. Only when day breaks can the astonished onlookers see that they have been delivered. It is not easy to date the passage; the old idea that Isaiah is speaking of the siege of Sennacherib has long been abandoned, for, when the prophet speaks of that event, he uses completely different terms. There can be little doubt that he was thinking of an event that could quite easily have taken place : but it also seems certain that the prophet was here making use of a tradition, and that neither the form of the story nor its various components were *ad hoc* creations.

The tradition which springs immediately to mind is that contained in the so-called Songs of Zion (Pss. 46; 48, and 76), for they belong specifically to Jerusalem – which means they have nothing to do with amphictyonic tradition. All three songs tell of Yahweh's mysterious defeat of royal armies which attack Zion – 'they saw it and were terrified, they were in panic and took to flight, trembling took hold of them there' (Ps. 48.6f. [5f.]). Before Zion 'he [Yahweh] broke the flashing bow, the shield, the sword, and the weapons of war', 'at thy rebuke, O God of Jacob, they lay stunned with their horses and chariots' (Ps. 76.4, 7 [3, 6]). The event upon which these poems draw has no ascertainable place in the history of the Davidic Jerusalem; neither, on the other hand, is the material mythological in the narrower sense of the term. Does it perhaps originate in the pre-Davidic Jerusalem? These psalms probably date from before the time of Isaiah : but their date is in fact of little importance; for their tradition of an unsuccessful attack on Jerusalem is quite certainly of very much earlier origin. Now, Isaiah's connection with this tradition of early Jerusalem is abundantly clear, particularly in the way, both moving and mysteriously allusive, in which the prophet depicts the divine intervention. This becomes even more obvious when we bring in further evidence from his writings, although, of course, in each case the prophet makes the old tradition into something entirely new. Thus, in Isa. 10.27b-34, a passage which may perhaps date from the same time as Isa. 17. 12ff., that is, c715, the picture of the enemies' onslaught is not in the least vague and featureless; instead, the text goes into full geographical detail, naming in order the towns and villages which were affected by the attack, until the point where the foe 'shakes his fist at the mount of the daughter of Zion'. At this point, however, Yahweh intervenes 'with terrifying power'. The cause of the enemies' destruction is Yahweh's own personal intervention, and not any battle. Here, too, deliverance comes only at the eleventh hour; the country districts of Judah are already overrun, and the enemy's power is only to be broken at the gates of Zion itself.

Isaiah shows the same calm assurance in connection with the revolt of the year 720 – he dismissed the ambassadors who certainly intended to incite the people of Jerusalem to join in the revolt with the calm words, 'Yahweh has founded Zion; in her the afflicted of his people will find refuge' (Isa. 14.28-32). Both in point of time and of subject matter there is a close connection between this prophecy and the one which announces the destruction of Assyria in Yahweh's own land (Isa. 14.24-27). Later in his career, when the prophet was waiting for Sennacherib's attack, there are no less than three more or less complete variations of this inherited *schema* and all its component parts. Of course, at the very beginning of the great poem on Ariel (Isa. 29.1-8), a highly paradoxical view is expressed : Yahweh himself is to rise up against Zion ('for I will distress Ariel. . . . I encamp against you round about'). This naturally alters the whole tone of the tradition; the event now means utter humiliation for Zion (v. 4). But it is followed by the turning-point of grace; Yahweh will intervene with storm and tempest, and the oppressors will become as chaff and dust that pass away. When the enemy first makes its assault on Zion, therefore, Yahweh takes part in the most personal way against her : but thereafter he turns against the enemy.

And it will be, as when a hungry man dreams he is eating,
and when he awakes, his hunger is not satisfied,
and as when a thirsty man dreams he is drinking,

and he awakes parched and longing for drink –
so will it be with the multitude of the nations that fight against
Mount Zion.

(Isa. 29.8)

In contrast with this, one of Isaiah's most powerful sayings (Isa. 30. 27-33) deals only with the repulse of Assyria, for which Yahweh appears in person, burning with his anger, letting his voice sound forth in majesty, and making the stroke of his arm plain. Finally, in Isa. 31.1-8, Yahweh turns against those who rely on alliances and armaments to meet the danger. Zion's protection is Yahweh himself. He will himself come down, 'he will protect and deliver, spare and rescue' (v. 5).

We must deal more fully with Isaiah's message in the earlier part of his career, during the Syro-Ephraimitic war. In the first place, Isa. 7.1-9 is completely different in form. The section is admittedly a narrative about a prophet, but this in turn only serves as the artistic framework into which are inserted a prophetic exhortation and an oracle of promise. What we then have is a rather unusual combination of two literary categories. Here too, in this exhortation to remain calm and fearless, and in this promise that the confederates' attack on Jerusalem will achieve nothing, the basic idea of the schema can again be easily recognized. But while in all the passages previously considered the interest was more or less exclusively concentrated on the external events, the attack and its repulse, in this case the inner feelings of the people in whose immediate neighbourhood so terrible and wonderful an event occurs are also important. They are asked whether they can hold out in 'faith' even in face of all these troubles; for only if they can will they be established (Isa. 7.9).[10]

This saying on faith seems to some extent to strike a solitary note in Isaiah, and this would suggest that it did not belong to any tradition. But in fact the very opposite is true; for it is precisely at this point that Isaiah is particularly clearly restoring an old tradition to use. We have merely to observe the very extensive use which he makes of ideas which derive from the old cycle of traditions about Yahweh's holy wars. Just as in bygone days Yahweh came from afar to these wars (Judg. 5.4f.), so now he will

[10] 'There is a play upon words here, which may be reproduced in English by the help of a North-England term : If ye have not *faith*, ye cannot have *staith*.' G. A. Smith, *The Book of Isaiah, I-XXXIX*, 1902, p. 106n. There is a similar play in the German (Tr.).

'come down to fight on Mount Zion'; and just as in bygone days he used to destroy the foe alone and without any help from men, so 'the Assyrian shall fall by the sword, no human sword and no earthly sword' (Isa. 31.4b, 8). Yahweh will draw near, he will let his voice ring out, and do battle 'with storm and tempest and hailstones' (Isa. 30.30); he will visit Zion 'with thunder, earthquake and great noise, with storm and tempest' (Isa. 29.6). In bygone days, in battle with the Canaanites, he threw stones down from heaven (Josh. 10.11), and in battle with the Philistines thundered with a mighty voice (I Sam. 7.10) and made the earth quake (I Sam. 14.15) – according to Isaiah's predictions, it will be exactly the same when Yahweh manifests himself at the final day. The demand for faith, too, has its home in this old cycle of traditional ideas about Yahweh's saving help. We have already discussed the part played by the demand for faith, even though the word itself is never mentioned, in the account of Gideon's struggle with the Midianites (Judg. 7). The account of the miraculous crossing of the Red Sea, which actually reads almost like a prefiguration of Isa. 7.1ff., not only contains the exhortation 'not to fear' and 'to be still' since present help is at hand, but also mentions that to some extent as a result of this Israel then 'believed' in Yahweh (Ex. 14.31). Thus there can be no doubt that in his own day and generation Isaiah gave fresh currency to the concept of the holy wars in which Yahweh both delivered his people and at the same time demanded faith from them, and that he did so with great vigour. We are not, of course, to think that in the process he went right back to the concepts current in the time of the Judges; the concepts which he took up were rather those which had become established at about the beginning of the period of the Monarchy. One of their characteristics is that they conceive the holy war as sheer miracle; Yahweh's saving act is entirely self-sufficient and does not allow any human co-operation.[11]

It is precisely at this point, the passionate elimination of all reliance on oneself, that Isaiah's zeal begins. That he saw a great act of deliverance lying in the immediate future was only one side of his message. Ahaz and the leaders in Jerusalem had to leave room for this act of God. And this is what Isaiah called faith – leaving room for God's sovereign action, desisting from self-help. Thus in Isaiah the demand for faith is actualized in an emphatically polemical and even negative sense – only do not now usurp God's place by your own political and military plans. For men, the only attitude appropriate to the situation was 'to be quiet' (Isa. 7.4). Isaiah reiterated the same thing many years later, in face of the threat from Assyria, in the paradox that 'being still' would then

[11] Cf. here von Rad. Der Heilige Krieg im alten Israel, pp. 43ff., 56ff.

be 'strength' (Isa. 30.15). When Isaiah speaks in this way of being
still, he is quite certainly not thinking only of an inward condition
of the soul, but also of an attitude which must be expressed in a
perfectly definite mode of political conduct.[12] The 'object' upon
which this faith should be based did not, however, as yet exist for
his contemporaries; it lay in the future. The astonishing thing was
therefore this: Isaiah demanded of his contemporaries that they
should now make their existence rest on a future action of God.
If they should succeed in taking refuge in Yahweh's future act of
deliverance, then they would be saved. Later, when it was all over,
when Jerusalem had capitulated and the land lay waste, Isaiah
once again balanced accounts with the people of influence in the
capital. In the matter of military protection, these men had left
nothing undone; every conceivable attention had been paid to the
city's fortifications and its water-supply:

> but you did not look to him who did it,
> or have regard for him who planned it long ago.
> (Isa. 22.11b)

'Looking to' Yahweh's action in history seems an odd expression;
yet it, too, comes from tradition; for, according to J's account,
Moses himself commanded the Israelites not to fear, to stand firm,
and to 'look to' the help of Yahweh (Ex. 14.13), and the story also
ends with the note that Israel 'saw the mighty hand of Yahweh'
(v. 31). The term, 'looking to the action of Yahweh', used just as
absolutely as that of 'faith', occurs elsewhere in Isaiah, and is

---

[12] The question as to whether this demand to be still should be described
as 'Utopian' from the standpoint of practical politics, or whether it was a
shrewd one even there, introduces viewpoints which are far from the
prophet's thoughts; for the question examines the practicability of his advice
from outside the situation. It is clear that we, who no longer see the co-
efficients of the forces which were then in play, can hardly decide it along
these lines. For Isaiah, being still was of course also the shrewder political
course, but only because Yahweh had commanded it! If the idea is correct,
that Isaiah saw the breach of faith with Yahweh as lying only in the appeal
to the Assyrians for help, and had no thoughts of ruling out all military
action, but on the contrary advised that the war should be undertaken in
quietness and confidence, this makes no essential difference, since, according
to all the relevant passages, Yahweh had promised even so to carry the
whole burden of defence. But since even the pre-Isaianic tradition shows
the increasing tendency to exclude all human participation in war, and since
Isaiah never speaks of such participation, but rather uses extreme language
to show that he looks to Yahweh's intervention to settle the whole issue,
this idea does not seem to me very probable.

almost a synonym for faith; at all events, like the term 'being still', it describes a very important aspect of what Isaiah calls 'faith'.

Isaiah's conception of faith, of being still, and of looking to Yahweh, must itself be set within still wider prophetic contexts, namely those connected with Yahweh's 'work' and with his 'purpose'.

Isaiah once attacked the careless revellers in the capital thus:

> But they do not see the work of Yahweh,
> nor do they regard the work of his hands.
>
> (Isa. 5.12)

This concept of a 'work' of Yahweh can scarcely originate in a sacral tradition; it really looks like an independent coinage of Isaiah himself. A few verses later, in another oracle of threatening, Isaiah quotes those who were saying:

> Let [Yahweh] speed his work, that we may see it;
> let the purpose of the Holy One of Israel draw near and be
> fulfilled, that we may know it.
>
> (Isa. 5.19)

It is perfectly obvious that these mocking words take up phrases used by the prophet himself in his preaching. Here the term 'purpose' of Yahweh is used more or less synonymously side by side with that of his 'work'. The former term is also very likely the prophet's own creation. It is quite secular in origin, and signifies the decision arrived at in a council. Very probably what is thought of is the royal council in heaven, in which a political project was discussed and then resolved upon (I Kings 22.19-22). This idea of a plan to which Yahweh gives effect in history is a new element in the preaching of the eighth-century prophets. In this connection, the present-day reader is well advised to lay aside all ideas of a general guidance of history by divine providence; for when Isaiah speaks of 'purpose', he is thinking of something planned for the deliverance of Zion, that is to say, of a saving work. Isaiah sets this saving act of Yahweh in the widest possible historical context, namely that of universal history. Nothing is improvised here: Isaiah says very definitely that Yahweh 'predetermined' his work 'long ago' (Isa. 22.11; cf. Isa. 37.26). This work of Yahweh thus enfolds the whole realm of world history as it was understood at that time; and the way in which the great world empires who were proudly strutting about on this very stage of history came into collision with God's plan is one of the great themes to which Isaiah returned again and again.

> Yahweh of hosts has sworn:
> As I have planned it, so shall it be,
>   and as I have purposed it, so shall it stand,
> to break Assyria in my land;
>   upon my mountains will I trample him under foot . . .
> this is the purpose, resolved concerning the whole earth,
>   this is the hand, stretched out over all the nations.
> For Yahweh of hosts has resolved it, and who can annul it?
>   His hand is stretched out, and who will turn it back?
>
> (Isa. 14.24-27)

In this passage, which apparently dates from the time when Assyria first became a serious danger, it is perfectly clear that Zion occupies the centre of the stage in Yahweh's plan. For her safety Assyria has to be broken in pieces 'upon the mountains of Yahweh'. This event, though it is concentrated on one tiny place, also involves the whole world; 'all nations' must bow before it; for none can bend back Yahweh's outstretched arm.

The same atmosphere pervades Isa. 10.5-19, a great passage which in respect of form alone is one of Isaiah's most powerful poems, and which is also unusual because of its baroque development of the diatribe, into which the prophet has packed so much as to give rise to a disproportion between it and the threat (vv. 16ff.). Assyria had been given a definite, though, in Isaiah's view, a strictly limited, commission by Yahweh: she was sternly to chastize his people. But she is about to exceed this commission. Nothing has happened as yet: but the very fact that she 'has it in mind' to exceed, that she 'intends' destruction, is sufficient reason for threatening her with punishment. There is hardly any other passage which so clearly shows the nature of the prophetic view of history. Isaiah does not consider the question of how the Assyrians came to have this task allotted to them, but he is in no doubt about the fact itself. Everything stands or falls on the precondition that the prophet claims to know the divine plan which lies behind an actual political event of his time, in this case the Assyrian invasion of Palestine. From this standpoint he sees the event divided up into its divine and its human constituent parts, and is able to distinguish between what Yahweh had intended and the guilty human addition, the element imported into it by man's high-handedness. The prophets did not use this way of interpreting history at its very deepest level, as Yahweh planned it, as a rational *modus operandi* which they could apply as they pleased. Yet in moments of great tension they claimed authority for such a view of it which they based on some unexplained inspiration.

The words, Yahweh 'will finish all his work on Mount Zion' are also found in this context (v. 12). Unfortunately they come at a bad place in relation to the whole passage, and therefore possibly derive from a different context; they may, however, be claimed without hesitation as Isaianic. They show more clearly than other references the way in which what Isaiah liked to call the 'work' of Yahweh, which fills the whole world of history, applies to Zion, and will also be brought to its consummation there.[13]

In the light of the passages so far examined, and particularly of Isa. 7.1ff. and 17.12ff., it would seem as though Yahweh would protect Zion from the Assyrians in all circumstances. In actual fact Isaiah said so quite plainly more than once. Nevertheless, he was never completely free from ambiguity in his view of this matter, least of all perhaps in his earliest period, when what he looked for from the coming of the Assyrians was almost entirely a devastating judgment and chastisement for Judah (Isa. 7.18, 20). At no time, however, did the prophet ever completely lose sight of this dark reverse side of the work of Yahweh. This aspect of it again becomes important in his later period – for example, in the Ariel poem which, as we have already noticed, sees Yahweh himself as the one who distresses Zion. There is to be 'moaning and lamentation', and Jerusalem is to be like a 'ghost' whose thin voice is 'to sound from low in the dust'. Such is the depth of humiliation which will precede the deliverance (Isa. 29.2, 4). Yahweh's work for Zion is here given a remarkable theological ambivalence: it judges and saves at one and the same time. Isaiah expressed the same idea in even stronger terms to the ruling classes in Jerusalem who believed that

[13] It would appear that Isaiah only once spoke in a very fundamental and theoretically didactic fashion about Yahweh's action in history, namely in Isa. 28.23-9 – that is, if the understanding of this text as a parable which alludes to a supernatural order, i.e., to Yahweh and his action in history, is correct. Perhaps, however, it is not altogether easy to believe that the text gives us no indication that it is not to be taken in the literal sense, but as parabolic discourse. In Vergil's *Georgics* there is a poem on the countryman's activities in the successive seasons of the year which includes a reference to the deity who taught the peasants (1.35ff.). Its only real difference from Isa. 28.23ff. is its compass, and it has never been understood as a parable.

they could make 'lies their refuge' in order to 'take shelter in falsehood'. He gave them this warning:

> For Yahweh will rise up as on Mount Perazim,
> he will storm as in the valley of Gibeon,
> to do his deed – strange is his action,
> and to work his work – alien is his work!
>
> (Isa. 28.21)

Here again we meet the concept of the 'work of Yahweh'; and this is the most remarkable of all the references to it. Its terms are once more allusive rather than direct, and leave a great deal open. The only thing certain is that Yahweh will rise up to do terrible battle; the words make one feel how even the prophet himself was seized with terror at the 'barbaric alien element' in this self-manifestation of Yahweh. Yahweh will rise up once again. The future act thus stands in a typological relationship to the one which once founded David's empire. Therefore the coming act will, like the former, in the end effect the deliverance of the city of God. What was this to signify for the 'scoffers'? For them, only the dark side of this appalling sudden appearance of Yahweh comes into the picture.

Who would be affected by the salvation which Yahweh's work was to bring? The usual answer to the question is to point to Isaiah's concept of the holy *remnant*; and in actual fact the prophet did on occasion put it in this way. The main reference to the remnant is the symbolic name Shear-jashub (a remnant returns) which he – no doubt at the command of Yahweh – gave to one of his sons (Isa. 7.3). Yet the concept as understood in this sense of a remnant to be saved at the *eschaton* is remarkably rare in Isaiah (Isa. 10.21 is post-Isaianic). As we have already seen, the remnant concept as such belongs to the language of politics, and describes what remained over of a people who had survived a campaign whose aim was their total destruction. This negative use is also found in Isaiah, as for example when he speaks of the remnant of Syria (Isa. 17.3, 5f.), of Moab (Isa. 16.13f.), of Kedar (Isa. 21.17), or of the Philistines (Isa. 14.30). Indeed, he sometimes employed it in this negative sense of a pitiful remnant with reference even to his own nation (Isa. 30.17, 1.9). Therefore it cannot be said that Isaiah made the remnant concept a leading one where his concern was his proclamation of salvation. Nor is it probable that in this matter he was basing himself on a fairly firmly defined prophetic tradition which he for his part resumed and developed in accord with his own ideas. If such a 'remnant tradition' did in fact ever exist, Isaiah echoes it only infrequently. There can be no doubt that the prophet envisaged a radical process of sifting: and if, for the sake of terminological simplicity, this is called a remnant concept, no exception can be taken to this. A reference to the remnant could then be seen in the Immanuel sign, and, more particularly, in the prophet's disciples (Isa. 8.16-18), or in the poor who are to find refuge in Zion (Isa. 14.32), etc. Nevertheless, it has to be remembered that Isaiah himself seldom used such an all-embracing term for the miraculous preservation of a minority. This could be said with much more truth of a number of post-Isaianic passages in which the remnant concept does in fact appear as a clearly defined idea (Isa. 4.3; 11.11, 16; 10.20; 28.5).

The reader of Isaiah who appreciates how the prophet's whole preaching is permeated from its very beginning by the theme of Zion threatened but finally delivered, is bound to sense something of the yearly increasing tension which must have burdened Isaiah until events finally reached a climax in the reign of Sennacherib. In 701 the Assyrians, who were never out of the prophet's mind his whole life long, did not simply make an appearance in Palestine; on this occasion they even marched into the hill country of Judah and surrounded Jerusalem. Hezekiah submitted to them – obviously after a short siege – and had to agree to pay a heavy tribute of silver and gold, and to cede part of his territory. He did not 'show faith', at least not as Isaiah conceived the term, but by an act of political common-sense saved the city from the worst possible fate. The sheer joy of relief expressed by the besieged inhabitants is easy to imagine; but Isaiah turned away ashamed and angry from the mob and its jubilation. This was the great moment to which he had looked forward for years – but Jerusalem was not equal to it.

> Look away from me; I must weep bitter tears.
> Insist not to comfort me for the ravishing of the daughter of my people.

> (Isa. 22.4)

This is one of the very few places where, in the midst of the austere atmosphere of his prophetic message, Isaiah's own human feelings assert their right and demand a hearing. He must have been shattered to the depths of his being when events turned out so completely different from what he had expected. Who could dare even attempt to comfort a prophet in the hour of his despair!

There is one other passage, Isa. 1.4-9, which, even if only indirectly, reveals in a rather unique way something of Isaiah's frame of mind in the period after the disaster which befell Jerusalem. It begins with a diatribe of unusual pungency ('a people laden with guilt', 'offspring of evildoers, sons who deal corruptly'). But these words of burning anger are not followed, as we should have expected, by the threat. As he describes the body of the people, so stricken by physical punishment that it really cannot be smitten any more, the prophet finds that he himself is caught up in the misery of it all: 'They [the wounds] are none of them pressed out, or bound up, or softened with oil' (v. 6b), and this now moves the prophet from anger to pity. His own personal pain drove from him his original intention to rebuke and threaten. He ends with a description – notice the metre, the lament – of the countryside devastated by the Assyrians, in which Jerusalem is left 'like a lodge in a cucumber field'. This passage probably belongs to the last phase of Isaiah's preaching, so far as records have survived.

In the light of what we have so far seen, the total result of Isaiah's work appears overwhelmingly negative. Not one of all his great sayings about Zion came true. The nation showed no faith, and Yahweh did not protect his city. Did the prophet demand too much of the people, or – a hard question – in prophesying the assured safety of Zion, did he encroach upon God's prerogative? It is beyond dispute that Isaiah's disappointment was very deep. On the other hand, there is no indication that the prophet was in any way puzzled by Yahweh. It was his fellow-men who puzzled him. This is one of the important differences between Isaiah and Jeremiah, whose relationship to Yahweh was much more critical. Isaiah apparently acquiesced in the failure of his work. This he could do, because for him the word of Yahweh with which he was charged was beyond all criticism. If his own generation had rejected it, then it must be put in writing for a future one. The very fact that Isaiah did write it down makes clear that in his eyes the prophetic message was far from being a dead letter even if it had failed. And had not Yahweh told him at the time of his call that he would have no success as a prophet? What was said then about the remnant is also found in Isa. 1.8f.; and so we have the right to say after all that even at the end of his work Isaiah had this comfort to cling to. Yet, whether he himself regarded his work as a failure, or whether he found comfort, is not so very important – and in any case we do not have the material to give a proper answer to such a question. It is much more important that his message was written down and handed on. More important still, successors took up the themes of Isaiah's message; they added prophecies in the Isaianic style to the old Isaianic texts, and thus kept the old message most vitally alive and made it contemporary for later generations.

Thus, for example, in Isa. 4.2ff. a word of grace was added to the oracle of judgment on the women of Jerusalem (Isa. 3.16ff.). It looks beyond the hour of punishment envisaged by Isaiah and speaks of ignominy washed away and of salvation on Mount Zion. As we now have it, the judgment pronounced on the Egyptians in Isa. 18.1-6 ends with a prospect of the blessings of the last time: the Egyptians are then to bring offerings to the God of Israel on Mount Zion. The 'spurious' addition (v. 7), though phrased in the style of the genuine prophecy of Isaiah, is certainly later. Again, the words, 'the proud crown of the drunkards of Ephraim' (Isa. 28.1) are repeated a few verses later, but are now given a saving and eschatological reference: Yahweh will himself be a crown and a diadem of beauty for the remnant of his people (v. 5). The Messianic prophecy in Isa. 11.1-8 was also subsequently enlarged. The Gentiles are to enquire about the shoot from the stem of Jesse: it is to become an ensign for the nations. Critical exegesis has no great opinion of these additions or of many others like them. In so far as this verdict is literary and aesthetic, one can largely agree. The difference in the form and in force of expression is in some cases quite unmistakable: the diction is more diffuse and less colourful, it heaps up the terms used, and the result is often enough the sacrifice of clarity. Nevertheless, we ought to exercise reserve in differentiating between what is original and what was added by successors, since the men of the ancient world were quite unfamiliar with such differentiations used as standards and measures of value. We must particularly remember that such judgments are quite meaningless as far as the theological adequacy of the additions is concerned. For how may we determine the rightness or wrongness of such subsequent actualizations of old Isaianic prophecy? All we can see is that the tradition of this prophet's message was not preserved in archives: it remained a living organism, speaking directly to later generations as it had done to its own, and able even of itself to give birth to new prophecy.

Finally, the subject of the continuing effectiveness of the message and also of the reinterpretation it was later given takes in the complex of narratives concerning the Assyrians' threat to Zion and their withdrawal (Isa. 36–38). Here themes recur which have an important place in our prophet's message – the question of the deliverance of Zion (Isa. 36.14, 18, 20; 37.12, 20), Yahweh's zeal (37.32), the remnant (Isa. 37.32), and above all the question of confidence and of what can be properly relied upon (Isa. 36.5-7; 37.10). At the same time, however, the differences from Isaiah are unmistakable. For these stories the Assyrian withdrawal is already a thing of the past. Accordingly they lack the specifically historical interest in the political aspect of the event which is closing in on Zion. For the narrator, the Assyrian king is little more than the type of the wantonly insolent foe of Yahweh; he could equally be called Nebuchadnezzar or Antiochus. Corresponding to this waning of interest in the saving history and its uniqueness, and in comparison with the real Isaiah, the demand for confidence is obviously more spiritualized. Faith is now on the way to becoming something almost divorced from history and belonging to the individual's encounter with his God.

2. YAHWEH'S ANOINTED ONE

If Isaiah's preaching had concentrated only on the threat to Zion and her defence it would have shown a single-mindedness unparalleled in the Old Testament, despite the astonishing number of variations the prophet played on this theme. But it contained another idea which, though it occupies less space, is expounded in texts of considerable scope and importance. This is the theme of David and the Messiah.

The idea that Yahweh had established David's throne in Jerusalem and made him far-reaching promises was current even during David's lifetime. It is not certain how large a part this played in the faith of the common people as opposed to the faith practised at court. In Deuteronomy indeed, which is later than Isaiah, we still find the deposit of a theology whose orientation was 'amphictyonic', and therefore expressly non-monarchical and non-Messianic. We do not know the attitude taken by the farmers and herdsmen of the Judean south : but in the royal city, the seat of the administration, the probable home of Isaiah, this sacral theology, stemming from the court, was very much alive. Our knowledge of it is derived chiefly from the so-called royal psalms; we do not, however, know it with enough precision to allow us to draw far-reaching conclusions about it by comparing Isaiah's utterances with the royal psalms – as, for example, about the particular nuances which each gave to the component concepts.

In Isa. 11.1-8, the Messianic theme is arranged under three headings. First comes the equipment of the anointed one for his office (vv. 2-3a). His authority is not conferred by one single *charisma* – as had been usual in Israel up to this time – but by a number of them. When Isaiah says that the possession of the spirit is to 'rest upon' the anointed one he probably intends to rule out the possibility that the possession should be temporary, as had so far always been the rule. In the second section (vv. 3b-5) we are shown the anointed one exercising his office in virtue of this gift of the spirit. His principal office is that of arbiter, in which he cares particularly for those whose legal standing is weak. Like the royal psalms – cf. particularly Ps. 72.12-14 – Isaiah regards the anointed one's commission as consisting pre-eminently in the establishment of the divine justice on earth. The prophet's insistence that the anointed one has at his disposal, both for his investigations and for punishing the guilty, such divine properties as omniscience and the power to cause instant death by word alone probably takes him beyond the traditional teachings of the royal theology. The third part (vv. 6-8), which agrees with traditional concepts, tells of the paradisal peace which is to accompany the reign of this anointed one, and to bring order even into the world of nature and to resolve its conflicts.

While Isaiah is here seen to be moving essentially within the traditional courtly concepts and adapting them to his own day, he did at one point abandon and break with these in an almost revolutionary way. He does not, as had hitherto been the case, attach what he has to say to a contemporary and present anointed one seated on the throne of David, but to one who is to come in the future, who is to spring from 'the root of Jesse'. The reference to the father of David makes it probable that Isaiah is not thinking simply of any future anointed one seated on the throne of David, but of a new David, at whose advent Yahweh will restore the glory of the original Davidic empire.[14] The Messianic prophecy of his contemporary Micah can hardly be taken in any other sense; for when Micah addresses the Ephrathites of Bethlehem, the clan from which David came, and prophesies that a 'ruler in Israel' (Micah 5.1 [2]) shall come forth from it, this can only mean that Yahweh is once more taking up his Messianic work from the beginning, in that he again starts at the very same place as he began in the past, namely in Bethlehem. Both passages are highly poetic in feeling; they are expressed in language remote from that of daily

[14] This alone makes the fact that Isaiah speaks of the root of Jesse comprehensible. Otherwise it would have been much more natural to speak of the line of David. Admittedly, it cannot be assumed for certain on the basis of Isa. 11.1 that Isaiah expected a new David; but since Jeremiah (30.9) and Ezekiel (34.23) explicitly make the assumption, and since Isaiah's contemporary Micah looks to Bethlehem and not to Jerusalem, it is very natural to presuppose that Isaiah also had the idea of David's return.

life, which, of course, makes it extremely difficult to analyse their concepts: but the fact that both of them look to the historical town and family from which David came, can only mean that they expect the new anointed one to appear from there. There is, however, one difference: for Micah this new beginning is bound up with the elimination of the old royal city, the total obliteration of Jerusalem from the pages of history (Micah 3.12), whereas, as we have already seen, Isaiah looks for a renewal of Jerusalem. In both cases, the contemporary monarch or monarchs of the Davidic line are dismissed by the prophets. The fact that they so expressly look for salvation in the anointed one of the future is tantamount to saying that the contemporary descendants of David have lost the saving function so emphatically attributed to them in the royal psalms. In this respect, they have relinquished all that caused the singing of their praises in favour of the coming anointed one. It is, of course, remarkable that our only guide in such an important matter is inference. We have no evidence that such a Messianic prophecy was badly received at court, or regarded as highly seditious – which, indeed, it was. All the evidence suggests, however, that these prophets increasingly wrote off the reigning members of the house of David of their own day, and even that they regarded the whole history of the Monarchy from the time of David as a false development. If they did not, what meaning could there be in their expectation that Yahweh would once again make an entirely new beginning? Was it only amongst their intimate friends that the prophets talked about these matters? The literary form in which these prophecies are clothed might suggest that this is so; for they do not look like open proclamations designed for a wider public; there is never any sign of an audience whom the prophet addresses, nor are they formulated as divine oracles, revelations made by Yahweh. Their literary category is really unique. Had they a somewhat esoteric character from the very beginning?

We must not think that the prophets only looked for the coming of an anointed one sometime in a vague future. Isaiah clearly envisaged the enthronement in the immediate future, that is to say, within the context of the Assyrian crisis and its defeat. His other great Messianic passage (Isa. 7.23b-9.6 [9.1b-7]) starts out from a definite, concrete contemporary situation, Tiglath Pileser's annexation of a considerable part of Israel's territory, and its incorporation into the Assyrian provincial system (II Kings 15.29). Cut asunder from the people of God, cast out into the darkness where there

can be no talk of history, these are 'the people that walk in darkness'; and 'the light which shines on them' is the fact that they are
given knowledge of two epoch-making events. First, Yahweh has
broken the yoke and rod of the oppressor, which is the might of
Assyria. This came about like one of the miracles of the old holy
wars – there is no explanation of the enemy's defeat; all that needs
to be done is to clear away and burn the bloodstained implements
of war still scattered round about (vv. 2-4 [3-5]). The other piece
of knowledge given is that of the accession of the anointed one
which, the prophet imagines, is to follow directly upon Yahweh's
act of deliverance. The child who is born, the son who is given, is
indeed no mere babe; he is the anointed one who, in terms of Ps. 2.7,
is at the moment of his 'coronation' brought into the relationship
of son to Yahweh. In Jerusalem, however, as everywhere in the
ancient east, a courtly accession ceremony was described in strictly
conventional language; therefore this text is the last place from
which we today may hope for personal information concerning
the anointed one. Isaiah's prophecy, too, is in the fixed language of
a characteristic ritual. Its interest lies in the questions of the office
of the anointed one and his authorization by Yahweh. Now, it is
very significant that this coming anointed one is designated as
'governor' and his rule as 'government'. A 'governor' is never an
independent ruler, but always an official commissioned by a higher
authority; even though he is like a king within his sphere of jurisdiction (Isa. 10.8), and has greater power than many who have no
one above them, he nevertheless remains himself a commissioned
official; in the language of the east, he is not sultan but vizier, and
as such is responsible to higher authority. The anointed one is
therefore not 'king', but is subordinate to a king, namely Yahweh,
to whose throne he is summoned as 'governor'. This deliberate
avoidance of the title of king – Micah too eschews the word 'king'
and speaks of a 'ruler' – may again involve an attack on the kings
in Jerusalem who were now emancipated from Yahweh and be-
having as independent rulers. When the anointed one is invested
with powers to govern in God's stead, he has also the customary
throne-names conferred upon him. Here the details are not all
equally clear. The first is particularly important, for when the
anointed one is called 'wonderful in giving counsel', the reference
is to the advice he receives from the universal king (cf. II. Sam.
16.23); he is in constant conversation with Yahweh about the
government of the world. The supports of his throne are justice

and righteousness, and 'there is no end of blessing' (Isa. 9.6) in his kingdom.

While nineteenth-century church traditions could still regard Isa. 7.10-17 as the Messianic prophecy *par excellence*, critical investigation since then has so complicated the understanding of the passage that, apart from the quite preliminary questions of the meaning of the words and of the various statements it makes, we are still very far away from any satisfactory agreement on it. Upon Ahaz' refusal to ask for a sign from Yahweh, Isaiah announces that Yahweh himself is to give a sign: the young woman will conceive, will bear a son, and will call him Immanuel. . . . Clearly, the first consideration here is the idea of the sign; and all interpretation of the passage must keep this firmly in mind. Where is the sign to be seen? In the child, in the strange food he is to eat, or in his name? The first idea that comes to mind is that the sign is the name given to the child, Immanuel. A prophetic symbolic name like Shear-jashub or the names in Hosea 1, it indicates salvation in the near future. Only we must notice that 'therefore' (v. 14), here as elsewhere in the Old Testament, should be understood in a threatening sense. Moreover, this message is spoken to Ahaz who has already cut himself off from the coming blessing by his refusal of a sign. The coming event therefore brings judgment for him. The alliance of the Syrians and Israelites, the danger which threatened Jerusalem and terrified her inhabitants, was soon to be broken (v. 16): but Ahaz, his royal house, and his people are to face hard times. Thus, as has often been pointed out, Isa. 7.10ff. seems to have close affinities with Isa. 8.1-4. Here, too, there is mention of a child who is still to come into the world, and who is to have a symbolic name, 'spoil is speedy, plunder hasteneth', while a time limit is also mentioned (Isa. 8.4), which corresponds to that of Isa. 7.16. This might suggest that we should think of the 'young woman' of Isa. 7.14 as the prophet's wife: Immanuel would then be a son of Isaiah's own, like 'a remnant shall return' and 'spoil is speedy, plunder hasteneth'. There is more to be said, however, for the interpretation of the incident, exactly like Isa. 7.1-9, entirely in terms of the concepts of the holy war, themes which were already touched upon in the prophet's utterance about the Syro-Ephraimitic war (Isa. 7.4-9), and which are now simply continued in the announcement of the sign (cf. Judg. 6.36ff.) and in that of the birth of the deliverer (cf. Judg. 13.5). In either case, the statement that the child is to eat curds and honey until he reaches the age of moral discernment, is extremely difficult. Does 'curds and honey' signify shortage of food, the sole products of a land ravaged by enemies (cf. Isa. 7.21f.), or does it on the contrary mean the mythical food of the gods, the food of paradise? Above all, however, does v. 15 form part of the original oracle? It is often regarded as an interpolation, and in

actual fact the logical connection of v. 16 with v. 14 is excellent.
In this case, it is the interpolator who shifted the centre of gravity
in the saying from the child's name to the child himself. In Isa.
8.8b too, though this verse is also to all appearance a later addition, Immanuel is spoken of as a person, the actual ruler of the
land. In face of this background, we have therefore to reckon with
the possibility that in Isa. 7.10ff. genuine words of the prophet
himself, in which he used the symbolic name Immanuel to prophesy salvation for believers and woe for unbelievers, have been
reinterpreted in a Messianic sense. Some commentators, of course,
introduce a much richer set of concepts deriving from the cult and
mythology and try to interpret the passage in their light.

As a result of this study, it can be said that the whole of Isaiah's
preaching is based on two traditions, the Zion tradition and the
tradition about David. Both are election traditions: that is to say,
they were adopted by court circles in Jerusalem as the basis of
their own legitimation before Yahweh. These men founded their
whole existence before Yahweh, their faith and their confidence
upon the God-given institutions of which these traditions were the
guarantee. Isaiah was also at home in these traditions: but he also
brought a completely new concept into them. The songs of Zion
were based on the fact of Yahweh's past choice of Zion, and the
royal psalms on Yahweh's past choice of David: Isaiah turned completely to the future – Yahweh is about to deliver Zion, he is about
to raise up the anointed one, the new David. It is here, in the
future event, and not in any historical event of the past, that
Jerusalem's salvation lies. Men must have faith in this future deliverance; for there is no other. We who have been brought up
with a European outlook find it strange to see how detached and
almost unconnected the two traditions are, even as late as Isaiah.
Yet this very fact has something important to tell us about the
kind of men these prophets were. Their message was not, as was
long supposed, an independent entity, based so to speak on its own
principles, and possibly of an entirely new kind. Instead, they regarded themselves as the spokesmen of old and well-known sacral
traditions which they reinterpreted for their own day and age.
Perhaps they were in their time the only ones who still took a firm
stand on the basis of these ancient Yahwistic traditions and were
conscious of their earth-shaking relevance.

13 The New Element in Eighth-Century Prophecy

CAREFUL consideration of the distinctive features in the prophecies of Amos, Hosea, Isaiah, and Micah might well lead us to
the conclusion that all comparisons are dangerous, because once we
have discovered the radical differences between them it is difficult
to avoid the temptation of going on and smoothing these out.
What, in actual fact, do Hosea and Isaiah have in common? Hosea
came from the farming world of the Northern Kingdom, he was
opposed to everything that in his day was implied by the word
'king'; of all the prophets, he was the most deeply involved in
patriarchal concepts deriving from the cult, and he paid particular
attention to problems in the sacral sphere and to cultic irregulari-
ties. Isaiah was a townsman, brought up in the traditions of the
royal city and a sharp-sighted observer of world politics; he explained all the changes in the political kaleidoscope as part of
Yahweh's rational scheme, he placed his confidence in the divinely
guaranteed protection of the city, and he looked for a king who
would bring peace and righteousness. Much the same can be said
of Amos and Micah. Amos was apparently quite unmoved by
Hosea's main topic, the threat to Yahwism from the Canaanite
worship of Baal; and he is also different from Isaiah, for he does not
inveigh against mistaken policies, against armaments and alliances.
Finally, there is absolutely no bridge between Micah and the hopes
cherished concerning Zion by Isaiah, his fellow-countryman and
contemporary; Micah in fact expected Zion to be blotted out of the
pages of history (Micah 3.12). Even the kind of prophetic office
surprisingly discovered in the state documents of Mari, which makes
it clear that the prophet could threaten even the king in God's
name, does not give us any standpoint from which to summarize
and categorize the prophetic role. If their close connection with
the king and their interest in political and military affairs is a particular characteristic of the 'prophets' of Mari, then Israel has com-

parable figures not only in Isaiah, but in a whole series of prophets beginning with Ahijah of Shiloh, including Micaiah ben Imlah and Elijah, and going down to Jeremiah. On the other hand, it is impossible to bring Amos into this category. Nevertheless, in spite of all these great differences, there is a great deal of common matter which links the eighth-century prophets to one another; for their religious ideas led them to an absolutely common conviction, one so novel and revolutionary when compared with all their inherited beliefs, that it makes the difference, considerable as these are, seem almost trivial and peripheral. We shall now make another attempt to find out which element in the prophets' teaching struck their contemporaries as being a departure from the religious standards of the time.

To begin with a very simple statement: these men were set apart from their contemporaries and they were very lonely. Their call gave them a unique knowledge of Yahweh and of his designs for Israel. We have already seen how, apparently to a much greater degree than any of their contemporaries, they are deeply rooted in the religious traditions of their nation: indeed, their whole preaching might almost be described as a unique dialogue with the tradition by means of which the latter was made to speak to their own day. Yet the very way in which they understood it and brought it to life again is the measure of their difference from all the contemporary religious heritage of their nation. When Amos said that Yahweh presided over the migration of the Philistines and the Syrians (Amos 9.7), he was departing pretty radically from the belief of his time. This novel and to some extent revolutionary way of taking the old traditions was not, however, the result of careful study or of slowly maturing conviction; rather, these prophets were all agreed that it was Yahweh who enlightened them and led them on from one insight to another. The reason for their isolation was therefore this – as they listened to and obeyed a word and commission of Yahweh which came to them alone and which could not be transferred to anyone else, these men became individuals, persons. They could say 'I' in a way never before heard in Israel. At the same time, it has become apparent that the 'I' of which these men were allowed to become conscious was very different from our present-day concept of personality. For first of all, this process of becoming a person was marked by many strange experiences of compulsion, and one at least of its characteristics – we have only to think of the 'be still' in Isaiah's demand for faith –

was passively to contemplate and make room for the divine action. Yet, at the same time, this opened up freedom upon freedom for the prophet. He could even break out into an 'exultation of the spirit' about this, as Micah once did when, as his *charisma* welled up gloriously within him, he became conscious of his difference from other people:

> But as for me, I am filled with power,
> [with the spirit of Yahweh],
>   with justice and might,
> to declare to Jacob his transgression,
>   and to Israel his sin.
>
> (Micah 3.8)

There is a very direct reflection of the prophets' attainment of personal identity and of their religious uniqueness in their style, the way in which they speak of God and of the things of God. During centuries of reverent speech Israel had created a language of the cult, and had devised a conventional phraseology for speaking about God; yet there were times when he might also be spoken of in the way these prophets loved to do – in monstrous similes, with an apparent complete absence of any feeling for dignity or propriety.[1] These were *ad hoc* inspirations, the provocative inventions of a single person, whose radical quality and extreme boldness was only justified by the uniqueness of a particular situation and the frame of mind of the people who listened to them.

Even if we knew still less than we in fact do of the way in which the concepts of Yahwism were still a living force at the shrines and among the broad mass of the people at the time when these prophets were active, one thing could yet be said for certain – the new feature in their preaching, and the one which shocked their hearers, was the message that Yahweh was summoning Israel before his judgment seat, and that he had in fact already pronounced sentence upon her: 'The end has come upon my people Israel' (Amos 8.2). The question has recently been asked whether the prophets did not base even these pronouncements of judgment on older tradition. Were there ceremonies in the cult at which Yahweh appeared as his people's accuser? So far nothing definite has materialized; and an answer to this question would not in any way be a complete answer to the other question: why did the prophets proclaim

---

[1] Yahweh, the barber (Isa. 7.20), the ulcer in Israel's body (Hos. 5.12), the unsuccessful lover (Isa. 5.1ff.).

this message? Moreover, the devastating force and finality of the prophetic pronouncement of judgment can never have had a cultic antecedent, for it envisaged the end of all cult itself.

For the proper understanding of what we have called this completely new note in the prophetic preaching, we have not least to remember the changing political situation, Assyria's increasingly obvious and steady advance towards Palestine. When in an almost stereotyped fashion Amos suggests that Yahweh's judgment will take the form of exile, this quite clearly reflects how much the Assyrians occupied his thoughts. The prophets are, however, obviously motivated not merely by one factor but by several. Let us simply say that these men spoke of the divine wrath as a fact, and designated as its proper object their contemporaries' whole way of life, their social and economic attitudes, their political behaviour and, in particular, their cultic practice. At all events, the favourite way of putting it, that this is simply the emergence of new religious ideas, and as such only a new understanding of the relationship between God and man, does not square with the fact that in this matter the prophets most decidedly took as their starting-point the old traditions of Yahwism. It was these that formed the foundation of their attack, and time and again the prophets took them as the basis of arguments with their audiences. Thus, as far as the old Yahwistic tradition was concerned, the prophets and their hearers were on common ground: but they differed in their interpretation of these traditions, which the prophets believed were far from ensuring Israel's salvation. The classic expression of this aspect of prophecy is in Amos' words – her very election made the threat to Israel all the greater (Amos 3.1f.)! This is therefore the first occasion in Israel when 'law' in the proper sense of the term was preached. This is most apparent in the prophets' castigations of their fellow-countrymen for their anti-social behaviour, their commercial sharp-practice. Here they do not in any sense regard themselves as the revolutionary mouthpiece of one social group. Time and again we can see them applying provisions of the old divine law to the situation. Isaiah uses much the same procedure when he measures the behaviour of the people of Jerusalem against the Zion tradition, and looks on armaments or security sought for in alliances as a rejection of the divine help. It is also used by Hosea when he takes the saving gift of the land, which Israel still completely failed to understand, as his starting-point, and uses it to show up the enormity of her faithlessness and ingratitude. Yahweh was known to be the judge of sinners in early Israel also; and early Israel was equally aware that a man's sin is more than the sum total of his several acts (Gen. 3). Yet, the prophets' zeal in laying bare man's innate tendency to oppose God, their endeavour to comprehend Israel's conduct in its entirety, and to bring out what, all historical contingency apart, might be taken as typical of that conduct – this was something new, especially since its purpose was to give reasons for Yahweh's judgment. Thus, for example, Hosea included and discussed the whole story of the relationship between God and his people in his poem on Israel's failure to understand that the blessings of the soil of Canaan were gifts from Yahweh. This was a great intellectual achievement. The prophets' chief concern was not, of course, to summarize human conduct under the most general concepts possible by the method of abstraction, though this does sometimes happen[2]; they reached their goal in a different way. For while they seem to be describing only a particular failure of a particular group of men in a particular situation, they have really depicted, by their use of a few characteristic traits, something that was typical of Israel's general attitude to God.[3]

If when the prophets spoke about man, they seldom used general theological concepts, this may also be connected with the fact that they regarded their contemporaries as the product of a definite history. They never took their hearers by themselves, standing in isolation in their opposition to God; those whom the prophets addressed were already 'the offspring of evil-doers, corrupt sons' (Isa. 1.4), and this did not excuse them, but made their case utterly hopeless.

The way in which the prophets' charges occasionally plumb the depths of history is particularly characteristic; and this gave them the opportunity of radically reviewing the history of God's people. Of course, these extreme ideas do not claim to be universally valid : but the very arbitrariness of their formulation, their concentration on a single idea, makes them a wonderful testimony to an independent conception and understanding of history. Thus, Amos recounts

[2] Here one might think, for example, of Isaiah's characteristic reproach of pride (Isa. 2.11, 17) or of Hosea's equally characteristic term 'spirit of harlotry' (Hos. 4.12; 5.4), or also of Amos' word about the 'pride of Jacob' (Amos 6.8). The comprehensive term 'return' and the statement that Israel does not return, also belong here.

[3] The courtly monologues which the prophets put into the mouth of foreign kings also belong to this tendency to make types, Isa. 10.8ff.; 14.13ff.; 37.24; Ezek. 28.2; 29.3, 9; 27.3.

a long series of divine interventions in Israel's history which caused
disaster – drought, famine, blight and mildew, locusts, and disasters
in war – all designed to bring the nation to its senses; but they
failed to move her to repentance (Amos 4.6-11). The series reads
almost like a parody of the saving history, as if Amos wanted to
contrast the generally accepted tradition with a completely different aspect of Yahweh's history with his people, one which, on this
interpretation, was also a succession of drastic historical acts. In
Isaiah Yahweh complains, in the manner of a father accusing his
rebellious sons (Deut. 21.18-21), that he had 'reared and brought up
sons' (Isa. 1.2). These few words open up great vistas in the divine
action in history. But the song of the vineyard is much fuller and
even bolder in its metaphorical dress. Here Yahweh appears as the
steadfast lover who devotes great care to his 'vineyard' – 'vineyard'
is the cypher for 'beloved' (Isa. 5.1-7). While we should not give an
allegorical interpretation to all his labours (digging the vineyard,
clearing it of stones, building a watch-tower and a wine vat), the
recapitulation of all that the lover did for his vineyard does give
the hearer some idea of the patience and sense of purpose with
which Yahweh tended Israel throughout her history. The picture
of Yahweh as father reappears in Hosea, this time the father who
taught Israel to walk like a little child and who loved her (Hos.
11.1ff.).

Yet these ways of picturing history, however bold and arbitrary
they were, are not in themselves new. What is new is the verdict
which the prophets passed on the history up to their own time,
namely, that it was one great failure, and that at whatever page it
was opened, it bore witness to Israel's refusal. These prophets did
not hesitate to include even the figure of the patriarch Jacob within
this revolutionary view (Hos. 12.4f., 13 [3f., 12]); indeed, they took
only the first steps along this road; Ezekiel, in particular, following
their example, was to take in very much wider vistas still (Ezek. 20).

Yahweh was, however, to have further dealings with Israel; he
did not intend to withdraw from her history because of this failure.
On the contrary, something tremendous was standing at Israel's
door. And this brings us to what is unquestionably the heart of the
prophets' message. As was said, one of prophecy's greatest achievements was to recapture for faith the dimension in which Yahweh
had revealed himself *par excellence*, that of history and politics.
Israel had always, of course, been occupied with the history of her
past, but since about the time of David, she had increasingly writ-

ten off Yahweh as her God as far as the present and the future were concerned; she had taken politics and the shaping of her future into her own hands. The saving history had come to a standstill; now it was rather a thing of the past to be looked back to with respect. We can therefore well imagine the perplexity which these teachings on universal history given by the eighth-century prophets must have caused. They most certainly did not revive the old patriarchal conception of Yahweh's action in history, as this is seen in the accounts of his holy wars in the Book of Judges. The old sacral conception of history, particularly after the development of historiography during the enlightenment in the time of Solomon, had been superseded by a new way of looking at it. One of the most interesting aspects of the prophetic theology is that these men brought the maelstrom of world politics, which involved all nations, great and small, into contact with Yahweh's actions. Even a glance at the verses of Amos mentioned above (Amos 4.6ff.) shows how completely the prophets were able to look on history in this new fashion – and it is most essentially history brought about by Yahweh; for these disasters (drought, famine, and plague) were acts of Yahweh, though in a different sense : they were not miraculous, and they did not break the concatenation of events by means of something completely new – drought and famine can happen everywhere. Such historical acts of Yahweh, one might inevitably conclude, are harder for faith to recognize, because they participate at a deeper level in the ambiguity of all historical phenomena. The prophets, however, would flatly have denied this. Amos's poem is full of growing amazement at Israel's failure to understand this language which her God spoke in her history. Isaiah went even further in asserting that Yahweh's action in history is plain to see :

'In that day it will come to pass that Yahweh will whistle for the fly which is beyond the streams of Egypt and for the bee from the land of Assyria, and they will come and settle all together in ravines, in clefts of the rock, on thornbushes and on all the watering places.
'In that day the Lord will shave with a razor hired and chartered from beyond the Euphrates the head and the pubic hair . . .' (Isa. 7.18-20).

There are two sayings from Isaiah's early period in which the prophet foretells the coming of the Assyrians to Palestine and the judgment which they will execute; and they can be regarded as characteristic expressions of classical prophecy, because their form

and content are quite different from those of all earlier ways of
speaking about Yahweh's action in history. The metaphorical dress
– Yahweh summoning an empire by whistling for it as if it were
an animal, Yahweh as a barber, borrowing a razor, an empire –
speaks of God's absolute power in history. This power is so absolute that it seems as if there is room for no other activity in
history.[4] When an ordinary individual is confronted with the might
of an empire he can see nothing beyond it, and so is faced with the
problem of reconciling its war-potential with God's omnipotence.
The prophet sees things quite differently. The empires on the Tigris
and the Nile are absolutely nothing; they are no more than a borrowed tool in the hand of Yahweh. Though it is true that from the
beginning of the monarchical period Israel began to take a more
secular and realistic view of history, this does not mean that history
had correspondingly moved away from God. On the contrary: in
the older historical tradition we look in vain for evidence of such
a conception of God as is given here, one in which he fills the whole
realm of history and reduces the mightiest factors of the political
world to insignificance ('I, even I, rend and go away, I carry off,
and none rescues,' Hos. 5.14).

We may therefore describe the characteristic feature of the prophetic view of history as follows: not only does it recognize most
clearly Yahweh's designs and intentions in history, it also sees the
various historical forces involved in quite a different light from
other people. The great powers which occupied the centre of the
political stage did not blind the prophets to God; these empires
shrivel up almost into nothingness before Yahweh's all-pervasive
power. It is the 'I' spoken by Yahweh that pervades the historical
field to its utmost limits. It is moving to see how Isaiah and his
subjective certainty about his own view of history came into collision – a proof of its completely undogmatic flexibility and open-
ness. As Assyria advanced, the interpretation he had put upon her
as an instrument of punishment in the hands of Yahweh proved to
be inadequate, or at least partial. The way in which she extermin-
ated nations and the danger that she would treat Jerusalem and

---

[4] There is, however, a slight difference between the two sayings. In the
first Yahweh calls, and the unclean flies come and spread over the land. In
the second Yahweh hires the razor and himself acts by its means. In the
second case, too, all trace of 'synergism' is ruled out. In the Ariel poem (Isa.
29) Yahweh is at the same time the one who attacks and humiliates Jerusalem (vv. 2-4), and the one who saves her (vv. 5-8).

Judah in the same way gave rise to a question: did she not intend also to overrun Zion? Nevertheless, Isaiah was still able to interpret Yahweh's design; he explained the difficulty by saying that the Assyrians were exceeding the task assigned to them. The scope of their commission was merely to chastise, not to annihilate (Isa. 10.5-7). This change in Isaiah's views is a further remarkable confirmation of the prophets' claim to be able to see history in its relation to God clearly and with perfect understanding. In Isaiah's view history can be analysed into the divine design and the coefficient of arbitrary human power. To come to this explanation – and we should make no mistake about this – Isaiah wrestled with the whole force of his intellect as well as of his faith. Written evidence of this expressly rational grappling with history is furnished by the generally accepted interpretation of the didactic poem in Isa. 28.23-9, in which Isaiah makes the multifarious and carefully considered actions of the farmer's sowing and reaping into a transparent parable of the divine action in history. 'Wonderful is his counsel and great his wisdom.'

So far, however, we have dealt almost too much with history in a general sense, with the result that misunderstanding could arise: it might be supposed that the prophets shared our concept of objective history. This is contradicted by the very fact that, as the prophets use the term, wherever history is spoken of, it is related in some sense to Israel. Even Isaiah's famous universalism still keeps to the idea that Yahweh directs history with reference to Israel. Yet, closer consideration of the prophecies of salvation shows that Yahweh's coming action in history upon Israel has still another peculiar characteristic. What comes in question here are not designs which Yahweh formed so to speak in perfect freedom, but only the fulfilment of promises he had already made to Israel in the old traditions. Whether we think of Hosea's prophecy that Israel will once more be led into the wilderness and once more be brought through the valley of Achor into her own land (Hos. 2.16ff. [14ff.]), or of the prophecy that Yahweh will once more gather nations together against Zion, though he is again to protect it, or of the prophecies about the anointed one who is yet to come in Amos, Isaiah, and Micah, we everywhere see to what an extent even the prophets' predictions of the future are bound to tradition; and this in the sense that on the prophets' lips the coming and, as we may safely call them, eschatological events of salvation are to correspond to the earlier events as antitype and type. Thus, even in what they say about the future, the prophets function largely as interpreters of older traditions of Yahwism.

At the same time they introduce a fundamentally new element, which is that only the acts which lie in the future are to be important for Israel's salvation. The old traditions said that Yahweh led Israel into her land, founded Zion, and established the throne of David, and this was sufficient. No prophet could any longer believe this; for between him and those founding acts hung a fiery curtain of dire judgments upon Israel, judgments which, in the prophets' opinion, had already begun; and this message of judgment had no basis in the old Yahwistic tradition. They believed, therefore, that salvation could only come if Yahweh arose to perform new acts upon Israel, an event which they looked on as certain – and they entreated those who were still able to hear not to put their trust in illusory safeguards (Micah 3.11), but to 'look to' what was to come, and to take refuge in Yahweh's saving act, which was near at hand. The prophets were therefore the first men in Israel to proclaim over and over again and on an ever-widening basis that salvation comes in the shadow of judgment. It is only this prediction of a near divine action, with its close relation to old election traditions and its bold new interpretation of them, which can properly be defined as eschatological. Everywhere there were pious hopes and confident statements about the continuance of the divine faithfulness. What the prophets foretold was something completely different theologically. They take as their basis the 'No' pronounced by Yahweh on the Israel of their day, her relationship to Yahweh which had for long been hopelessly shattered. They were sure, however, that beyond the judgment, by means of fresh acts, Yahweh would establish salvation; and their paramount business was to declare these acts beforehand, and not simply to speak about hope and confidence.

Summing up, it may be said that in regard to both their 'preaching of law' and their proclamation of salvation, the eighth-century prophets put Israel's life on completely new bases. The former can only be seen in its true light when it is considered in relation to the latter. We have already emphasized the fact that the prophets did not derive their conviction that Yahweh purposed judgment from any special revelation, independent of his saving acts, but from the old saving traditions themselves; thus, they interpreted the message in a way different not only from their contemporaries but also from all earlier generations. For them the traditions became law. Yet, they were not precursors of legalism; they did not reproach their fellows with not living their lives in obedience to law; their reproach was rather this, that as Yahweh's own people they had continually transgressed the commandments and not put their confidence in the offer of divine protection. How little the prophets' work was aimed at a life lived under the yoke of the law is made particularly clear in those places, which are, of course, few in number, where they go beyond negative accusations to positive demands. 'Seek good, and not evil; hate evil, love good!' 'Seek Yahweh, that you may live!' (Amos 1.14f., 6). This is not the language of a man who wants to regulate life by law. In Amos' view, what Yahweh desires from Israel is something very clear and simple; if not, how could he have described it by the perfectly general term 'good' (cf. also Hos. 8.3; Isa. 5.20; Micah 3.2)? And listen to Micah. The prophet answers the excesses in the performance of legal and cultic rites to which Israel's anxiety was driving her: 'He has showed you, O man, what is good and what Yahweh seeks from you: to do justly, to love kindness, and to walk humbly before Yahweh' (Micah 6.8). This is the quintessence of the commandments as the prophets understood them. There is no demand here for 'ethics' instead of a cult, as if the prophet's desire was to lead men from one set of laws into another. No, something quite simple is contrasted with the arduous performance of works which can end only in destruction – a way along which men can walk before God. Exactly the same is true of the verse in Hosea which 'reads like the programme of an opposition party', to the effect that what counts with Yahweh is not the offering of the proper sacrifices, but 'loyalty to the covenant and knowledge of God' (Hos. 6.6). The vow which this same prophet puts into the mouth of those who turn to Yahweh is given in negative terms, doubtless because it follows a literary category used in worship, but in principle it takes the same line. It does not expect the fulfilment of a legal demand:

Assyria shall not save us, we will not ride upon horses;
and we will say no more 'Our God' to the work of our hands.
(Hos. 14.4 [3])

Isaiah says practically nothing about the inner disposition of the purified remnant, with the result that it is not easy to imagine what this is. The remnant is composed of those from whom Yahweh has not hidden his face (Isa. 8.17), those who have had faith. On one occasion he calls those who take refuge in Zion 'the poor of his people' (Isa. 14.32).

The eighth-century prophets were, of course, only the first to tread this new theological path. Their successors were to go further along it, and in particular were to have still more to say about the question of the new obedience. In general they were to take up the topics they inherited and to develop them in their own way; but they were also to enrich the prophetic preaching with new topics which for eighth-century prophecy had not as yet appeared on the horizon.

14 The Transition to the Babylonian Era

Nahum, Habakkuk and Zephaniah

THE Assyrian empire, which had for so long threatened the Kingdom of Judah, finally collapsed ninety years after Jerusalem capitulated to the army of Sennacherib. To those who witnessed it, the collapse was extremely swift; for in c664, which saw the subjugation of Egypt, Assyria seemed to have reached the zenith of her power. In 612 Nineveh fell to a coalition of the Babylonians, who had sometime earlier thrown off Assyria's yoke, of the Medes, who had recently appeared on the political scene, and of a horse-riding people from Scythia. To be sure, Assyria was not dashed in pieces before the gates of Zion, as Isaiah imagined that she would be; on the other hand, she never came to the point of incorporating Judah into her provincial system. It would be perfectly astonishing if such an epoch-making event as the downfall of Assyria remained unechoed in the pages of the prophets, the keen-sighted observers of all the changes in the political scene.

The man who was first inspired by this event was *Nahum*, and in some poems of more than ordinary magnificence he celebrated it as a judgment of Yahweh on the 'bloody city' (Nahum 3.1). The little book is perfectly attuned to the mood of joy and satisfaction evoked by Yahweh's manifestation of himself in the world as the avenger of wrong. The book contains only a single word directed to Judah herself, and this by the 'messenger who brings good tidings', who exhorts her to be aware of the hour of feasting before Yahweh (Nahum 2.1 [1.15]). Nahum has often been accused of being unlike his near contemporaries among the prophets in saying not a word about the sins of the people of God itself. This would only be remarkable if the prophets as a body were the spokesmen of a single idea – that of ethical monotheism, or of a general moral relationship between God and man. But if we understand that their preaching was completely dependent on the historical events of the hour, this criticism does not apply to Nahum, just as when times of cultic feast are distinguished from those of cultic fast, those to be presumed responsible are the men who thus interpreted such specific times. Nahum is the only prophet who may possibly have had a function within the framework of the cult. His message, too, though it has at least intimate connections with the literary category of oracles against foreign nations, can be seen as following the traditional threats against the enemies of God's people used in a sacral ceremony. As far as the absence of words of judgment against his own people is concerned, it must also be remembered that Nahum's prophetic message very probably dates from the time of Josiah, and in the period after the 'discovery' (II Kings 22f.), that is, after the reform, a time which perhaps the prophets as well as the king looked on as having made a return to Yahweh which held promise for the future.

It is easy to see in retrospect that this joyous hour was soon over. In 609 Josiah was defeated and killed by Necho; Judah was thus brought under Egyptian domination for the first time, though we know next to nothing about the political effects of this. Only a few years later, in 605, the Egyptians were defeated by Nebuchadnezzar, and this victory made the neo-Babylonians masters of Palestine too (II Kings 24.7). Jehoiakim, the successor of Josiah, was, however, an unreliable vassal, and as a result his land suffered greatly at the hands of the Babylonian armies (II Kings 24.1f.).

It is very probably within this period, that is, 609–597, that *Habakkuk* was active. The first part of his prophecy (Hab. 1.2–2.4) consists of an almost liturgical dialogue between the prophet and Yahweh. The prophet twice lays a complaint before Yahweh, and Yahweh twice answers him. The first complaint tells of wrongs and violence; the *torah* 'grows cold', and the wicked lie in wait for the righteous (Hab. 1.2-4). It is hard to say whether this complaint is a reference to oppression by enemies within or by enemies without. It is given a most surprising answer : Yahweh says : Be astounded! now am I arousing a terrible people, the Chaldeans (the neo-Babylonians, Hab. 1.5-11). The prospect here opened up by the divine words, that worse is still to come, that the enigmas of the divine guidance of history are to grow even darker, takes the prophets completely by surprise. This leads to a further complaint : how can Yahweh behold so much iniquity and not intervene? In this case the 'wicked' who swallows up the 'righteous' is certainly a foreign power. Men fall into his nets like fish. The way in which he makes idols of his instruments of war ('therefore he sacrifices to his net and burns incense to his seine,' v. 16) is absurd. Yahweh again answers, with a word which is to be written down, because it is not to be fulfilled at once; indeed, postponement of fulfilment is to be reckoned with from the very start; whatever happens, 'the righteous shall live by his faith' (Hab. 2.1-4). Recent critics have argued that this cannot be the full account of a 'vision' which was given such an elaborate introduction and which was obviously very comprehensive, and they suggest that the theophany described in ch. 3, a tremendous picture of Yahweh arising to do battle with the nations and with the wicked one (v. 13), should also be considered.

Apart from one or two unsolved problems, Habakkuk's prophecy yet shows several characteristic features. The reader who comes to it by way of Amos, Micah, or Isaiah cannot but be surprised at the change which has come over the prophet's relationship to Yahweh. The roles seem to be reversed: the initiative lies with the prophet, for it is he who is discontented and impatient, while Yahweh is the one who is questioned. It is, of course, possible that prophets who were commissioned to act primarily within the cult always made intercession and were recipients of divine answers: but it is open to question whether Habakkuk's prophecy can be classified as cultic. One thing is certain: the way in which he puts his questions and the kind of trials he suffered show Habakkuk to be a child of his own age. The topics of the relationship between Yahweh and the Monarchy during its final period and of the prophetic attitude to theological problems of the time are ones to which we must return later. Meanwhile we must consider the answer Habakkuk received to his complaint. In the first place, it is not in any sense a comforting one (has Yahweh destroyed an old cultic form here?). Yahweh is on the point of shaping history even more ominously. (In Jeremiah we shall meet with a similar instance of cavalier treatment given to a prophet's question.) But those who hold fast to Yahweh will be saved. What Habakkuk says here about the saving power of faith sounds like an echo of the prophecy of Isaiah, particularly since Habakkuk also speaks mysteriously of Yahweh's imminent 'work' (Hab. 3.2), and thus suggests that Yahweh will appear to do battle with his foes. But Habakkuk differs from Isaiah in that he mingles the very ancient *motif* that Yahweh will appear from the south with a *motif* taken from Canaanite mythology – Baal-Hadad's battle with the powers of chaos.

Zephaniah also is chiefly concerned with the imminent advent of Yahweh and a universal battle against the nations on this day: but with him very much more emphasis is laid upon the resulting judgment of Jerusalem and threats against the complacent (Zeph. 1.10-13).

There was, however, a contemporary of Habakkuk and Zephaniah whose preaching covered a very much wider field, and whose task it was to explore new realms in the relationship between Yahweh and Israel and to mark out new theological horizons such as Israel had never before suspected.

15 Jeremiah

JEREMIAH received his call to be a prophet in the year 627–626, and, characteristically, there is a close connection between this and events on the world political scene – trouble was to come from the north and to threaten Palestine, among other places (Jer. 1.13ff.). It is uncertain whether this is an early reference to the neo-Babylonians who, in 625 under Nebopolassar, had made themselves independent of Assyria. In actual fact, thanks to Assyria's collapse and the appearance of the Scythians and the Medes, the situation in Mesopotamia had become dangerously fluid. From the very beginning of his life as a prophet this foe from the north was a determinative factor in Jeremiah's predictions, and it continued to be so amid all the many political exigencies of which the Babylonians were the authors in the years that followed, right down to the time when Jeremiah fell silent. This is the first factor upon which the prophecy of Jeremiah depends. The other derives not from politics, but from tradition. Jeremiah came from a priestly family which lived in Anathoth. Near relatives of his were land-owners there (Jer. 32.6ff.). Though the village lay only a few miles north-east of Jerusalem, it belonged to the tribe of Benjamin. Benjamin was the son of Jacob by Rachel. Yet if she, and not Leah, was the ancestress of Jeremiah (Jer. 31.15), we may at once assume that the traditions cherished both in Benjamin and in Ephraim were those specific to Israel, those of the Exodus and the covenant at Sinai, which we have to differentiate from the traditions of Judah. Once aware of this distinction, the reader who comes to Jeremiah from, say, Isaiah enters a different theological world. The Zion tradition which was determinative for the whole of Isaiah's prophecy has no place whatsoever in Jeremiah; in contrast, what resounds there – even in the prophecies of salvation – are the Exodus, Covenant, and Conquest traditions. No doubt, after his call the scene of Jeremiah's work was Jerusalem; here he had to deal even with kings, and here he also met the sacral tradition of David. He took this seriously, and he used it from time to time in his prophecy. But the limited way in which he employs it, as compared with the predominance of Israelite traditions, makes it plain that here was something quite alien to Jeremiah. There is a further factor. In his early years, Jeremiah was dependent on Hosea. This dependence extends even to his choice of words, and far transcends what was traditional among the prophets, which was at most a dependence in subject matter. This forces us to assume that Jeremiah had close contacts with Hosea's disciples, and possibly even that he had a thorough knowledge of the writing which Hosea left behind. And, as we have already seen, Hosea stood exclusively within the Israelite tradition.

Had these two basic preconditions of Jeremiah's prophecy been all that had to be taken into account, then – making due allowance for various special features either personal or historical – we should have expected from Jeremiah a message fundamentally similar on the whole to that of Isaiah, Micah, or Amos. But this is far from being the case. The actual differences need more than a sentence to describe them; they go to the very heart of this prophet's message and find the most varied forms of expression in specific passages, with the result that we can only proceed step by step to their nearer definition.

One way of determining the special elements in Jeremiah's prophecy is, again, by the examination of literary categories. In fact, the radical differences between the form of Jeremiah's preaching and that of earlier prophets is in itself enough to justify the conclusion that the substance of his message must also have been peculiarly his own. The category of diatribe and threat, which was formerly the prominent one, falls into the background – it is quite remarkable how seldom Jeremiah delivers a message he has received from God tersely and objectively, as for example in the 'messenger formula' form. Further, the line which previously had been so clearly drawn between the prophet's own words and the actual words of God begins to disappear. Jeremiah makes much freer use of divine words spoken in the first person; he makes Yahweh launch forth into long complaints, and in other places he raises his own voice to utter most comprehensive complaints. Where is this to be found in Isaiah or Amos? We meet in Jeremiah – perhaps for the first time – with what we today should describe as lyric poetry. It is because of this as much as anything that his preaching has such a uniquely personal note. To put it briefly: in Jeremiah all the forms of expression to be found in classical prophecy are obviously breaking up. It would, of course, be stupid to view this process solely from its negative and destructive aspect, and then go on to describe Jeremiah as 'in decline' as compared with Isaiah. It is far more important to discover the co-efficient in Jeremiah's prophecy which provides the background for these changes in form, what it was that brought them about, that demanded the creation of new forms for its proper self-expression.[1]

1. Jeremiah's preaching in his early years (Jer. 1–6) may be summarized thus: disaster is coming from the north upon an Israel which has forsaken the worship of Yahweh and given herself up to the worship of Baal. We must, however, notice particularly the outward form which Jeremiah gave this message, for such a statement of its content is far from giving an idea of its real characteristic quality.

The very first major unit (Jer. 2.1-13) is quite characteristic. Yahweh remembers the time of Israel's first love: he defends himself, just as a man on trial might do, by appealing to the kindnesses he did her as he led her through the wilderness into the promised land (vv. 5-7). After the settlement, however, Israel forsook Yahweh. But who has ever heard of a people changing its God? The passage culminates in the paradox that Israel's apostasy runs absolutely contrary to common sense. There is no precedent for it in the whole world (vv. 10f.). In the next two units also (Jer. 2.14-19, 20-8), Jeremiah again starts from the fact that Israel has forsaken her God. This apostasy has its roots in the far distant past (v. 20a). This same point of view – the divine – is again expressed in the image of the choice vine planted by Yahweh: what Israel ruined was a design with a far-reaching historical effect; by falling away to Baal she has put herself outside the reach of all that Yahweh has been trying to do for her. Yet, how was this possible? Can a maiden forget her ornaments? 'Yet my people have forgotten me days without number' (v. 32). In human marriage a woman who forsakes her present husband is legally forbidden to go back to her former one; how then could Israel annul her divorce from Yahweh (Jer. 3.1-5)? There is in fact still something belonging to a more primitive time in the way in which the young Jeremiah

---

[1] A relatively large strand of the Jeremiah tradition bears the marks of the influence of Deuteronomy and the Deuteronomists; i.e., it is dependent on the Deuteronomistic terminology and is in prose. For prophetic diction, the latter suggests in principle secondary redaction. The passages in question are: Jer. 7.1–8.3; 11.1-14; 16.1-13; 17.19-27; 18.1-12; 21.1-10; 22.1-5; 25.1-14; 34.8-22; 35.

places Israel's whole failure in the sphere of the cult, at the altar,
and how he still thinks in cultic categories. (For example, in Jer.
3.2f. the reasoning is still completely sacral – the land was polluted
because of worship which was an abomination to Yahweh, with
the result that in return the rain was withheld from it.) Much less
space is given to reproof for breaking legal enactments than to
complaints against Israel's cultic apostasy (Jer. 2.8b; 5.1f.; 6.6b;
7.27f.; 13.27). Jer. 4.5–6.30 is a collection of prophecies, in the
form of discursive poems, speaking of an enemy from the north,
a mysterious horse-riding people which is to chastise the nation's
forgetfulness of God and punish the many offences it has committed in the sight of Yahweh.[2]

In trying to grasp the precise content of Jeremiah's preaching in
the first phase of his activity we come upon one remarkable fact –
political prediction and the threat of judgment which earlier prophets had outlined so clearly is very much less prominent. In Jer.
2.1-13 it is entirely absent; all that the passage contains is Yahweh's complaint, and reflections on the incomprehensibility of
Israel's apostasy. In Jer. 2.14-19 it is certainly said that Judah is
bringing chastisement upon herself by her apostasy (v. 19), and in
Jer. 2.36 that Yahweh will also disappoint the confidence that was
being placed in Egypt. Not, however, until we come to the war
poems in Jer. 4.5–6.26 do we find genuine prediction in the old
prophetic style concerning a nation running headlong towards
judgment (Jer. 4.5f., 13; 5.15-17); yet these show at the same time
a particularly clear impression of Jeremiah's own characteristic
stamp. Strange to say, the express threats cannot be called the
climax of these poems, or their real subject. This is clear from the
very fact that they do not come at the end, as the goal to which
everything is moving. Rather, they are embedded in cries of alarm,
descriptions of the misery which the war brings over the land,
laments, exhortations to repent, and reflections on the enormity
of the nation's offences, and they form an inseparable whole with
all these. If, then, we ask what these poems say, it is at once
apparent that they contain very much more than invective or the

---

[2] Even today these poems are still sometimes connected with the 'Scythians', though it has become more and more a question whether they can
be connected with what appears to be the rather legendary account given
by Herodotus (1.105) of the Scythians' incursion into Palestine (between
630 and 625). The enemy envisaged by Jeremiah is quite uncertain. It may
be that he thought of a speedy advance of the Neo-Babylonians into Palestine.

announcement of impending judgment. Jeremiah's speech has a strong tendency to become diffuse, and it has epic and even drama- tic qualities. No doubt both in their diatribes and their threats, Amos or Isaiah, like Jeremiah, not only announced what was to come, but also on occasion gave a very graphic description of it, even if it was generally only a thumbnail sketch. With Jeremiah, however, first this descriptive element occupies a much larger place, and secondly – this is still more important – it has a very characteristic theological tendency: the dominant feeling is that of complaint and suffering. In Jer. 2.1-13 there are utterances on the subject of God's feelings of yearning for his lost people, his sense of injustice, and his emotions of dismay at the exchange of gods. Thus, what is said about Israel's apostasy is not said directly, but we derive knowledge of it rather at second hand, from the divine complaint, and this is all that there is to it. The complaint is therefore in no sense the prelude to a word of judgment, but stands in its own right. The case is practically the same with the war poems in chs. 4.5–6.26, the only difference being that here it is the prophet's own pain that serves as a mirror.

> My anguish, my anguish! I must writhe in pain!
> Oh, the walls of my heart! My heart is beating wildly;
>   I cannot keep silent;
> My soul hears the sound of the trumpet, the alarm of war.
>   (Jer. 4.19)

This is a cry with which Jeremiah interrupts the description of the coming war, but in fact it is not a real interruption at all, for elsewhere also the distress is portrayed through the medium of the prophet's soul and its suffering.

> I looked on the earth, and lo, chaos . . .
>   I looked on the mountains, and lo, they were quaking . . .
> I looked, and lo, there was no man . . .
>   I looked, and lo, the fruitful land was desert. . . .
>   (Jer. 4.23-6)

Here, too, the future is described wholly from the standpoint of a man who is feeling its pain before it takes place, and it is as much as he can bear. Compared with this, how objective and detached the earlier prophets' announcements seem, even when they were spoken with very deep feeling! In Jeremiah we are conscious of a prophet's feeling of solidarity with his people in their danger, and even with the land itself in hers, such as we shall never meet with again.

Finally, it must be said that in this first phase of his activity, Jeremiah was still far from regarding Yahweh's relationship to Jerusalem and Judah as broken for good and all. He envisaged severe testing. Yet, be the danger ever so great, Yahweh had so far 'not torn his soul away from Jerusalem'. Because of this, the prophet's task was 'to give Jerusalem warning' (Jer. 6.8). We therefore find the literary category of 'exhortation' used more frequently in this earliest section than anywhere else. Jerusalem is to wash her heart from wickedness, and then she will be saved (Jer. 4.14). What is needed is that the fallow ground be broken up, and no seed sown among thorns – or rather, the circumcision of the heart (Jer. 4.3f.). Jeremiah attached particular hopes to the 'repentance' of the Northern Kingdom (Jer. 3.6ff.), though in this he perhaps shared a hope which everyone cherished during the reign of Josiah.

2. There is good reason for believing that Jeremiah was silent in the years which followed Josiah's reform (621). We may well assume that his attitude at this time was at least one of goodwill, all the more so since this was the king of whom he was later to speak in more than usually appreciative terms (Jer. 22.15f.). The reason for this break in his activity is not, however, sufficiently clear to allow us to take it as the basis for definite conclusions as to his attitude towards the 'Deuteronomic' reform.[3] After Josiah's ill-starred death Jehoiakim succeeded to the throne, and he was unhappily in every respect the very reverse of his predecessor. Immediately we find Jeremiah active once more. To a people which pays no heed to the decalogue, even the temple itself has no security to offer – so Jeremiah proclaims in his famous temple address (Jer. 7.1-15). Yahweh has earlier shown that he can utterly destroy a shrine with a long and honourable history (Shiloh). What worth does a shrine have if men who hold Yahweh's command-ments in contempt think that they can find security there! This ruthlessness, which does stop short of criticizing the holiest of things, and shatters in pieces all pious attempts to attain security,

---

[3] The situation is rather different in the case of the much discussed ques-tion of Jeremiah's attitude to Deuteronomy. It is unlikely that Jeremiah could have come out forthrightly against the digest and 'codification' of the will of Yahweh as ancient tradition had handed it on and as this was pub-lished in Deuteronomy.

sets Jeremiah completely in line with the classical prophecy of the eighth century. But while the source which gives Jeremiah's own words does no more than report the address itself, a further account by a second hand adds a number of details, in particular those concerning the perils and hostility incurred by the prophet as the result, and from which he was only delivered by the intervention of certain Judeans from the country districts (Jer. 26.10). This is the one case in the prophets where we have the benefit of both a prophet's own account of an incident and that of a narrator. The conjunction is not, however, coincidental; for this shift of the centre of interest from the message to the messenger is in fact characteristic of the whole tradition connected with Jeremiah. The earlier prophets had also been repeatedly exposed to hostile threats. With Jeremiah these apparently took on a more menacing aspect. This is not itself important. What is important is the change in the idea of what went to make a prophet; and from this arose a growing interest in the prophet's life as well as in his message, and in the complications in which his message involved him. It began to be appreciated that the two were very closely connected. Jer. 19.1–20.6 is a good example of this new interest.[4] Jeremiah had broken an earthen flask in the sight of certain men, and had said that Yahweh would break the nation and the city in exactly the same way. The narrative goes on to report that as a result of this incident Jeremiah was beaten by the chief officer Passhur and put in the stocks for a night.

Though the temple address was in the form of an exhortation directed to a nation which wanted to find safety in an illusory security, its ending leaves open only the prospect of complete rejection. The verses which follow also forbid the prophet to intercede, for Yahweh is to reject the 'generation of his wrath' (Jer. 7.29); even those who survive the catastrophic events will long for death (Jer. 8.3). This has a much sterner ring than anything in Jeremiah's earlier prophecies. In the same way also, the liturgy for the great drought ends with an appalling word of judgment which leaves all pleas for mercy unheeded (Jer. 15.1ff.). The oracle on the jars says that it is to be Yahweh himself who fills the nation, even the priests and prophets and kings, with drunkenness, so that they end by destroying themselves (Jer. 13.12-14). In this connection, Jeremiah was thinking of events that were soon to come to pass, plundering by enemies (Jer. 17.3), slaughter of

---

[4] Vv. 2b-9 and 12-13 can be seen to be later additions.

the young men (Jer. 15.8f.), and exile (Jer. 10.18; 13.8-10; 17.4).

Yet, even although Jeremiah realized that Jerusalem was apparently to be finally rejected, this did not prevent him from occasionally speaking as if there were still hope, as if it were still possible for the nation to be reached, as though there could still be a decision 'before it grows dark, before your feet stumble on the twilight mountains, while you hope for light; but he turns it into gloom' (Jer. 13.16). Jeremiah's revelation at the potter's workshop also belongs here. For Yahweh's words as the prophet watched the potter knead the spoiled vessels together in order to remould new ones from the lump, 'can I not do with you as this potter has done?', are really only a question and they leave the door still open for the call to repentance (Jer. 18.1ff.).

In this last passage, the content is somewhat obscure, and this detracts from its impressiveness. In the opening verses Jeremiah is dealing with his own people who, by being shown the immense freedom at God's disposal, are to take warning. Then, however, it suddenly passes over into general terms. If Yahweh has purposed evil against a particular nation, and it 'turns', then he repents of the trouble he intended to cause; and if he has purposed good for another nation, but it is disobedient, then he will alter his design and punish it. This part, too, is meant to indicate Yahweh's freedom as he directs history, but it does this in an oddly theoretical way by giving imaginary examples which are quite contrary to the sense of the passage, for they almost make Yahweh's power dependent on law rather than on freedom. This middle passage (vv. 7-10), after which Judah is once more addressed, should probably be regarded as a theological expansion.

Jeremiah did not threaten only his own nation with disaster. There is a collection of oracles in which he prophesies the destruction of a number of foreign nations (the Egyptians, Philistines, Moabites, Ammonites, Edomites, Syrians, Arabs, Elamites, and Babylonians).[5] The disasters which these oracles picture are always those of war: but, oddly enough, the power which is the source of such destructive effects remains almost completely obscure.[6] These oracles thus all the more emphatically see Yahweh at work; it is he himself who acts; his is the sword that is to rage against these nations. Since these oracles contain still further elements

---

[5] Jer. 25.15-38; 46–51. In the latter, the oracles against Babylon (Jer. 50f.) are certainly post-Jeremianic.

[6] According to 47.2, the enemy comes from the north; only in 49.2 is Nebuchadnezzar mentioned by name.

which derive from the usage of the old holy wars, it becomes all
the more probable that this form, the war oracle, belongs to the
earliest prophetic tradition. This was the way in which the prophets of Israel who functioned in these wars had once actually
spoken when Israel – or rather, Yahweh – went into battle against
the foe. The passage of time had brought considerable changes
over the category, and it had become detached from its original
context, Israel's sacral warfare; its horizons widened to embrace
universal history, for it now addresses nations with whom ancient
Israel had never had dealings in her wars. Jeremiah's oracles against
foreign nations very nearly comprise a judgment on the whole
world. The element of reproof of the arrogance and godless self-
confidence of the foreign nations (Jer. 46.7f.; 48.1f., 7, 14, 42; 49.4)
probably only derives from the ideas of a later period, that of
classical prophecy, but others which come down from the earliest
tradition have maintained their place with an astonishing tenacity.
This early tradition is the only possible explanation of the prediction that Yahweh is to do battle in person and of the vague
language used in the poems to speak about the human instrument
of judgment – Babylon was undoubtedly in Jeremiah's mind.

Thus, like his predecessors, Jeremiah looked into the future and
noticed the movements on the horizon of universal history. Nor
does he fall short of them in the boldness with which he interpreted events, or the certainty with which he saw Yahweh taking
the most direct action. However, while with Amos or Isaiah we
can grasp all the essentials of their preaching simply by looking
at what they have to say about the future, with Jeremiah the case
is different; for, as well as predictions, there are a great many
passages which deal exclusively with the present, and which are
particularly characteristic of this prophet.

> Grief rises within me,
>   my heart is sick within me.
> Hark, cries for help of the daughter of my people from the
>   length and breadth of the land:
> 'Is Yahweh not on Zion,
>   is her king not in her?'
> Why have they provoked me with their images,
>   their foreign vanities?
> The harvest is past,
>   the summer is ended and no help has come for us.
> Because of the wound of the daughter of my people am I
>   wounded.

I mourn, and dismay has taken hold of me.
Is there no balm in Gilead,
    is there no physician there?
Why is there no healing for the daughter of my people?
O that my head were waters,
    my eyes a fountain of tears,
that I might weep day and night for the slain of the daughter of
    my people!

(Jer. 8.18-23 [8.18–9.1.])

It is impossible to classify this passage under any specific literary
category. There are certainly echoes of a community lament and
of something like an answer from Yahweh (v. 19); but these are
perceived only, as it were, from the outside; whereas the very
first sentence places us inside Jeremiah's thought, and this is where
all the essential action takes place. Here, first, is the realization
of a calamity overtaking the land; the prophet looks for deliverance; then it becomes clear to him that all is lost; and he finally
expresses the wish that he could weep out his eyes in tears of
grief. This is the 'event' of which we are told! How far is this
prophetic proclamation? Verses such as these in fact come very
close to being what we describe as free lyric poetry. This again
shows us that Jeremiah is much more keenly inflamed, and in an
entirely novel way, by a poetic impulse which exists quite independently from prophecy. It also raises the question of how
we are to evaluate this remarkably large increase of the element
of pure poetry. The answer might, of course, be that the essential
element of prophecy in Jeremiah was weakened by his yielding
to the poetic impulse: it could also be that this apparent weakness gave his words a new strength. Those who took the view
that these passages mark the first appearance of a free, personal
ego and that Jeremiah is the father of free, personal prayer, found
this question relatively simple; and there is, of course, an element
of truth in their theory. But it is very doubtful whether it does
justice to the special character of these passages. Because of the
special nature of God's relationship with Israel, and particularly
with Jeremiah, it is probable *a priori* that the specific form of
these passages and their message can only be understood in the
light of their specific preconditions.

3. This also comes out, much more clearly, in those passages
which, while still being laments, do not remain pure monologue,
but rise to the level of conversation with Yahweh. They are usually

called *Jeremiah's Confessions*. In form and content, of course, they vary considerably. Their common factor is that they are not addressed to men, as is the case with divine oracles, but are a result of Jeremiah's own musings with himself and with God. It has long been recognized that the form and style of these most private utterances of the prophet are more or less closely linked with the ancient literary category of the individual lament.[7] It is therefore quite fascinating to watch the way in which, as occasion arose, Jeremiah interpenetrated the conventional usage of the old cultic form with his own concerns as a prophet, and transformed it. The poem which most closely adheres to the traditional usage is Jer. 11.18-23. It contains a complaint about attacks on the prophet himself, and a plea that the one to whom he has committed his cause should protect him. It is a prayer which might have been made by anyone suffering persecution. This cannot, however, be said of the prayer contained in Jer. 15.10-18. This, too, includes many of the conventional requests: but they are so intimately expressed that they can only have come from Jeremiah's personal experience.

> Words coming from thee were found, so I ate them.
> Thy word became to me a joy and the delight of my heart;
> I was called by thy name, Yahweh, God of hosts!
> I do not sit rejoicing in the company of the merrymakers,
> bowed down by thy hand, I sit alone;
> for thou hast filled me with indignation.
>
> (Jer. 15.16-17)

God then answered this complaint. This itself corresponded with the normal order of events in the liturgy; for there, through the mouthpiece of the priest, Yahweh answered a prayer of lamentation with an 'oracle of salvation'. Here, however, where it is no longer a cultic ritual form, there is a change – Yahweh answers with a rebuke; indeed, when Yahweh reaffirms the great promise he made to Jeremiah at the time of his call – on condition that the prophet returns to him – he tells Jeremiah that he has betrayed his prophetic calling. But if he does return, Jeremiah may once more 'stand before God' and 'serve [him] as his mouthpiece' (v. 19).

Jer. 12.1-5, too, contains a question-and-answer conversation between God and the prophet. Jeremiah wants to plead his case before Yahweh; yet, in the very first words, he gives up his whole

---

[7] Jer. 11.18-23; 12.1-6; 15.10-12, 15-21; 17.12-18; 18.18-23; 20.7-18.

case – 'Yahweh is always in the right'. The prophet's subject is
the prosperity of the godless, whose chain of success seemed
secure in every link. Here Jeremiah is undoubtedly contributing
to a question which occupied his whole generation. How is the
individual's share in Yahweh's gifts apportioned? The question has
become personally important for Jeremiah, for he has burnt his
boats far more than others, and his dependence on Yahweh has
made his life one of danger and solitude. Here, too, God's answer
is a stern one:

> If you run with men on foot, and they weary you,
>   how can you compete with horses?
> And if you only feel safe in a land at peace,
>   how will you fare in the jungle of Jordan?
>
> (Jer. 12.5)

Yahweh demolishes the prophet's question with a counter-ques-
tion. The answer shows amazement that Jeremiah is threatening
to founder on such difficulties, for they are as nothing compared
with what he ought to be able to bear. It is pointed out that he
is still only at the threshold of his trials, and that, as Yahweh's
prophet, he ought not already to be complaining about such
problems.

Jeremiah probably discussed the trials of his office with Yahweh
in this way throughout his life. He was given special commissions:
for example, he was appointed a gleaner (Jer. 6.9), that is to say,
he was to look for the unnoticed fruits of goodness. His answer
was that it was useless to make such a search. On another occasion
God gave him the task of going about amongst his people as an
assayer, to test, as is done in a refinery, whether the dross could
be separated from the pure metal; but again his answer was that
it was impossible (Jer. 6.27-30). One thing stands out – both the
passages in which Jeremiah holds converse with God and those
in which he alone is the speaker always shade off into darkness,
the impossibility of the prophet's task. There is not one single
instance of hope, no occasion when he gives thanks to Yahweh for
granting him redemptive insight or for allowing him some success.
What a difference from the defiant boasting of Micah! Reading the
passages in the order in which they occur – and they are best taken
as arranged according to the course of the prophet's life – one is
haunted by the impression that the darkness keeps growing, and
eats ever more deeply into the prophet's soul. It is no accident

that the last two passages of this kind also describe the extremity of Jeremiah's despair. Israel's language when she addressed God in prayer, and particularly in the prayer of lamentation, was never exactly timid: she was not afraid to use positively audacious expressions. But here Jeremiah went far beyond anything in the traditional form of lamentation which, though freely expressed, did keep more or less to conventional cultic language.

Thou hast deceived me, Yahweh; and I let myself be deceived.
Thou wast too strong for me, and prevailed over me.
Now I have become a laughing-stock all the day:
everyone mocks me. . . .
Yet, if I thought, I will know no more of him
and speak no more in his name,
then it was in my heart like a burning fire,
shut up in my bones.
I tried to hold it in, but I could not.
(Jer. 20.7, 9)

The word which we have rendered as 'deceived' in fact designates the act of enticing and seducing a young girl – 'you took advantage of my simplicity' (Rudolph). The prophet cannot really blame himself: his power and Yahweh's were too unequal. He admits that he attempted to escape from this intolerable service: but the word with which he was inspired was like fire in his breast. Therefore he had to continue to be a prophet. But what is to become of him as a result! His days are to end in shame (v. 18). And so finally – and this is the supreme consequence – Jeremiah curses the complete abandonment of his life (vv. 14f.). These last passages are soliloquies – the God whom the prophet addresses no longer answers him.

The confessions are central for the interpretation of Jeremiah. They must be understood as the written testimony to an intercourse between Yahweh and his prophet that is both striking and unique. The external circumstance of the order in which they appear in itself outlines a road which leads step by step into ever greater despair.[8] Each one of these passages tells of a separate experience. The areas in which these experiences were made are also different. Yet, the passages all point alike to a darkness

[8] This would of course still remain substantially true even if the order of the texts as given does not correspond to the succession of the incidents in the prophet's life; for what is important is not the phases of his passion in which Jeremiah had these experiences, but the fact that he did have them.

which the prophet was powerless to overcome, and this makes them a unity. It is a darkness so terrible – it could also be said that it is something so absolutely new in the dealings between Israel and her God – that it constitutes a menace to very much more than the life of a single man : God's whole way with Israel hereby threatens to end in some kind of metaphysical abyss. For the sufferings here set forth were not just the concern of the man Jeremiah, who here speaks, as it were, unofficially, as a private individual, about experiences common to all men. In every instance these confessions grow out of his specific situation as a prophet; what lies behind them is a call to serve in a quite particular way, a relationship of particular intimacy with Yahweh, and therefore they have in the highest degree a typical significance for Israel. This does not, of course, mean that commentary on Jeremiah should pay no attention to the human side of the matter. The intimacy of spiritual intercourse with God here revealed, the maturity of self-expression, and the freedom in admitting one's own failure and making no concealment of God's censure, is a manifestation of the human spirit at its noblest. But here we are particularly concerned with the circumstances in which this phenomenon occurred and the place in Israelite prophecy occupied by these confessions and what they add up to. When they are set in this wider context, their most striking feature is seen to be a questioning reflection. We should not think of the earlier prophets as unconscious organs of the divine will in revelation, but what happened with Jeremiah was an increasing inability to see where he was going. It was not merely that he pondered on the lack of success which attended his work. The failure was not only an outward one, stemming from other people, it was also personal, in that the prophet was no longer at one with his office and his tasks – at all events, he now called the first in question. With Jeremiah, the man and the prophetic task part company; indeed, serious tensions threaten the whole of his calling as a prophet. As a result of this parting between the man and the prophet, the prophetic calling as it had been known up to Jeremiah's own time entered upon a critical phase of its existence. As the child of his age, it was no longer possible for Jeremiah to resign himself to the will of Yahweh; he had to question, and to understand. In his sensitiveness and vulnerability, his feeling for the problems of religion, he was certainly at one with many of his contemporaries He was undoubtedly very much more spiritually complex than

Amos or Micah. Thus, there was also a large element of the refractory in him, a rebellion against decrees of the divine will which earlier ages, more secure in their faith, would probably have accepted with greater submissiveness. On the one hand, he was bound to Yahweh and remained subject to him more than any other prophet; on the other, however, he had to let his thoughts have free range. And the seriousness with which he took this intellectual state, which of course lay outside his prophetic calling proper, is shown precisely by the wide range of his reflection on theological problems.

There is no doubt that from this point of view Jeremiah is to be regarded as a late-comer in the prophetic series. At the same time, he is completely conscious of his spiritual ancestry – he speaks more than once of the prophets who preceded him.[9] During his lifetime, there was certainly something very like a tradition even among the free prophets. This included not only the subjects and topics traditional in prophetic preaching, but also the experiences and disappointments of many generations. There was certainly also an awareness of an unchanging pattern of failure, to be found only amongst these free prophets and transmitted by them alone. If it is only with Jeremiah, and not earlier, that the earthly vessel broke, the reason is primarily that the prophetic office assumed by Jeremiah was far greater in its range and depth than that of any of his predecessors. In proportion, he also required the continuous support of God. At the same time, however much we attempt to place Jeremiah in the correct historical framework of his age, and this is essential, a great deal remains that we cannot explain. It is still Jeremiah's secret how, in the face of growing scepticism about his own office, he was yet able to give an almost superhuman obedience to God, and, bearing the immense strains of his calling, was yet able to follow a road which led ultimately to abandonment. Never for a moment did it occur to him that this mediatorial suffering might have a meaning in the sight of God. Again, if God brought the life of the most faithful of his ambassadors into so terrible and utterly uncomprehended a night and there to all appearances allowed him to come to utter grief, this remained God's secret.

4. Surprisingly enough, beside the confessions, the book of Jeremiah contains another source which traces the prophet's steps. This is the *narrative of Baruch* (Jer. 37–45). However, just as the

[9] E.g., Jer. 7.25; 26.5; 28.8.

confessions are confined to the development of the prophet's inner life, so the Baruch narrative is only concerned with describing the outward circumstances of this *via dolorosa*. Although it does sometimes contain oracles spoken by the prophet, the accounts given here are not to be understood, as in many other cases (e.g., chs. 26–29), as no more than the narrative framework for the oracles; no, the subject described here is the dramatic events in which the prophet was involved and which brought him into greater and greater dangers. Baruch begins with Jeremiah's imprisonment and dispassionately traces the subsequent events, recording the prophet's various conversations and ending with his exile in Egypt. Jeremiah's death apparently formed no part of this account. The narrator's strict concentration on events in space and time is made clear in the résumés with which he likes to round off his description of the various stages in the story.[10] The man who so exactly describes the stations of Jeremiah's cross was obviously most closely associated with the events, then can therefore be no doubt that his description is trustworthy. Yet, what can be said of his intention? To what end did he make a written record of the events? What was it he wanted to document with such a circumstantial account? The author in fact gives the true cause of all Jeremiah's suffering.

As is well known, it was Jeremiah's firm conviction that, at this time, by the instrumentality of Nebuchadnezzar, God was about to effect great changes in the international situation, and that he would bring Judah also under the dominion of the Babylonian empire (cf. Jer. 27.5f.). Consequently, during the months when the danger from Babylon was at its greatest, all that Jeremiah could prophesy was that the capture of the city was certain (Jer. 37.8, 17; 38.3; cf. 34.2), and his advice was to capitulate as quickly as possible (Jer. 38.17). This conviction, which Jeremiah also expressed in public, was therefore the reason for the prophet's sufferings, for the nationalists in Jerusalem found a man with such convictions quite intolerable.

Jeremiah's sufferings are described with a grim realism, and the picture is unrelieved by any divine word of comfort or any miracle. The narrator has nothing to say about any guiding hand of God; no ravens feed the prophet in his hunger, no angel stops the lion's

---

[10] 'So Jeremiah came into the vaults of the cistern, and remained there many days' (Jer. 37.16). 'So Jeremiah then remained in the court of the guard' (Jer. 37.21; 38.13, 28). 'So Jeremiah came to Gedaliah at Mizpah and remained there with him' (Jer. 39.14).

mouth. In his abandonment to his enemies Jeremiah is completely powerless – neither by his words nor his sufferings does he make any impression on them. What is particularly grim is the absence of any good or promising issue. This was an unusual thing for an ancient writer to do, for antiquity felt a deep need to see harmony restored before the end. Jeremiah's path disappears in misery, without any dramatic accompaniments. It would be completely wrong to assume that the story was intended to glorify Jeremiah and his endurance. To the man who described these events, neither the suffering itself nor the manner in which it was borne had any positive value, least of all a heroic value: he sees no halo of any kind round the prophet's head. On the contrary, Jeremiah sometimes appears in situations which even a reader in the ancient world might have regarded as somewhat dubious (Jer. 38. 14-27).[11]

As with all the rest of Israelite narrative writing, the actual theological substratum in the account of Jeremiah's sufferings is fairly slight. Its author is not one who is aware of connections between things and the necessity which brings them about. On the other hand, he does give some leads. It is only to be expected that in a writing which is so uncommunicative in the matter of theology, a particular hermeneutical significance should attach to its conclusion, and this has been rightly emphasized in recent literature. The conclusion here has something special about it, since Baruch tells of an oracle which Jeremiah spoke to him himself regarding his complaints:

'You said, "Woe is me! Yahweh adds sorrow to my pain; I am weary with groaning, and can find no rest." . . . Thus hath Yahweh said: "Behold, what I have built I am breaking down, and what I have planted, I am plucking up" . . . and do you seek great things for yourself? Seek them not! For, behold, I am bringing great evil upon all flesh, says Yahweh, but to you I give your life as a prize of war wherever you may go' (Jer. 45.3-5).

Here we meet again with the idea of the reorganization of world-history and of the destruction it is to bring with it. An undertone of sadness accompanies Yahweh's words: they hint almost at feelings of pain at this work of pulling down what his own hands built up. At this time of judgment, when God has to tear down his own work in history, no human being can look for any good

---

[11] For an example of an entirely opposite idea, cf. the way in which the martyrs were made heroes in II. Macc. 7.

for himself; it is no wonder if the prophet and those about him are drawn in a quite exceptional way into this demolition. Thus, the reason why Baruch so conscientiously traces all the details of this *via dolorosa* is that the catastrophic events into which the prophet was drawn do not after all come by chance; instead, they bring about the divine destruction; here a human being has in unique fashion borne a part in the divine suffering.[12]

5. The oracle just mentioned ended with the mysterious words that Baruch was to preserve 'his life as a prize of war', that is to say, he was to survive the destruction following this judgment. The saying naturally leads us to ask about the special features of Jeremiah's *prophecies of salvation*. Prophecy of this kind is not, of course, to be looked for in the early part of his activity, for, as we have already seen, at that time he hoped that Israel could still decide for or against Yahweh. In his final period, however, during the reign of Zedekiah, the case was completely different. The Babylonians had already administered one shock – in 598 the young king Jehoiachin was deported, along with his officials and members of the upper class. Even those who had never before considered the question were now asking what action Yahweh would take next. We have already seen that Jeremiah expected the Babylonians to win a complete victory. But his was an isolated position, opposed to an overwhelming war party and, still more serious, a group of prophets who stirred up religious ferment and prophesied that Yahweh would speedily intervene for the honour of his people and of his pillaged temple. Jeremiah's clashes with his own colleagues were probably among his hardest battles (Jer. 23.9ff., 28). He seems at times almost to have been overwhelmed by the problems thus raised. We can see him searching deliberately for practical criteria to identify the false prophet. At one moment he compares the content of their message with the prophetic tradition, at another he is suspicious of the forms in which they received their revelations, because they appealed to dreams, and not to a word from Yahweh, and were therefore in danger of self-deception. Further, their offensive conduct spoke against them. The very fact

[12] Even if the addition of Jer. 45 is not to be attributed to a particular purpose which Baruch wished to serve – it could indeed also be regarded as a rather chance appendix, since the event it records is twenty years earlier than what is recorded in the chapter immediately preceding – even so, the word is still of great importance for the Baruch narrative, because it so clearly defines his place within the divine destruction of history: he cannot stand outside it.

that Jeremiah could not point to any criterion that might in principle answer the question – who was the false prophet and who the true – showed him the full difficulty of the problem; for there could be no such criterion in respect of form or content. Just because Yahweh was not 'a God at hand', but a God 'far off' (Jer. 23.23), there could be no standard method of any sort by which he granted revelation. On the other hand, it is surprising to see a prophet so troubled with a problem. At times in his famous encounter with Hananiah, Jeremiah's arguments are almost groping (Jer. 28.5-9). The splendid certainty and straightforwardness which characterizes the way in which classical prophecy saw things was no longer vouchsafed to Jeremiah in the same measure. Two centuries before, the problem of prophets who contradicted one another was given a completely different solution by Micaiah ben Imlah. Micaiah did not look for criteria to deal with his opponents. He saw the whole matter as lying in the transcendent sphere, in the council of Yahweh, who himself inspired the false prophets in order to entice Ahab (I Kings 22.21ff.). With such a point of view he could accept his opponents' *bona fides* and their subjective certainty of having been commissioned much more calmly than did Jeremiah.[13]

This last decade of Judah's independence thus constituted a high water mark of prophetic activity in which Jeremiah's message of doom made his position very difficult. But perhaps even greater difficulty was caused by his message of salvation, for, of course, it was entirely different from that of his colleagues. The letter which he sent to those exiled to Babylon in 598 was written in a spirit of calm certainty. It was aimed at their faithless feelings of

---

[13] Deuteronomy, too, tries – not very successfully – to draw up objective criteria by means of which the false prophet might be recognized (Deut. 18.21f.). The contradiction between prophet and prophet, each speaking in the name of Yahweh (cf. Jer. 27.4; 28.2), must have been particularly confusing in the final period of the Monarchy. As far as we can see from the relevant texts, their colleagues' proclamation of salvation was particularly suspect in the eyes of the 'true' prophets (I Kings 22.11ff.; Micah 3.5ff.; Jer. 6.14; 14.13; 23.9ff.; 28.5-9; Ezek. 13.16). It is probable that the false prophets and their predictions of salvation coincided with the interests of the national cult. But even this is no assured criterion. Did not what they predicted coincide with the faith of Isaiah? The falsity cannot be seen either in the office itself, or in their words themselves, or in the fallibility of the man who spoke them. It could only be seen by the person who had true insight into Yahweh's intentions for the time, and who, on the basis of this, was obliged to deny that the other had illumination.

depression and their equally faithless fervent hopes, and clearly reveals the tension between the two.

'Build houses and live in them, plant gardens and eat their produce. Take wives and have sons and daughters. Take wives for your sons, and give your daughters in marriage, that they may bear sons and daughters, that you may multiply there and not decrease. Seek the welfare of the city where I have sent you into exile, and pray to Yahweh on its behalf, for its welfare is also your welfare' (Jer. 29.5-7).

Here is solitary exhortation to sober thinking and an attack on fervent high hopes fostered by religion. The exiles were obviously quite unable to appreciate the real seriousness of the situation, and therefore Jeremiah counselled them to do what lay to hand and prepare to settle down. This meant, of course, a change in the deportees' attitude to Babylon. She is no longer the enemy. She carries the people of God upon her bosom, and therefore it was fitting for prayer to be made for her. Times had changed. Prayer for Babylon is now a prayer for the people of God. For the latter has still a future in his sight.

'For I know the thoughts I have for you, says Yahweh, thoughts for welfare and not for evil, to give you a future and a hope' (Jer. 29.11).

In this passage it is possible that Jeremiah's whole message on Yahweh's will for the salvation of Israel is contained in the two words 'future and hope', for v. 14b, which speaks of a return from among all the nations, is perhaps an interpolation. He was more explicit about the nation's future on the occasion when he was ordered to purchase a field, for in the context of this piece of family business he received a word from Yahweh. Jeremiah had the deed of purchase duly witnessed and placed in safe keeping at a time when besiegers were already throwing up earthworks against the city and famine was raging within it, as a symbol that 'houses and fields and vineyards shall again be bought in this land' (Jer. 32.15). In this glance towards the future Jeremiah had in mind equally the exiles of 598 and those who still remained in Jerusalem. In the vision of the two baskets of figs, however, those in exile are now ranked much higher than those still in the land of Judah. They alone are the subject of the promise:

'Thus hath Yahweh, the God of Israel, spoken: Like these good figs, so do I regard as good the exiles from Judah, whom I have sent away from this place to the land of the Chaldeans, and set my eyes upon them for good. I will bring them back to this land, I will build them up and not tear them down, I will plant them and not uproot them, and I will give them a heart to know that I am Yahweh, and they shall be my people and I will be their God, for they shall return to me with their whole heart' (Jer. 24.5-7).

The eschatological salvation which Yahweh purposed for his people is therefore this. Both the exiles of 587 and those of 721 are to return home. Jerusalem is to be rebuilt (Jer. 33.4ff.), people will once more buy fields and vineyards, and there will also be Rechabites who take upon themselves particularly rigorous vows of abstinence and serve Yahweh in this strange way (Jer. 35.18f.). This picture of the future is almost disappointingly sober. Jeremiah has nothing to say of any changes in the natural world of the land where God's chosen people are to dwell; and nothing of any paradise-like fertility. All he says is that, in the land which at the moment is lying waste, conditions will return to normal and life will go on again. Pilgrimages to Jerusalem will be arranged once more (Jer. 31.6), and laughter and rejoicing be heard in the villages (Jer. 30.18f.; 33.10f.). Of Yahweh it is said that he will look upon them 'for good' (Jer. 24.5). This apparently rounds off the picture of Israel's new life before Yahweh and, reading it, one might feel that the time of salvation of which Jeremiah speaks is in all essentials a restoration of previous conditions. The truth is quite the opposite. With Jeremiah, the gulf between old and new is far deeper than with any of his predecessors among the prophets, for in our account of these prophecies of salvation we have still to consider the statement that Yahweh is to give his people a heart to know him (Jer. 24.7). If we neglect this we never grasp the characteristic feature of the salvation envisaged by Jeremiah, for here is his prophecy of the new covenant compressed into one sentence.

Jeremiah addressed his words about the new covenant to the exiles of the former Northern Kingdom (Jer. 30.1-3), but the saving event which he had in mind was certainly to be shared by the whole of Israel, in particular by the exiles of 721 and 598.[14] What is important, and towers right above any previous prophetic prediction, lies in the *prophecy of a new covenant* which Yahweh

---

[14] The date of the 'little book of comfort for Ephraim' (Jer. 30f.) is a matter of controversy. The fact that Jer. 31.31ff. bears a direct resemblance to both Jer. 24.7 and Jer. 32.37ff. makes it probable that this prophecy belongs to the later period of the prophet's activity.

intends to make with Israel. This is clearly something quite different from Yahweh's saying that days were coming when he would
again remember his covenant which he made with Israel. No, the
old covenant is broken, and in Jeremiah's view Israel is altogether
without one. What is all important is that there is no attempt here
– as there was, for example, in Deuteronomy – to re-establish Israel
on the old bases. The new covenant is entirely new, and in one
essential feature it is to surpass the old. To us today, however, the
greatness of the difference between the two ordinances is not at
once obvious, and so we must take the much-interpreted passage
Jer. 31.31ff., examine it with particular care, and safeguard it
against some common false expositions.

The content of the Sinai covenant was the revelation of the
torah, that is to say, the revelation of Israel's election and appropriation by Yahweh and his will as expressed in law. This *torah*
is also to stand in the centre of the new covenant which Yahweh is
going to make with Israel 'in these days'. Thus, as far as the content of Yahweh's self-revelation is concerned, the new covenant
will make no change. Jeremiah neither says that the revelation
given at Sinai is to be nullified in whole or part (how could a revelation given by Yahweh ever be nullified or taken back!), nor does
he in any sense suggest any alteration or expansion of its content
in the new covenant. The reason why a new covenant is to ensue
on the old is not that the regulations revealed in the latter have
proved inadequate, but that the covenant has been broken, because
Israel has refused to obey it. And here is the point where the new
factor comes into operation – there is to be a change in the way
in which the divine will is to be conveyed to men. At Sinai, Yahweh had spoken from the mountain top, and the Elohist – thus
early – reports that Israel could not endure this address, and begged
Moses to receive the revelation of the divine will in her stead (Ex.
20.18ff.). If we understand Jeremiah correctly, the new thing is to
be that the whole process of God's speaking and man's listening
is to be dropped. This road of listening to the divine will had not
led Israel to obedience. Yahweh is, as it were, to by-pass the process
of speaking and listening, and to put his will straight into Israel's
heart. We should completely ignore the distinction between outward obedience and obedience of the heart, for it scarcely touches
the antithesis in Jeremiah's mind. As we have already seen, every
page of Deuteronomy, too, insists on an obedience which springs
from the heart and conscience. It is at this very point, however,

that Jeremiah goes far beyond Deuteronomy, for in the new covenant the doubtful element of human obedience as it had been known
up to date drops out completely. If God's will ceases to confront
and judge men from outside themselves, if God puts his will
directly into their hearts, then, properly speaking, the rendering of
obedience is completely done away with, for the problem of obedience only arises when man's will is confronted by an alien will.
Now, however, the possibility of such a confrontation has ceased
to exist, for men are to have the will of God in their heart, and
are only to will God's will. What is here outlined is the picture
of a new man, a man who is able to obey perfectly because of a
miraculous change of his nature. It is very significant that Jeremiah, writing comparatively late in Israel's history, should lay so
much emphasis on the anthropological side of Yahweh's work of
salvation.

Behold, days are coming, says Yahweh, when I make a new covenant
with the house of Israel < >, not
like the covenant which I made
with their fathers when I took them
by the hand to bring them out of
the land of Egypt, which they
broke, so that I had to show myself
as lord, says Yahweh. But this is to
be the covenant that I will make
with the house of Israel after these
days, says Yahweh: I will put my
instruction within them and write
it upon their hearts, and so I will
be their God, and they shall be my
people. Then no man needs any
longer to teach his neighbour, and
no man his brother, saying, 'Know
Yahweh,' but they shall all know
me, from the least to the greatest,
says Yahweh, for I will forgive their
iniquity, and I will remember their
sin no more. (Jer. 31.31-4)

Behold, I will gather them from all
the countries to which I drove them
in my anger and my wrath and in
great indignation, and will bring
them back to this place and make
them dwell in safety. They shall be
my people, and I will be their God,
and I will give them a heart and a
way, that they may fear me for
ever, for their own good and the
good of their children after them.
And I make an everlasting covenant
with them, that I will not turn
away from doing good to them.
And I will put the fear of me in
their hearts, that they may not turn
away from me. And I will have joy
in doing them good, and I will plant
them in this land in faithfulness,
with all my heart and with all my
soul. (Jer. 32.37-41)

These two passages almost read like two targums on a text. At
any rate, they are so alike in content that we ought not to miss
the opportunity of amplifying the exposition of Jer. 31.31ff. by
comparing them. Both texts have the same event in view, but there
are considerable differences in the way in which they describe it.
We cannot say very much about their literary relationship. We
can be certain that Jer. 32.37ff. is not simply a copy or twin of
Jer. 31.31ff. The phraseology of the second passage is too distinc-

tive, and the distinctions occur at the central points of the argument. If Jer. 32.37ff. is to be regarded as later than Jeremiah
himself, then it might be taken as something like an interpretative
paraphrase of Jer. 31.31ff. But the dependence is not close enough
for this. Furthermore, even Jer. 31.31ff. can hardly be the form
of the oracle as it was originally spoken by Jeremiah, for he, like
the other prophets, usually gave his oracles a verse form. Jer. 31.
31ff. is, however, prose, though there are one or two places where
the outlines of an original verse form can still be recognized. The
best explanation is, therefore, that Jeremiah spoke of the new
covenant on two different occasions, both times in a different way,
and that each of the passages as we now have them has been subsequently worked over.

God's promise to put his will in men's hearts is only slightly
altered in Jer. 32.37ff. – he is to put the 'fear' of him 'in their
hearts'. Here we have only to recall that in the Old Testament the
expression 'the fear of God' is the equivalent of obedience to the
divine will. As a result of this creative grafting of the will of God
on the hearts of men, all theological teaching offices become un-
necessary and there is no further need for admonition. This agrees
with ch. 32.39, where it is said that in their fear of Yahweh men
are to have one heart and one way. The will of God is one, and
each man is to know it in his heart. In the same way, too, it was
prophesied in ch. 24.7 that, when the Israelite tribes of the North
return home, Yahweh will give them a heart to know him. This is
Jeremiah's way of speaking of a future outpouring of God's spirit,
for what he thinks of is nothing other than a spiritual knowledge
and observance of the will of God. Ezekiel after him is to speak
in the same sense of the spirit's being planted in what had hitherto
been the stony heart. The fact that Jeremiah never actually employs the word 'spirit' means nothing when we remember the very
concrete terms in which he describes the way in which this transfer takes place. (The word 'covenant' does not occur in Ezekiel.)
There is nothing in the second passage corresponding to the forgiveness of sins in the first.

The road whose end Jeremiah glimpsed when he spoke of the
new covenant is a long one. In terms of prophetic speech it might
be called Israel's full and final return to her God. Had the prophets
been preachers of revival, we should expect to find their statements on conversion in the form of exhortation. But that is not
the case, for they are found rather amongst their preaching of
judgment. What the prophets have to say on this subject is that

contemporary Israel is not returning to Yahweh,[15] and by the word
'return' they mean not so much our individualistic and spiritual
idea of 'conversion' as the nation's turning back to the serenity
of its original relationship with Yahweh. Jeremiah also takes up
the complaint that Israel refused to return (Jer. 8.5); indeed, on
occasion he went so far as to say that a return to Yahweh was
actually inadmissible, for it would contravene the law (Jer. 3.1).
Yet, in spite of this, it is precisely with this prophet – and in
speeches of exhortation at that – that the call to return is suddenly
found on a broad basis.[16] In Isaiah (Isa. 7.3) and Hosea (Hos. 3.5;
14.2ff. [1ff.]) Israel's return was a subject of promise; but just for
that very reason Hosea could also exhort Israel to return, call upon
her to close with God's offer (Hos. 14.2 [1]). Here again, therefore,
Jeremiah is Hosea's disciple. The call bulks larger with him, however, inasmuch as he recognized – and in this he goes far beyond
Hosea – that such a return was Yahweh's work upon Israel (Jer.
24.7). So far, then, there is no essential difference in basic theology
between Isaiah and Hosea on the one hand and Jeremiah on the
other, for in all alike what is said about returning is found within
the proclamation of salvation. Where, however, the later prophet
does differ from his predecessors is in the much greater emphasis
he places on the human side in the divine saving work. Jeremiah is
also the prophet in whose preaching one constantly comes across
reflections on whether man's disposition can or cannot be changed.
God appointed him an assayer (Jer. 6.27), and he knew that the
human heart was 'deceitful' and 'incurable' (Jer. 17.9). As he thus
meditated on the nature of man, he arrived at a very profound
understanding of elements in it. His thoughts constantly revolve
round the tremendous bondage in which man is the prisoner of
his own opposition to God. It is simply not in his power to determine his way; to no one is it granted to direct his own steps (Jer.
10.23). Any attempt to make oneself clean in God's sight would
be even less successful – man would still remain stained with his
guilt (Jer. 2.22).

> Can an Ethiopian change his skin
> or a panther his spots?
> Then also even you can do good
> who are accustomed to do evil.
>
> (Jer. 13.23)

[15] Amos 4.6, 8, 9, 10, 11; Isa. 9.12 [13]; 30.15.
[16] Jer. 3.12, 14, 22; 18.11; 35.15.

It is only in the light of this devastatingly negative judgment on the possibility of Israel's setting her relationship to God aright again by her own efforts that one can understand not only what Jeremiah says about the new covenant, but also his imploring entreaty to return. Jeremiah gained ever-increasing insight into man's actual condition, and for this reason he did not unthinkingly demand that man should follow a road on which he would again inevitably come to grief. His appeals to return increasingly emanate 'from God's decision to save'. They urge the nation to settle for what God has promised to do for it. No matter how many reservations we may have about interpreting a prophet's message in terms of his own psychology, we may nevertheless assume in the case of Jeremiah that he constantly reflected on the problem of man; that is to say, he reflected on the question of what must come about in man as man if God is to receive him into a new communion with himself. If God is again gracious to him, how can he in any way stand before him as man without once again coming to grief because of his heart's opposition to God? The answer which Jeremiah received to this question was the promise that God would himself change the human heart and so bring about perfect obedience. No prophet before Jeremiah was so much at pains to provide a basis for the human side of God's saving event. None the less, Jeremiah was not the only one to wrestle with this particular set of theological problems, and because of this we shall have later to consider his prophecy of the new covenant not merely as something isolated, but as set within still wider contexts.[17]

6. So far as we have found Jeremiah's prophecy to have roots in tradition the case is clear – Jeremiah stands and acts upon the Exodus-Sinai tradition, and this gives his preaching a very broad foundation. He shows his indebtedness to tradition both when he looks back (Jer. 2) and when he looks forward (Jer. 31.31ff.). At the same time, however, it is perfectly obvious that Jeremiah also took up the *Messianic tradition associated with David*. Linked with a diatribe against the nation's useless shepherds comes the following prophecy – the connection between the two literary categories is not altogether clear:

[17] This peculiar prophetic interest in what may be called the eschatological man who is justified in God's sight also lies behind the prediction in Zeph. 3.11-13 : God himself will remove the proud boasters; 'you shall no longer be haughty in my holy mountain, for I will leave in the midst of you a people humble and lowly, that seeks refuge in the name of Yahweh, the remnant of Israel.'

> Behold, days are coming, saith Yahweh, when I will raise up
>   for David a righteous branch.
> He shall reign as king and deal wisely,
>   he shall execute justice and righteousness in the land.
> In his days Judah will be saved
>   and Israel will dwell securely.
> And this will be the name by which he is called:
>   Yahweh is our righteousness.
>
> (Jer. 23.5-6)

The fact that the oracle employs the terminology which had long
been conventionally applied to the monarchy is, of course, no
reason for suggesting that it does not come from Jeremiah himself.
The designation of the king as shepherd, the special significance
attaching to his throne-names, and the righteousness and wisdom
of his rule, all form part of the language of the court. Nor should
Jeremiah's authorship be questioned on the grounds that the prophecy may be felt to show a certain colourlessness, a lack of that
personal emotion which almost everywhere else characterizes his
diction. The impress of his own personality on a piece of old traditional matter, so as to make a new thing of it, varied from case
to case, nor was there always the same need for the prophet to
alter: there were cases when it was enough for him to actualize
the tradition in the form in which he received it. It is, of course,
remarkable that in ch. 23.5f. he speaks of an anointed one of the
line of David, but in ch. 30.9 of the return of David himself. In
the complex of prophecies concerning the lost Northern Kingdom
(Jer. 30–31) there is, however, an oracle on the subject of the
coming of the anointed one in which we meet with something
special that Jeremiah had to say.

> His ruler shall come forth from his midst;
> I will make him draw near to me, that he may walk before me;
> for otherwise who would risk his life to draw near to me? says
>   the Lord.
>
> (Jer. 30.21)

Of the many powers and functions of the anointed one, only one
is here singled out; however, it is apparently the most important,
as it is also the hardest – Yahweh is to 'make him draw near' to
himself. Since the term 'to draw near' is a technical term of the
priesthood, its use here might indicate a sacral and specifically
priestly function of the anointed one. Yet, on the basis of traditional Messianic concepts, it is much more probable that the ex-

pression here indicates a specific privilege at court. The anointed one is Yahweh's representative on earth; as such he shares the throne with him (Ps. 110.1), and has most personal converse with him. Among the things which testify to and emphasize the intimacy of the anointed one's association with Yahweh, and his part in the divine government of the world, is included the right of free access to Yahweh. What Jeremiah means is that the anointed one deals directly with Yahweh: he has access to the most secret counsels of the ruler of the world.[18] However, the special feature of this prophecy lies pre-eminently in its reflections on the uniqueness of this access. It can only truly be attributed to this one person, the anointed one. No one else would be ready 'to give his heart in pledge'. This expression comes from the legal sphere, and denotes the deposit of a pledge or the giving of security. Thus, the rhetorical question that so strangely interrupts the prophecy is meant to suggest that this access on the part of the anointed one to Yahweh is only possible on the condition that he yields up his life. No indication is given as to where Jeremiah thought the particular danger lay. The commentaries think of early Yahwism's belief that the one who sees God must die.[19] It seems to me to be extremely characteristic that even in a Messianic prediction, Jeremiah is particularly interested in the preconditions of the saving event as these affect the person involved. In his view – and here again we recognize Jeremiah – the most important thing is that the anointed one risks his life, and in this way holds open access to God in the most personal terms possible. 'Who is it who gives his heart in pledge to come near to me?' This is one of the hardest questions that was ever put in ancient Israel. What knowledge of God and of man was required for it even to be asked!

---

[18] The word 'approach' occurs with this specifically courtly sense in II Sam. 15.5. It is significant that the verb is also used when the 'son of man' is presented to the council of the king in heaven (Dan. 7.13b). In this connection, when the prophecy speaks not of the king, but of the 'ruler', this is perfectly correct, for Yahweh is the king. Cf. here also Zech. 3.7b.

[19] Judg. 6.23f.; 13.22; Isa. 6.5. The prophecy ends in v. 22 with the old covenant formula, an indication of how strands of tradition with completely different origins are now beginning to be woven together.

16 Ezekiel

THE fact that Jeremiah and Ezekiel were more or less contemporaries has always led to their teachings being compared. Even a child can see that, although both came from priestly families, they are extremely different not only in temperament, but especially in their way of thinking, speaking, and writing. But to be able to pin-point the difference, to define Ezekiel's specific standpoint as a prophet and his use of traditional material as opposed to those of Jeremiah, would be to solve not only the unusual measure of perplexities in Ezekiel's message but also those in Jeremiah's. As far as the outward course of Ezekiel's life is concerned, intensive research has made clear that the reasons which led some critics to deny that the scene of his work was the exile are inadequate. To divest his message of its exilic dress and assume that he worked exclusively in Jerusalem before 587 entails a radical criticism which makes deep inroads into the very nature of the prophecy which affect the text. We may therefore start by supposing that Ezekiel arrived in Babylon with the first deportation in 598, that he was there called to be a prophet in 593, and that he exercised his office from then on until about 571. The great interest with which he followed the course of events in Jerusalem – so great that at times he even seems to be living with the people in the homeland rather than with those around him in Babylon – is something he has in common with exiles of all times. The very careful arrangement of his book (chs. 1–24 oracles of doom against Jerusalem and Judah, chs. 25–32 oracles against foreign nations, chs. 33–48 oracles of salvation for Judah) is beyond all doubt due to fairly complicated redaction, but present-day criticism once more thinks of a considerable basis of genuine prophecy. This conviction rests not least on the autobiographical form in which his work has come down to us and the careful dating of many of the oracles, for these, with recognizable exceptions, must derive from the prophet himself.

Like all his predecessors, Ezekiel followed events on the political scene with a keen interest. Assyria had left the stage (Ezek. 32.22f.). The two empires in whose sphere of influence Palestine now lay were Babylon and Egypt. In grave danger from the former, Judah sought help from the latter, and was bitterly disappointed (Ezek. 17.1ff.; 30.2of.). After this the prophet follows the advance of Nebuchadnezzar (Ezek. 21.23ff. [18ff.]). The Babylonian emperor is first of all to deal with Tyre, and Ezekiel is very well informed about conditions there (Ezek. 26–27). After this the Babylonians advance against Judah and Jerusalem, whose fall a messenger announces to the exiles (Ezek. 33.21). Similarly, the prophet is aware of the hostile attitude of the lesser neighbouring peoples, the Ammonites (Ezek. 25.2ff.) and the Edomites (Ezek. 25.12ff.). As has already been said, there is nothing surprising in the fact that Ezekiel was *au fait* with all that went on in the homeland, even in detail, for this is how exiles have behaved down through the ages.

In matters of general knowledge and culture alone Ezekiel's intellectual horizons were unusually wide. More detailed consideration of his knowledge of the traditions connected with the saving history and with sacral law will be given later; this fell within the more restricted sphere of his professional knowledge as a priest. Yet, his casual remark about the exceptional ethnic position of early Jerusalem is amazing: 'as to your origin, your father was an Amorite and your mother a Hittite' (Ezek. 16.3), because the two terms exactly fit the actual historical conditions which obtained in Jerusalem before the time of David – a Canaanite population and a 'Hittite' governing class.[1]

As well as possessing such historical knowledge, Ezekiel was familiar with a variety of traditional material of a mythological or legendary kind (the primeval man, Ezek. 28.11ff.; the foundling, Ezek. 16.1ff.; the marvellous tree, Ezek. 31.1f.), which can hardly have been common or general at the time. At least, the use which he makes of this material, and the way in which he grafts and fuses it into the quite dissimilar elements in his preaching, point to an unusual intellectual ability to integrate material. When we further notice that Ezekiel is as well-informed about the technical details of shipbuilding as about the places from which the necessary materials had to be imported (Ezek. 27.1ff.), we arrive at a picture of a man of not only all-round general culture, but of intellectual powers of the first rank. For Ezekiel, more even than Jere-

[1] Ezekiel also knows of the consequences of the disasters of the year 701, the transfer of Judean territory to the Philistines (Ezek. 16.26f.).

miah, needed to express his prophetic message in writing – in an ordered form. He makes scarcely any use of the shorter units of expression, the diatribe and the threat, which classical prophecy had employed. When he speaks, the results are as a rule literary compositions, even large-scale discussions, for example, the literary category of the dirge, which he develops to almost baroque proportions.[2] In these compositions which, as we have said, are often considerably extended in length, Ezekiel more than any other prophet likes to reduce his subjects to a figure or type. The prophets had from the very first stimulated their hearers' attention by use of the 'parable' or the 'riddle' with the veiled element which they contain. With Ezekiel, however, the disguised form of expression no longer derives from the prophet's public dispute with his audience; it is much more a question of an artistic literary form. To this category belong the parable of the vine, which approximates more closely to the parable proper (Ezek. 15.1ff.), the allegory, called a 'riddle', of the two eagles and the topmost twig of the cedar tree (Ezek. 17.1ff.), that of the girl whom Yahweh first found and later espoused (Ezek. 16), the two laments over Zedekiah (Ezek. 19.1-9 and Ezek. 19.10-14, the lioness and the vine), and again the allegories in Ezek. 21.2ff. [20.46], and 24.3ff. A different but just as characteristic indirect method appears where Ezekiel uses typical cases to shed light on problems and point the way to their solution. The three successive generations in Ezek. 18.5ff. are a schematic abstraction, and the three intercessors Noah, Daniel, and Job (Ezek. 14.12-23) are equally types serving as examples. Imagery of this kind and the tendency towards abstractions and types enable Ezekiel to some extent to stand back from his subject – his expositions largely have an air of cool didactic detachment: and, where the prophet allows himself to be coarse and even shocking in his descriptions, this can have a positively icy effect. Here the difference from Jeremiah, whose preaching is so shot through with the emotions of his own troubled heart, is particularly great. In fact, Ezekiel must have been a man of completely opposite temperament. None the less, this very coldness and hardness upon which the commentators all remark, produces an impression of grandeur and aloofness. It would, of course, be completely wrong to see in Ezekiel the detached judge of his age and its abuses, for within this man glowed a strange fiery zeal, not merely for Yahweh, but also for Israel. What is really remarkable and intriguing, how-

[2] Ezek. 19.1ff., 10ff.; 27.1ff.; 28.1ff.; 31.1ff., 32.1ff.

ever, is that Ezekiel finds a place for rational reflection beside the visionary and inspired elements in his work. No other prophet feels so great a need to think out problems so thoroughly and to explain them with such complete consistency. In other words, Ezekiel is not only a prophet, but a theologian as well. And this double office was essential for him, because he confronted a presumptuous and indeed rebellious generation for which a prophet's preaching was not enough: he had to debate and argue with it.

1. The account of Ezekiel's call at the river Chebar (Ezek. 1.4–3.15) is itself a complex of traditions of baroque proportions. It is built up of several kinds of traditional material, but none the less is meant to be a unity in its present form. Ezekiel sees the 'glory of Yahweh' coming down from heaven, and then receives his commission in the form of a kind of state paper written in heaven. The message which he is to preach as an 'ambassador' is handed to him in a roll. Each part of this unit has a long history of tradition behind it; and this applies not least to the disclosure that in the exercise of his prophetic office he must preach to deaf ears and dwell among scorpions (Ezek. 2.6). The burden of no prospect of success laid on the prophet in the first hour of his ministry must continue to increase; this, too, is traditional.[3] But Yahweh arms him for this road on which he will find opposition too great for any human power to support – he makes the prophet's face harder than flint. Yet the message of doom which Ezekiel is given to eat – it is written in a book which exists already in heaven – tastes as sweet as honey to him. This means that from now on he is entirely on God's side; the prophet and his message are the same. Unlike Jeremiah, therefore, he does not rebel against it.

The roll which the prophet had to eat had 'lamentations and mourning and woe' (Ezek. 2.10) written on both sides of it; thus, his commission, like that of all his predecessors, was 'to declare to Jacob his trangression and to Israel his sin' (Micah 3.8). Our task must now be to understand what is peculiar to Ezekiel's conception of Jacob's transgression and to his method of argument.

Even a cursory reading of the text makes one thing plain. Where Ezekiel speaks of sins, he thinks in particular of offences against sacral orders. Complaints about transgression of the social and moral commandments are very much less prominent. For Ezekiel,

---

[3] Heedlessness of the prophet's message must have taken curious forms; there even seem to have been people who gave him the kind of hearing that a singer with a beautiful voice receives (Ezek. 33.32).

the cause of Israel's approaching fall lay quite indubitably in a failure in the sphere of the holy. She had defiled the sanctuary (Ezek. 5.11), turned aside to other cults (Ezek. 8.7ff.), and taken idols into her heart (Ezek. 14.3ff.) – in other words, she had 'rendered herself unclean' in the sight of Yahweh, and this is the reason for her punishment.[4] The richest quarries for information are, of course, the great historical retrospects in chs. 16, 20 and 23. There is no mistaking that these are written from a priestly point of view. No doubt, Ezekiel is above all else a prophet, but the world of ideas in which he lives, the standards which he applies, and the categories according to which he sees Israel's existence ordered before Yahweh, are expressly those of a priest. Another outcome of a priestly, sacral way of thought is the importance which Ezekiel attaches to the land of Israel and its cultic status (Ezek. 36.17). Indeed, to the prophet the people of Israel and its land are so closely united that he often speaks to 'the land of Israel' or the 'mountains of Israel' as if they were Israel herself.[5] The standard by which Ezekiel measures Israel's conduct is that of the 'ordinances', the 'judgments', which Yahweh gave to his people (Ezek. 5.6, etc.).[6] When Amos accused Israel he, too, was concerned with transgressions of the commandments. The difference in Ezekiel, however, comes out characteristically in the remarkable changes in the forms he uses. Exact analysis of Ezek. 14.1-11 has made it clear that while the unit begins as a prophetic diatribe, this form is presently abandoned, and the discourse proceeds in the impersonal form used for regulations in sacral law ('Any man of the house of Israel who cherishes his idols . . .' v. 4). The same thing is found with the threat. After the usual 'therefore', God speaks in the first person in v. 6, but again the words pass over into the form characteristic of the language of sacral law ('Any one of the house of Israel, or of the aliens that sojourn in Israel, who separates himself from me . . .' v. 7). This is not simply the prophet arrogating an alien form, applying it *ad hoc*, and then dropping it. Such a remarkable use of forms is much more than just a casual game with an unaccustomed form; it points to a profound difference in Ezekiel himself. Not only does he make use of the old sacral ordinance in the diatribe; what is of greater import is that, when he

---

[4] Ezek. 20.30f., 43; 23.7, 13, 30; Ezek. 22.26; 23.39; 26.22f.
[5] Ezek. 7.2; 21.7f. [2f.]; 36.6; 6.2f.; 35.12; 36.1, 4, 8.
[6] Texts like Ezek. 18.5ff. or 33.25 allow us to see the 'ordinances' which the prophet has in mind.

announces the punishment, again, without further ceremony, he
uses the wording of the old ordinance and the punishment it prescribed. He does not give a judgment based on his own prophetic
outlook: here it is enough for him to cite the age-old penalty
prescribed in the ban – this is an old sacral formula – in the words
of the old ordinance. This gives an important clue towards answer-
ing the question of what traditions form the basis of Ezekiel's
preaching, and so helps us to a better understanding of him. Ezekiel's roots are in the sacral tradition of the priesthood. It is from
this that he took these basic categories by which all sacral thought
understands the world, the categories of the holy and the secular.
At the same time the sacral tradition also supplied him with a
number of standards still then in existence by which those who
were in contact with the holy had to live. Ezekiel had, of course,
no priestly function. His message went far beyond priestly theology, and, indeed, can easily be shown to have shattered its bases
at certain points. Ezekiel's relationship to this sacral tradition is
curiously ambivalent: he was dependent on it, and yet free from
it. The effect of this attitude on his prophecy was that this sacral
understanding of the world shaped even the prophecies of the
new Israel.

2. It is to this priestly tradition that Ezekiel also owes his *picture
of the history* of Israel's origins. Like others, Ezekiel summoned
up history to demonstrate her lost condition and sinful depravity.
He drew up three such indictments, basing them on a broad historical foundation (Ezek. 16, 20 and 23). The recapitulation, in ch.
20, of the history from the time when the nation was first elected
down to her taking possession of the land is of particular interest,
because here the prophet follows on the one hand an ancient and
well-known *schema* of the saving history long ago established in
tradition – though it was apparently not that of any of the source
documents which form our Hexateuch – while on the other he
gives the traditional material a completely new twist by means
of a highly individualistic interpretation and arrangement of it.
The election, that is to say, the beginning of this history of Israel's
dealings with Yahweh, took place in Egypt with the revelation
of the name Yahweh and the giving of the first commandment.
Yet here, right at the very start, we at once meet with novel features in this historical survey. Even in Egypt the people refused
to obey this revelation: they did not forsake the cults practised
there, and even in Egypt Yahweh all but rejected them (vv. 5-10)!

Then a second phase follows – Yahweh leads Israel into the wilderness and reveals the commandments to her. However, this attempt to bind the nation to himself also failed (vv. 11-14). The result is the third phase – Yahweh urged his commandments on the second generation as well; again, of course, without meeting with any obedience (vv. 15-17). In the fourth and last phase Yahweh gives his people commandments 'that were not good', in particular the commandment to offer up their first-born sons, because of which Israel was inevitably defiled in God's sight (vv. 18-26). Here the description ends – more or less at the point designated by the traditional summaries as the conquest. We cannot say for certain that details of this account of the sacred history were not found in tradition; yet this travesty of it, a succession of divine failures and acts of chastisement, must be exclusively the work of Ezekiel. The prophet has made the venerable tradition into a monstrous thing, and he shows a quite paradoxical mixture of close attachment to it on the one hand and audacious freedom in its interpretation on the other. He divides the history into four phases, each of which has four acts (1. Yahweh reveals himself; 2. Israel disobeys; 3. Yahweh acts in wrath; 4. Yahweh spares Israel). It is easy to see that the prophet was working with material which did not really lend itself to his interpretation. This is, of course, particularly true of the passage dealing with the commandments which were 'not good', where prophetic interpretation reaches its boldest limits.[7] It is also quite clear that the traditional material has had an alien *schema* forced on to it, where it is said that on each occasion Yahweh was obliged to refrain from pouring out his wrath 'in order not to profane his name in the sight of the nations' (20.9, 14, 22). The first three phases of the history close by saying that Yahweh restrained his anger out of 'pity' for his people, and resolved to go on leading Israel (vv. 9, 14, 17). This enabled the prophet to make the link with the earlier summaries which, of course, only recounted the actual facts of the way by which Israel was

[7] Theological interpretations of this commandment are also to be found in the priestly tradition (Num. 3.12ff.; 8.16). In Ezekiel this meaning put upon a commandment which, while it was certainly recognized as having been given by Yahweh, had, however, for long ceased to be taken literally, is an extremely bold one. Since, however, Ezekiel too understood the commandments given at Sinai as commandments by whose observance men live, this interpretation of an isolated commandment does not allow us to draw radical conclusions as to the theological significance of the commandments in Israel. Ezekiel himself describes the thing as exceptional.

led. In the final phase this refrain is lacking. This phase, therefore, which really lasts down to the prophet's own time, is still open.

It cannot, of course, be denied that Ezekiel's intellectual mastery of this history led to a slight distortion of its real nature. The prophet schematized it and divided it into phases: but these, with the exception of the last, have an absolutely cyclical course, for each returns to the point where the one before it ended. The old summaries, compact as they are in detailing the history, had an element of progression in each phase: here, however, divine action is characterized by repetition. This, of course, makes the question of how Yahweh will act in this final and still open phase all the more exciting.

Such, then, is Ezekiel's understanding of the canonical saving history – on Yahweh's part a series of unsuccessful actions, and on Israel's a constant failure to comply with the divine will. The one thing which allowed the whole story to go on was a lasting divine 'inconsistency', namely, God's regard for the honour of his name among the nations. Ezekiel's real intention in making these historical excursions is this – what can be expected of a people with such a pre-history, a people that all this long time had been wearing the patience of its God to shreds? Moreover, the history of Yahweh's dealings with Israel has actual prophetic force, for, just as it was a history of divine judgment, so Yahweh will again bring his people into the 'wilderness of the peoples', in order there again to enter into judgment with them (vv. 35f.). However, this judgment again will not exterminate Israel: it is to be a purifying judgment.

Ezekiel also reviewed the history of the monarchical period. But here he had far less documentary material on which to draw than for his recapitulation of the 'canonical' saving history. Excerpts from annals did not supply his needs: what he needed was a conspectus which again considered the age not from the political angle, but as the story of God's action; and this did not yet exist, for the Deuteronomic histories only came into being after the time of Ezekiel. He was therefore thrown back on his own resources, and had to depend on such recollections, either of his own or of his contemporaries, as were still available. The consequence was one with which we are already familiar – factually, the account of this period proves to be much less vivid, with actual historical events much less clearly set down and described, than was the case with the earlier saving history. In both chapters the prophet chose the form 'allegory', though, of course, he continually abandons metaphorical language to speak directly of historical events. In ch. 16 he represents the history of Jerusalem as the story of a girl exposed at birth but ordered by Yahweh, as he passed by her, to live: she grew up to marry him, but thereafter broke her covenant with him by her continual unfaithfulness. Such a picture of the history is again as black as it can possibly be. Even when we bear in mind that in Ezekiel's time people were particularly conscious of their unworthiness in the sight of Yahweh ('you are the fewest of all people', Deut. 7.7), the cutting pungency of his description of the paradox of the divine act of election far transcends anything that had ever been said hitherto. Judah-Jerusalem was like an abhorred foundling, on whom not the slightest care had been bestowed: but Yahweh, who saw her 'weltering in her blood', commanded her to live; he bathed her, washed off her blood, clothed, and adorned her; but when she grew up, she lapsed into harlotry. Now Yahweh is about to summon her lovers; they are to execute a ghastly judgment upon her who was once the bride of Yahweh. The verdict passed in the other allegory, that of the two sisters Oholah and Oholibah, who are the two kingdoms with their capitals Samaria and Jerusalem (ch. 23), is even more sweeping. Although they played the harlot even in Egypt, Yahweh took them to wife, and they bore him children; but they never gave up their harlotry. Oholibah-Jerusalem was the more corrupt. Now Yahweh has had enough of her also, and the end is the same as in ch. 16 – the lovers are to come and execute judgment.[8]

These three reviews occupy a special place in Israel's conception of her own history. Leaving aside the Chronicler's history, they add a final and completely new version to Israel's long series of pictures of her history. Israel's view was never a heroic one. It was never herself she glorified, but the deeds of Yahweh. Yet Ezekiel brought everything connected with the human factor under Yahweh's judgment in an entirely unprecedented way. With him the human partners – and they are men who had been called into fellowship with Yahweh – are shrouded in utter darkness. Hardly anything more could be said than is done here about Israel's unfaithfulness, her indifference to the love of God, and her inability to render the slightest obedience. For a proper understanding of

[8] Here and in ch. 16 Ezekiel uses the term 'whoring' in a double sense. He understands it as cultic apostasy to the nature deities, but he sometimes uses it with reference to politics, seeking security with the great powers.

this, however, we have to notice the theological standpoint of the message. Two things need to be kept in mind. Ezekiel speaks as he does in order to give the reason for a divine judgment which is to come about in the very near future. He also speaks in the light of a saving event, whose outline he can already discern, an event which Israel is to take to herself and which is entirely unmerited on her part. In a sense even these three sombre chapters are the prelude to the glory of Yahweh's saving act, a glory which is all the greater simply because it cannot be based on any merit of Israel herself.

Ezekiel thus brings a new direction to the old prophetic task of exposing sin. He is, perhaps, more concerned than his predecessors were to demonstrate its total dominion over men. These digressions on the history are intended to make clear that it is not a matter of separate transgressions, nor simply of the failure of one generation, but of a deep-seated inability to obey, indeed of a resistance to God which made itself manifest on the very day that Israel came into being. What makes Ezekiel's pictures of Israel's history so unvarying is that in his eyes the end is no better than the beginning. There is no difference, no moment of suspense – the same state of affairs exists in every age of her history. Now, however, Yahweh is making an end to this: he revokes his historical design. Proof of his intentions can be seen in an event which at one and the same time is both catastrophic and magnificent for the saving history – the prophet sees the 'glory of God', that manifestation of Yahweh which mysteriously dwelt with Israel, solemnly leaving the temple and soaring up in the direction of the east (Ezek. 10.18f.; 11.22ff.).

3. All that has been said so far might give the impression that despite its difficulties Ezekiel's task was basically simple because it was to inform people of their lost condition. Surprisingly enough, we here come upon one of the prophet's most complex functions, for it was Ezekiel's particular task to show great quickness of mind by getting right inside his hearers' exceptional religious situation. His call to be a prophet had, as it were, a supplementary clause, in terms of which his office was extended in a special direction – he was appointed a 'watcher' for the house of Israel.[9] His office was thus modified to the extent that he had not only to deliver a

---

[9] The connection of the prophet's office as watchman (Ezek. 33.1-9) with his call (Ezek. 3.16-21) is due to redaction. The intention was to make the entrusting of the former to him a part of his call.

divine 'word'; when he received a message of doom, he had also, like a sentinel on a city wall, to 'warn' the inhabitants when danger threatened. However, the comparison is defective at the most important point. A watcher's duty is a simple one – he gives warning of the enemy; but Ezekiel's position is more complicated. Indeed, it is almost contradictory, since it is Yahweh who both threatens Israel and at the same time wishes to warn her so that she may be saved. Here, therefore, the delivery of the message entails a second task for the prophet, that of giving Israel a chance to 'turn'. The prophet's failure to warn the 'wicked' will be followed by the latter's death: but Yahweh will hold the prophet responsible. The kind of activity in particular involved in this office of 'warning' is not immediately apparent from ch. 33.1-9 (3.16b-21). Elsewhere, however, there are two detailed examples of this special function which clearly show how the prophet thought of this office.

In ch. 18 Ezekiel is dealing with people who were suffering because the divine dispensation took no account of the individual, and who opposed the old collective idea according to which the generations form a great organic body, which is also a single entity in the sight of God. They deny God's right to punish them for the sins of their fathers. The prophet helps them to think these problems through, and tries to comfort their troubled hearts by saying that every life is in a direct relationship of its own with God. A father's wickedness cannot prevent his son from approaching Yahweh, nor can a wicked son reap the benefit of his father's righteousness. Indeed, even in the life of one individual there is no casting of accounts – Yahweh does not average out a man's life; for the wicked, the way of turning to him is always open, and when he does turn, all his previous wickedness will no longer incriminate him.

The second passage (Ezek. 14.12ff.) also takes as its starting-point religious questions which became acute – perhaps to those in exile, too – because of the inevitable calamity threatening Jerusalem. In this case, of course, the question apparently worked the other way round – in the general collapse, will it be possible for someone whom Yahweh spares to save his children, too? Ezekiel's answer is that in a city under so great a threat even men of exemplary righteousness, like Noah, Daniel, and Job, could save only their own lives.

In both cases Ezekiel accomplishes his task by handling the problem abstractly and quite impersonally – he lifts it on to a purely theoretical and didactic plane, and works it out by means of exaggerated typical examples. This is in keeping with his priestly way of thinking: but we must not therefore lose sight of the fact that these expositions are based on a quite independent consideration of the problems, and that the solution offered by Ezekiel, whose eyes are fixed on an imminent act of God, is one which could only be given by a prophet. Here Ezekiel entered upon a completely new sphere of prophetic activity. The subject to which the prophets of the classical period directed their messages was Israel, i.e., a rather general audience. They then left it to each individual to take out of them what applied to himself. Even Jeremiah, who was himself so highly individualistic, did the same. Only with Ezekiel does this change. He was the first prophet consciously to enter this new sphere of activity, which may be described as a 'cure of souls', provided we remember that it corresponds to the New Testament *paraclesis*, the promise, an address of warning and comfort. His discussions are not intended to satisfy a speculative need, but speak instead to a man's will, and sometimes at the end pass over into personal appeal (Ezek. 18.30f.; 33.11). The precondition of such a pastoral activity had been given quite automatically by the emergence of the individual from the group, and this process had assumed particularly aggressive forms in the later monarchical period. At that time each generation was consciously distinct from that of its fathers, and the problem of the individual's relationship to Yahweh was being discussed as never before; and it was against this background that the prophets were for the first time given the task of caring for individuals as well as for the nation, of thrashing out their problems with them, and of impressing on each of them his own personal situation in the eyes of God. In doing this, it was Ezekiel's special endeavour to hunt men out in their secret fastnesses of religious security and their assumed 'righteousness'. The individualism of his own day suited his purpose perfectly, because it helped him to bring a man face to face with the living God. The royal word of Yahweh, however, determined the whole basis of his pastoral activity and its direction: 'As I live, I have no pleasure in the death of the wicked, but that the wicked turn back from his way, and that he stay alive' (Ezek. 33.11).

This pastoral office meant much more for Ezekiel than simply an extension of his prophetic calling, or a special nuance given to it. It was his duty to live for other people, to seek them out, and place himself and his prophetic word at their disposal, and this task affected his own life in deadly earnest, for Yahweh had made him responsible for the souls of these individuals: if he allowed the wicked to die unwarned, Yahweh threatened to require their lives of the prophet's own hands. Yahweh had thus imposed on the prophet a special mediatorial office which already entailed suffering. And this is not the only instance of the kind; there are other passages as well which show how for Ezekiel the prophetic office was a matter of life and death, and how the offence of the message he was charged to deliver reacted first upon his own person, and had sometimes to be most strangely and painfully expressed in symbolic actions.

'And you, son of man, groan! With trembling loins and bitterness shall you groan before their eyes!' (Ezek. 21.11 [6]).

Things of this kind were not cheap play-acting. Here the coming disaster, the destruction of Jerusalem, is casting its shadow before it and harnessing the prophet, body and soul alike, with a hard yoke of suffering. Yet Yahweh had so decreed, for Ezekiel was to be made 'a sign for Israel' (Ezek. 12.6b). He was not to present a symbolic action which did not involve him personally; his own condition was to pre-figure the suffering of the coming judgment (see also Ezek. 12.17ff.). The other symbolic action which compelled him to lie for a considerable time first on one side and then on the other, in order to bear the guilt of the house of Israel (Ezek. 4.4-8), must have affected the prophet's inmost being even more profoundly. Here there is as yet no idea of a vicarious bearing of guilt, for what happens to Ezekiel is above all a prediction, a drastic prefiguration of what is about to come. It is very significant, however, that the method of prediction is not confined to oral communication, but that Yahweh draws the prophet's whole being into the disaster as its sign, and in the 'days of his siege' makes him the first to suffer what is to come. We shall have to discuss later how near Ezekiel's mediatorial office comes to that of the servant in Isa. 53, and how it yet falls short of it. Ezekiel himself once gave a very clear statement of what he reckoned to be the heart of the prophetic service. It was made when he was dealing with false prophets. He reproaches them that, at the time when the threat from Yahweh was grave, they 'did not go up into the breaches' or 'build a wall round the house of Israel' (Ezek. 13.5). The picture indicates war, siege, and extreme peril for the people of God. In Ezekiel's view, the prophet's task is to set himself in the

front line before Yahweh, in order to protect the people with his
life. In this conception of the prophetic office Ezekiel again has
affinities with the mediatorial office of the servant of Deutero-
Isaiah.

4. The abrupt juxtaposition of *predictions of doom and predictions of salvation* in classical prophecy which, as is well known,
raised so many misgivings in the minds of more than one generation of scholars, does not occur to the same degree in Ezekiel, because even before the destruction of Jerusalem he spoke of the
possibilities of deliverance. It was his theological 'individualism'
which above all else gave his preaching a more flexible form; for
he was free to allow men a considerable latitude in their decision
for or against Yahweh. With Ezekiel, then, the transition from
doom to salvation is apparently much more intelligible from a
logical point of view – those who receive salvation are those who
have remained true to Yahweh, who 'sighed and groaned over all
the abominations' that were committed in Jerusalem (Ezek. 9.4), or
at least those who at the eleventh hour took warning from the
prophet and repented. The fact that Ezekiel sometimes expressly
envisages the judgment as a purging (Ezek. 20.37f.; 22.17ff.; 24.11)
seems only to reinforce this. Yet the point is not as easy as this
for the logic of religion. On the contrary, it may be said that no
other prophet tore open so deep a gulf between doom and salvation, or formulated it in so radical a fashion. The guardian 'glory
of God' departed from the temple before men's eyes (Ezek. 11.22f.);
Israel is dead in the true sense of the term (Ezek. 37.1ff.). These are
the theologically relevant events which the prophet believes to lie
between doom and salvation. Such a prospect makes the continuance of Israel's life in Palestine – which does not surprise the
historian – seem possible only as the result of a miracle.

Whenever Ezekiel speaks of the lot of the new Israel, he always
assumes an historical, and also a political, existence for God's
people within their own ancestral land. Their members are to be
enrolled in the register of Israel's citizens and to return to the land
of Israel (Ezek. 13.9). Yahweh will then multiply the nation and
bless the land with fruitfulness (Ezek. 36.9, 29f., 37). In this connection, Ezekiel compares the once desolate land with the Garden
of Eden (Ezek. 36.35), but clearly the prophet was not envisaging
any mythological 'paradise-like' conditions, or some kind of
Elysian fields. Farmers will till the land for the future (Ezek. 36.34),
and the cities will even be refortified (Ezek. 36.35).

Though these external conditions are important and even essential for the new Israel, it is the saving event which Yahweh is to bring about in the heart of man that is of the greatest moment.

'I will take you from the nations and gather you from all the countries and bring you into your own land. I will sprinkle you with clean water, and you shall be clean from all your uncleannesses, and from all your idols will I cleanse you. A new heart I will give you, and a new spirit I will put within you. I will take out of your flesh the heart of stone and give you a heart of flesh. My spirit will I put within you, and cause you to walk in my statutes and be careful to observe my ordinances. Then you shall dwell in the land which I gave to your fathers and be my people, and I will be your God' (Ezek. 36.24-8).

The best starting-point for interpreting this passage is the last of the verses quoted, for in 'you my people, I your God', it contains the old formula of the covenant, and this puts it beyond all doubt that Ezekiel is speaking of a saving appointment of Yahweh analogous to the making of the old covenant. The fact that the word 'covenant' is not mentioned here means nothing – there are other passages where he did designate the saving event as covenant (Ezek. 34.25; 37.26) – for the content of the passage shows it to be closely parallel, feature by feature, to Jeremiah's pericope on the new covenant (Jer. 31.31ff.). Here, too, the purpose of God's saving activity is the re-creation of a people able to obey the commandments perfectly. Here, too, this is connected with a forgiving expurgation of previous sin (Jer. 31.34b=Ezek. 36.25); above all, however, with both prophets the saving work consists in God's making men capable of perfect obedience by as it were grafting it into their hearts. Ezekiel, of course, goes into very much greater detail over the human aspect than did Jeremiah – God takes away their hardened heart and gives in its stead a 'new heart', a 'heart of flesh'. Moreover, God will bestow his spirit on Israel, and thus equipped she will be able to walk in the path of the divine ordinances. There are striking parallels with Jer. 31.31ff.; one feels that Ezekiel must somehow have had Jeremiah's prophecies in front of him (in particular, Jer. 32.37ff.). Jeremiah's wording, 'I will put my law in their hearts', seems almost too undefined compared with the theological precision with which Ezekiel describes the process of renewal. There is another feature, concerned not with the process itself but with its result, where Ezekiel goes far beyond Jeremiah – when in her completely transformed state Israel looks back on her evil past and remembers it, she will loathe herself (v. 31).

5. This remains, however, an incomplete account of Ezekiel's picture of the new Israel, for God's people are once more to be led by a monarch. Even the grievous harm done to the royal office by those who had last worn the crown did not vitiate the prophet's hope that Yahweh would redeem the promise attached to the *throne of David*, 'until he comes whose right it is' (Ezek. 21.32 [27]). Thus mysteriously – with silence rather than speech – did Ezekiel once speak of the anointed one to come. At another time he expressed himself with somewhat greater clarity, in the parable of the twig which Yahweh was to plant on the lofty mountain of Israel; this twig (cf. Isa. 11.1) is to become a great life-giving tree, and Yahweh is to make the dry tree sprout again (Ezek. 17.22-4). Twice, however, Ezekiel took up the topic of the Messiah directly. In Ezek. 34.23-4 a shepherd is mentioned whom God is to set over his people, his 'servant David', and in Ezek. 37.25ff. the prophet again speaks in exactly the same way of the shepherd, the servant David, who is to rule over 'Judah and Joseph', now finally re-united as one nation. There is, of course, no mistaking the fact that in Ezekiel also the topic of the Messiah and the traditional concepts specific to it are not altogether properly drawn. He is strangely unable to expound the Davidic tradition. One looks in vain in Ezekiel for an exposition of the subjects connected with it: instead, in both passages he slips over into the wording of the Exodus-covenant tradition. In Ezek. 34.23f. the formula belonging to the Sinai covenant – I their God, they my people – follows upon the heels of what is said about the Messianic advent of the king, and in Ezek. 37.23 it immediately precedes it. How, then, is the covenant concept which appears in both places to be understood from the point of view of the history of tradition? Is it a renewal of the covenant with David, or of the Sinai covenant? Undoubtedly the latter. We have just seen how little Ezekiel expounds the once-widespread Messianic-Davidic tradition. Thus Ezekiel fuses the Sinai tradition and the David tradition which Jeremiah still kept essentially separate. But the Sinai tradition dominates his thought – under the new David, Israel will obey the commandments (Ezek. 37.24).

Ezekiel sometimes looked at this whole saving work from a theological viewpoint which is highly characteristic of his whole message. By gathering Israel and bringing her back to her own land,

'Yahweh manifests his holiness in the sight of the nations'.[10]
This 'manifestation' is therefore much more than simply something inward or spiritual; it is an event which comes about in the
full glare of the political scene, and which can be noticed by
foreign nations as well as by Israel. Yahweh owes it to his honour
that the covenant profaned by all the heathen should be re-
established. There is an unmistakable element of reason in this
method of argument. In order to make the whole saving work
theologically comprehensible, Ezekiel takes the radical course of
relating it to Yahweh's honour, which must be restored in the
sight of the nations.

'Therefore say to the house of Israel: Thus says the Lord Yahweh: It is not for your sake, O house of Israel, that I act, but for
the sake of my holy name, which you have profaned among the
nations to which you came. I will vindicate the holiness of my
great name, which has been profaned among the nations, and
which you have profaned among them; and the nations will know
that I am Yahweh — oracle of Yahweh — when through you I
vindicate my holiness before their eyes' (Ezek. 36.22-3).

These words remind us that in Ezekiel Yahweh concludes many
of his predictions of coming events with the words: 'that they
may know that I am Yahweh'. The final goal of the divine activity
is therefore that Yahweh should be recognized and worshipped by
those who so far have not known him or who still do not know
him properly.

[10] Ezek. 20.41; 28.25; 36.23.

17 Deutero-Isaiah

SCHOLARS have had to invent a name for the prophet whose mouth Yahweh filled with words of an unparalleled splendour which charm the reader and carry him forward. The anonymity of the message meant that its derivation from a special kind of prophet was only recognized by biblical criticism. The messenger himself – a man who would be of the greatest interest to scholars – is completely hidden behind his message, so completely that we do not know his name, the place where he worked (though this is generally believed to have been Babylonia), or anything else about his life. His literary style, too, is quite different from that of, say, the first Isaiah. The latter's style led us to believe that he was no ordinary man: but the high emotional tone of Deutero-Isaiah's words, and the richness of his language, which leaves the reader spell-bound, are closely linked with the diction of the hymn and other cultic forms and therefore are less personal. On the other hand – and this is also characteristic of a prophet of Yahweh – it is easy to recognize the new epoch upon which the history of Israel was about to enter, and which this prophetic voice sets itself to interpret. Cyrus was on the throne of Persia and rising to power, and his successive victories were convulsing the world. His career naturally aroused great interest among the deportees in Babylon, as everywhere else. He did, in fact, later demolish the neo-Babylonian empire.[1] The preaching of Deutero-Isaiah is most intimately connected with these events which, after a period of fairly peaceful transition, changed the face of contemporary history.

Before considering his message, however, it is perhaps once more worth while to make ourselves familiar with the theological

[1] The subjugation of Lydia (Croesus) c547/6, which has always been regarded as taking place about the time when Deutero-Isaiah appeared, was an event of particularly far-reaching significance. It may be taken as certain that Deutero-Isaiah's preaching preceded the collapse of the Babylonian Empire. Anything but a general date is, however, hypothetical.

traditions in which Deutero-Isaiah stood and lived. It is now, of course, apparent that when the prophets spoke of coming events, they did not do so directly, out of the blue, as it were; instead, they showed themselves bound to certain definite inherited traditions, and therefore even in their words about the future they use a dialectic method which keeps remarkably close to the pattern used by earlier exponents of Yahwism. It is this use of tradition which gives the prophets their legitimation. At the same time, they go beyond tradition – they fill it even to bursting-point with new content or at least broaden its basis for their own purposes. The three election traditions (of the Exodus, of David, and of Zion) which are constitutive for the whole of prophecy are all, we find, taken up by Deutero-Isaiah and used by him in striking poems. On the whole, however, in his view of the future, the most prominent tradition is undoubtedly that of the Exodus.[2] The position of the Exodus in Yahweh's saving activity for Israel is such a central one that this prophet can only imagine the new saving acts in the form of another Exodus. We shall have more to say about this later. Since Deutero-Isaiah was familiar with the Exodus tradition, it is not surprising that he sometimes also speaks of the election of Abraham (Isa. 41.8; 51.1ff.), and touches on the dim figure of Jacob (Isa. 43.22), for the patriarchs were, of course, the starting-point of that saving history which led on to the Exodus.

Besides what he owes to this, the oldest and most important of all Israel's 'election traditions', Deutero-Isaiah is also indebted to the Zion tradition; for the Exodus, of course, leads to a city destined to be rebuilt, guaranteed by Yahweh (Isa. 44.26; 45.13; 49.14f.; 54.1ff., 11ff., etc.), and the future home of God's scattered people and even of the Gentiles (Isa. 49.22ff.; 45.14). Deutero-Isaiah's thoughts dwell continually on Zion. He likes to use the term, which is, after all, simply a place name, to address God's people as a body.[3] In his predictions about a pilgrimage to be made by the nations to the holy city, it is easily seen that Deutero-Isaiah took up traditional matter of a peculiar kind (Isa. 45.14f.; 49.14-21, 22-3; 52.1-2). In point of the history of tradition, these prophecies belong to a complex which overlaps the Zion tradition proper, for they occasionally appear in later prophecy. Their characteristic is the idea of the eschatological coming of the nations to Jerusalem, and they

---

[2] Isa. 43.16f., 18-21; 48.20f.; 51.10; 52.12. Abraham is mentioned in Isa. 41.8; 51.2, and Jacob in Isa. 48.28.

[3] Isa. 41.27; 46.13; 49.14; 51.3, 11, 16; 52.1, 7, 8.

form a remarkably self-contained body of prophetic concepts. They will therefore be discussed later.

On the other hand, Deutero-Isaiah's relationship to the David tradition is a very strange one. He mentions it once and, using a traditional description, grandly calls it 'the sure and gracious promises made to David' (Isa. 55.3; cf. II Chron. 6.42). He does not, however, interpret Yahweh's promises concerning the throne of David and the anointed one of Israel in the traditional way, for he understands them to have been made not to David but to the whole nation. It is, therefore, for all Israel that the promises made to David are to be realized: Israel is to become the 'sovereign ruler' of the peoples (Isa. 55.4). In thus 'democratizing' the tradition, Deutero-Isaiah actually robbed it of its specific content. Indeed, the Messianic hope had no place in his prophetic ideas. This bold reshaping of the old David tradition is an example, though admittedly an extreme one, of the freedom with which the prophets re-interpreted old traditions.[4]

Very surprisingly, however, there is still another tradition in Deutero-Isaiah, one upon which no previous prophet had called. It deals with the creation of the world by Yahweh. Because Yahweh had the power to subdue chaos, appeal could also be made to him to help his people in times of tribulation in the historical realm (Isa. 51.9f.); and because Yahweh created the ends of the earth, the message which he is now sending to Israel is also trustworthy (Isa. 40.27ff.). A special feature in Deutero-Isaiah's thought about creation is, of course, that he does not regard creation as a work by itself, something additional to Yahweh's historical acts. Indeed he seems to make no clear distinction here – for him creation is the first of Yahweh's miraculous historical acts and a remarkable witness to his will to save. The conclusive evidence for this 'soteriological' conception of creation is the fact that Deutero-Isaiah can at one time speak of Yahweh, the creator of the world, and at another of Yahweh, the creator of Israel.[5] Yahweh is Israel's 'creator' in the sense that he called this people in its whole physical existence into being, yet he is creator in particular because he 'chose' Israel and 'redeemed' her. When the prophet speaks of Israel's 'creation', however, he is thinking of the historical acts which the old Exodus tradition had ascribed to the God of Israel,

---

[4] The same reinterpretation in the collective sense is seen in Ps. 105.15 ('Touch not my anointed ones!').
[5] Isa. 43.1, 7, 15; 44.2, 21.

and especially of the miraculous crossing of the Red Sea. In Deutero-Isaiah, 'to create' and 'to redeem' can be used as entirely synonymous.[6] When, taking the literary form of the hymn, he pictures Yahweh as the creator and redeemer of Israel, he does not allude to two separate activities, but to a single one, the saving redemption from Egypt (Isa. 44.24; 54.5). The fact that this saving act is never mentioned for its own sake, but only because it is the type and pattern of one to come, will be dealt with later.

We thus see in Deutero-Isaiah a remarkable combination of two traditions which originally had nothing to do with one another. The reason for this sudden incorporation of the creation tradition into the prophets' preaching is to be found in the new situation in which Israel was placed. Abruptly confronted with the Babylonians and with the power of so great an empire, appeal to Yahweh and his power needed to range more widely than it did in the days when Israel was still more or less living a life of her own. If this explanation is correct, then it again presupposes that the prophet used considerable freedom in his handling of the creation traditions. His relationship to the old saving traditions seems to have been even freer still. Deutero-Isaiah could choose among them, he could combine them, and sometimes he could even interpret them in a new way. This almost eclectic attitude is also something new, as form-criticism bears out. It has long been recognized that Deutero-Isaiah makes particular use of the literary category of the priestly oracle of response for his proclamation of salvation. This was the cultic form in which God's help was promised to a suppliant. Such characteristic expressions as 'fear not' and 'I redeem, I strengthen you, I help you, I am with you' or 'you are mine' (Isa. 41.10, 13f.; 43.1, 5; 44.2, etc.) belong to this category, but the discourses which speak of Yahweh as the creator of the world and of Israel, with which these are combined, certainly do not. Deutero-Isaiah has thus moulded the contents of the old traditions into a form of his own choice which was originally alien to them. Here again it is instructive to glance back to Isaiah: when he, too, proclaimed salvation for Zion, he kept the form of the old Zion tradition.

But was Deutero-Isaiah really a prophet in the specialized sense of the word? Is it not more likely that this great unknown, whom it is so difficult to imagine speaking in public, was not a prophet

---

[6] In Isa. 44.1f. Israel's creation is co-ordinated with her election.

but a religious writer of the greatest skill?[7] The question is easily
answered, for the pivot on which his whole preaching turns is an
awareness of the reality of Yahweh's creative word. At the time
of his call a voice from heaven pointed him to the word of Yahweh, which 'stands' for ever. He finds it important to be able to
think of himself as in the succession of earlier prophets (Isa. 44.26;
45.19). What they prophesied long ago is now beginning to be fulfilled (Isa. 48.9ff.; 44.7; 45.21), and in the case of the words which
are put into his own mouth, realization will follow in their wake
(Isa. 55.10ff.). Indeed, Deutero-Isaiah sees the whole course of
world-history from the viewpoint of its correspondence with a
previously spoken prophetic word. In this he reminds us strongly
of a near contemporary, the author of the Deuteronomic history,
the only difference being that with Deutero-Isaiah this theological
aspect of history has much more practical application – he uses it
for apologetic purposes, to counter the anxiety that in the long
run the Babylonian gods may prove to be more powerful than
Yahweh. In fact, Deutero-Isaiah puts in bold relief the question of
who is the controller of world-history, and the answer he gives
almost takes one's breath away – the Lord of history is he who
can allow the future to be told in advance.[8] This is something the
gods of the heathen cannot do, and therefore they are 'nothing'.
In Yahweh's contest with the idols, the power to foretell proves
his specific difference from them. Of course, in the arena of history,
which is the scene of the mighty contest, Yahweh is thrown back
on his people, for Israel is his witness. Poor as this witness is (Isa.
42.19), it can at least perform this service:

> All the peoples are gathered together and the nations assembled;
> Who among them declared this, and tells us the former things?
> Let them bring their witnesses, that they may be justified,
>   let them tell it, that we may say, It is true.
> You are my witnesses, says Yahweh, and my servant,
>   whom I have chosen.

(Isa. 48.9-10)

[7] The dangerous political situation of the time is not really a satisfactory
explanation of the anonymity of the Deutero-Isaiah tradition. On the contrary, ought he not to have been remembered, and his name all the more
dutifully connected with his message, some decades after he appeared, and
after the great change in the situation which he foretold? Did Deutero-Isaiah
appear in public? Or did he work only indirectly, as a 'writer'? It is better
to assume that the messages of Deutero-Isaiah, especially his oracles of salvation, had their place in liturgical services of lament held by the exiles.

[8] Isa. 41.25ff.; 48.14.

The power of Yahweh's word in history is shown particularly in its shaping of the future of God's people (Isa. 55.10ff.). Deutero-Isaiah has the almost gnostic vision of the word of Yahweh as the only source of creation. History and all its peoples are the realm of the transient (Isa. 40.6-8). Yet it is a sphere where prophecy is genuinely fulfilled, the battlefield where the witness borne by the servants of the true God is ranged against the presumptuous powers of the heathen gods and their prophecies (Isa. 44.25). Everything depends simply upon the word of God. Surely such a vision carries with it the title prophet. The fact that theological reflection and rational argument, almost prolix on occasion, occupy a large space even with Deutero-Isaiah, corresponds with the spiritual climate of his age, and links him with Jeremiah and Ezekiel.

I. THE NEW SAVING EVENT

On the first occasion when Deutero-Isaiah heard Yahweh speak to him, he was given the content of his message in a nutshell – Yahweh's advent is imminent; but he is not only to reveal himself to Israel: this time his advent is to be a final theophany for the whole world; he is to reveal his glory in the eyes of all the nations. In Israel only one man knows this, but in heaven the angelic beings are already astir – they are already summoned to the task of preparing the miraculous highway for this advent of Yahweh the king (Isa. 40.3-5). The new turn given to world-history by Cyrus has set events in motion that are swiftly leading to the end. 'My deliverance is near, my help draws nigh' (Isa. 51.5; 46.13). Yahweh has already bared his arm before the eyes of the nations (Isa. 52.10); a wonderful event is about to take place. Deutero-Isaiah has a variety of ways of alluding to the new political direction given to history by Cyrus, and, contrary to the custom of the older prophets, he twice mentions him by name.[9] It is Yahweh himself who

[9] It is certainly remarkable that Yahweh calls Cyrus 'his anointed' (Isa. 45.1), but this is no more than a rousing rhetorical exaggeration inspired by the actual situation. How could Deutero-Isaiah have meant more than this, since Cyrus was not of the line of David, and since the prophet had already imparted to his nation his prophecy concerning David (Isa. 55.1ff.)? Cyrus was Yahweh's instrument in basically the same way as were the Assyrians for Isaiah of Jerusalem. So, his emotions kindling as he spoke, Deutero-Isaiah applied to Cyrus that title which his own preaching had left without any rightful bearer. If Cyrus had a *charisma*, its activity is exclusively restricted to the political field.

makes Cyrus the centre of attention not only for Israel but also
for the whole world. Yahweh has 'stirred him up' (Isa. 41.2, 25), he
addresses him in the courtly language of the ancient east as the
one whose hand he has grasped, whom he accompanies as friend,
whom he has called by name, and whom he loves.[10] Yahweh has
now given Cyrus a free hand in world history; he is to cut asunder
bars of iron, and unsuspected treasures are to fall to him (Isa.
45.2f.). The words are reminiscent of Jeremiah's thoughts about the
dominion over the world which, at that time, Yahweh had given to
Nebuchadnezzar (Jer. 27.5ff.). His day is past, and it is now Cyrus
who, as master of the world, accomplishes the will of Yahweh. Yet
again Israel is and remains the object of these world-wide historical
designs of Yahweh : it is for her sake that Cyrus has been 'stirred
up', and it is for her sake that he must be furnished with a world
empire (Isa. 45.4). For it is he, Cyrus, who is to vanquish Babylon
and to allow the captives to return home 'without price or reward'
(Isa. 48.14; 45.13).

This could be described as the sole topic of the prophecy of
Deutero-Isaiah, or at all events as a relatively self-contained set of
ideas concerned with the impending historical events. What we
have seen is, however, only the preparations, knowledge of which
is given to the prophet, by whose means Yahweh mobilizes history
for the real subject. The saving event proper is the departure of the
exiles from Babylon and their return home, and the advent of
Yahweh himself, who is to accompany his people. It is only now
that the prophet's message reaches its climax and his language
soars to the highest flights of passion. The stir of emotion, the
quiver of excitement felt in these passages is almost unmatched in
the whole of prophecy. At one moment he calls upon the exiles to
touch no unclean thing, to make ritual preparation for the departure, because Yahweh in person accompanies them on the march
(Isa. 52.11-12; 48.20), at another he speaks of the miraculous conditions which are to attend this march through the desert.

> They shall not hunger or thirst,
> neither scorching wind nor sun shall harm them,
> for he who has pity on them will lead them,
> and by springs of water will he guide them.
>
> (Isa. 49.10)

[10] Isa. 45.1-3; 48.14. Notice has always been taken of the parallelism with
the courtly form of language used on the so-called Cyrus cylinder about the
relationship of the god Marduk to Cyrus; J. B. Pritchard, *Ancient Near
Eastern Texts relating to the Old Testament*, 1955, pp. 315f.

Those who go forth will not hunger or thirst (Isa. 48.21). The road will not be hard for them, for all obstacles are to be removed, so that they will travel on a level highway (Isa. 49.11). Myrtle trees are to grow instead of thorns (Isa. 55.13), and Yahweh is to turn darkness into light (Isa. 42.16); indeed the whole of nature is to take part in the beatitude of this saving event – the mountains are to break forth into singing and the trees to clap their hands (Isa. 49.13; 55.12), when the redeemed of Yahweh return 'with everlasting joy upon their heads' (Isa. 51.11). On another occasion Deutero-Isaiah shows us these same events from the standpoint of the holy city, telling how the 'messenger of good tidings' speeds before the marching column, and how the watchmen see him and break out into songs of joy.

How beautiful upon the mountains are the feet of him who
    brings good tidings,
who publishes salvation, who brings tidings of good, who
    publishes deliverance,
who says to Zion, 'Your God has become king'.
Hark, your watchmen lift up their voice, together they sing for
    joy;
for eye to eye they see their delight at the return of Yahweh to
    Zion.
Break forth and rejoice together, you waste places of Jerusalem,
for Yahweh has comforted his people, he had redeemed
    Jerusalem.

(Isa. 52.7-9)

Thus, as the prophet understands him, this man is an 'evangelist' (Isa. 52.7, LXX): a messenger of joy who makes speed before the advent of the Lord and proclaims the dawn of God's kingly rule! In another place Deutero-Isaiah entrusts this office of herald of victory to Zion herself. As yet the wonder is all unknown to men; only on Zion is there knowledge of it; therefore she has the duty of proclaiming the tidings of Yahweh's advent far and wide throughout the land (Isa. 40.9-11).

However, the proper significance of the event only becomes clear when it is seen within that context of the saving history in which Deutero-Isaiah himself set it. There can be no doubt that the prophet regards the exodus of the redeemed from Babylon as the counterpart in the saving history to Israel's departure from Egypt in the far off past. He in fact stresses the parallel course of the two events – Yahweh is once more to go forth as a warrior

(Isa. 42.13), as he then did against the Egyptians, and at the new exodus, as at the first, he is miraculously to make water flow from the rock for his people to drink (Isa. 48.21). At the same time, the new exodus will far surpass the old in wonders, for this time they are not to depart in 'haste' – an idea which formed an important element in the old tradition (Ex. 12.11; Deut. 16.3) – but Yahweh is to lead them in person (Isa. 52.12). One must be clear about what is implied here. In referring as he does to the new exodus, Deutero-Isaiah puts a question mark against 'Israel's original confession'; indeed, he uses every possible means to persuade his contemporaries to look away from that event which so far had been the basis of their faith, and to put their faith in the new and greater one. Does this mean, then, that Deutero-Isaiah thinks that God's saving activity for his people falls into two phases? As a matter of fact, the prophet stated this in plain terms by drawing such a sharp distinction between 'the new', that which is 'to come to pass hereafter', and 'the former things'.[11] By 'the former things' he can hardly mean anything other than that saving history which began with the call of Abraham and the exodus from Egypt and ended with the destruction of Jerusalem. Deutero-Isaiah attaches great importance to the fact that the events in this history were all foretold, and came to pass accordingly; for they plainly show the importance Yahweh attaches to his word, and this allows men to put their trust in the new event prophesied. In the idea that all saving history is history foretold by Yahweh, Deutero-Isaiah agreed with his contemporaries – cf. the Deuteronomist. By the 'new' event he means the saving act about to come after a long pause in the saving history, and which he as a prophet can foresee from the course of secular history. A remarkable aspect of Deutero-Isaiah's message is that on the one hand he so depicts the departure of the exiles from Babylon as to recall the first exodus from Egypt and the miracles which accompanied it; yet he is also aware that Yahweh's new revelation is something which cannot possibly be represented – no one is to imagine that he knew of it and anticipated it on the basis of the earlier event (Isa. 48.7f.). And because the task Yahweh is now undertaking is so marvellous and will so completely eclipse his previous ones, Deutero-Isaiah be-

[11] 'The former things' Isa. 43.18; 'the former things' Isa. 41.22; 42.9; 43.9, 18; 46.9; 48.3; 'the new thing(s)' Isa. 42.9; 43.19; 48.6; 'what is to come hereafter' Isa. 41.23.

lieved that his contemporaries should concentrate all their thought upon it and turn away from the events which had previously given their faith its content. On one occasion he stated this very bluntly, in words which the pious in particular must have felt to contain an element of blasphemy:

> Thus says Yahweh, who made a way in the sea, a path in the mighty waters,
> who brought forth chariot and horse, army and warrior together
> – they lie there, they rise not up, they are extinguished, quenched like a wick! –
> 'Remember not the former things, nor consider what is past!
> Behold, I am doing a new thing, now it sprouts forth, do you not perceive it?
> Yea, I make a way in the wilderness. . . .'
>
> (Isa. 43.16-19a)

The verses first make clear that by the former things Deutero-Isaiah means the act of deliverance at the Red Sea on which the saving history was based, and the exodus from Egypt. We may conclude from the style of vv. 16f. that the account of the saving act with which Deutero-Isaiah was familiar was one given in hymns used in worship. From now on, however, Israel is to turn her back on this venerable tradition of Yahwism. This can mean one thing only – Yahweh's first dealings with Israel have come to a full circle. As the prophets viewed history, the exile was an end; as a threat which had received fulfilment, it was the end of a road leading from prophecy to fulfilment. Now, however, in Deutero-Isaiah's eyes, the 'new' event is on the point of beginning, for its first dawning rays are already visible. 'The first has passed away' and only remains valid as a type of the new. Never before had a prophet so sharply marked off the inauguration of the *eschaton*, nor so strictly dissociated it from all Yahweh's previous actions in history. In actual fact, there was also a great danger inherent in this sharp discrimination. Must it not have meant for the prophet's hearers that Yahweh's action was completely torn in two, with the result that justifiable doubts must have arisen about the credibility of the new prophecy? If there was no sort of continuity between the old and the new, was it really the self-same Yahweh who was at work in both parts? This caused Deutero-Isaiah no trouble, however, for the new as well as the old had been foretold long ago. This give his message its legitimation: it was legitimized by the continuity of prediction.[12]

This proof from prediction, which Deutero-Isaiah is conspicuously eager to use, has a wider significance than for Israel only. As we have already seen, its strength depends on the theological judgment passed on the power – or rather, the lack of power – of the heathen gods. Indeed, there is something absolutely new in the way in which Deutero-Isaiah always pictures Yahweh's total saving action as at the same time relating to the heathen, 'the nations', as well as to Israel, that is, as relating to the influences which these acts upon Israel are to have on the political world round about her. Deutero-Isaiah is firmly convinced that their effects will be on a world scale. Once Yahweh has performed his work upon Israel, there will be a universal 'twilight of the gods' among the nations, for the heathen will realize the impotence of their idols. The heathen will be put to shame (Isa. 41.11; 42.17; 45.24), they will come to Yahweh; indeed, because they are convinced of the greatness and glory of the God of Israel, they will even bring home the Lord's scattered people (Isa. 45.24; 49.22f.). 'Kings shall see it and arise, princes, and prostrate themselves' (Isa. 49.7). True, again by Deutero-Isaiah's lips, Yahweh can make a direct appeal to the nations to avail themselves of this hour of the dawn of salvation: 'Be saved, all the ends of the earth' (Isa. 45.22); 'let the coastlands put their hope in Yahweh and wait for his arm' (Isa. 51.5). This ought not, however, to be called a 'missionary idea', for when Deutero-Isaiah describes Israel as a 'witness' for the nations (Isa. 43.10; 44.8; 55.4), he is not thinking of her sending out messengers to them. In the prophet's mind Israel is thought of rather as a sign of which the Gentiles are to become aware, and to which, in the course of the eschatological events, they will resort of their own accord. They will come to Israel and confess that 'God is with you only, and nowhere else, no god besides him'; 'only in Yahweh are salvation and strength'; 'truly, thou art a God who hidest thyself' (Isa. 45.14f., 24).

Did people believe the prophet when he said this? The question introduces us to another peculiar side of his activity, his discourse with those of little faith and those who had grown weary, for

---

[12] Isa. 44.7f.; 45.21. It is not easy to say what Deutero-Isaiah is thinking of as he speaks of this already fulfilled prophecy. Is he thinking of earlier oracles against Babylon such as Isa. 13 or 14? Or did he, perhaps like his predecessor Hosea, understand the old saving history as prophecy? He obviously believes that he stands himself in a prophetic tradition.

whom reality wore a very different appearance, because they felt themselves forsaken by God and were unable to believe that Yahweh cared about their 'way'.

Why do you say, O Jacob, and speak, O Israel,
'My way is hid from Yahweh, and my right is disregarded by my God'?

(Isa. 40.27)

Fear not, for I am with you, look not in dismay, for I am thy God.

(Isa. 41.10)

But thou, Zion, sayest, 'Yahweh has forsaken me, my Lord has forsaken me'.
Can a woman forget her sucking child, that she should not have compassion on the son of her womb?
Even if these forget, yet will I not forget you; see, I have graven you on my hands. . . .

(Isa. 49.14-16a)

For a brief moment I forsook you,
    but with great compassion I will gather you.
For mountains may depart and hills be removed,
    but my grace shall not depart from you,
    and my covenant of peace shall not be removed.

(Isa. 54.7, 10)

Never before had Yahweh spoken in such a way by the lips of a prophet. Never before had he come so close to his people when he addressed them, laying aside anything which might alarm them in case he should terrify one of those who had lost heart. In these dialogues the prophet brings every possible means of persuasion into play. He appeals now to reason, now to emotion. He gives arguments and proofs. As Deutero-Isaiah entices and woos the heart of Israel, hardened by excessive suffering, he uses terms which expose the heart of his God almost shamefully. He almost makes light of the divine wrath which lies upon Israel and of the judgment that has been executed. Israel has already made too great expiation (Isa. 40.2); or, the wrath lasted only a brief moment, and it is now past (Isa. 54.7). To be sure, Yahweh kept silent when the enemy exulted over his people. Yet, how he had to restrain himself and hide his pain (Isa. 42.14)! No one is to think that Yahweh has rejected his people in wrath for all time. 'Where is the bill of divorce?' There is none (Isa. 50.1)! And if the question be put, why does Yahweh still hold on to this people, the answer is, 'because you are precious in my eyes, and honoured, and I love you' (Isa. 43.4). And if the further question be put, why the accusations which were so prominent in the pre-exilic prophets fall into the background with Deutero-Isaiah, and why it is only with him that the message of Yahweh's invincible love bursts out with such mighty power, the answer is that Yahweh has forgiven his people. The prophet looks upon this forgiveness as an unlooked-for event which it is his task to voice in this special hour of history.

2. THE NEW SERVANT

The Servant Songs are discussed separately, perhaps because we cannot fully understand them. We see that, both in diction and in their theological subject-matter, they have much in common with the rest of Deutero-Isaiah – for there is no reason to think that their author is not Deutero-Isaiah himself. On the other hand, we still cannot dovetail these songs smoothly and successfully into the prophet's ideas as outlined above. For all their close connection with his preaching, they still stand in a certain isolation within it, and have their own peculiar enigmas enshrouding them. Not a few of the questions which are of importance for their understanding can no longer be answered – or at least, the expositor ought to allow that, in places, more than one answer is possible.

> Behold, my servant, whom I uphold, my chosen, in whom I delight.
> I have put my spirit upon him, he will bring forth truth to the nations.
> He does not cry, or lift up his voice, or make it heard in the street.
> The bruised reed he will not break and the dimly burning wick he will not quench.
> Faithfully does he bring forth justice, he is not extinguished nor broken,
> till he has established truth in the earth; and the coastlands wait for his teaching.
>
> (Isa. 42.1-4)

In this first song, the speaker throughout is God. Yahweh introduces his Servant, and he does so in a form apparently borrowed from the court. This is the way in which, on some solemn occasion, an emperor might have presented one of his vassal kings or a provincial governor to his nobles and legally defined the new

official's duties and powers.[13] After the presentation, a statement
is made about the equipment received by the official to help him
in the discharge of his grave responsibilities – that is to say, his
charisma. Then comes a brief description of the responsibility
itself – he is to bring forth 'truth' to the nations who, indeed,
already await his teaching. Finally, we are told something about
the way in which he is to work. There is nothing violent about
it : it is something that spares, something that saves. The meaning
of the word 'justice', or 'truth', which occurs three times, is important for the understanding of the passage. It could be taken as
meaning a 'pronouncement of judgment', that is to say, the clem-
ent judgment which the Servant has to speak to the nations. A
more probable view, however, is that the word has a very general
sense, and means the God-given fixed orders for cult and life. It
could in fact be equated with true religion.[14]

Listen to me, you coastlands, give heed, you peoples from afar.
Yahweh called me from the womb, from the body of my mother
  he named my name.
He made my mouth a sharp sword, in the shadow of his hand
  he hid me;
he made me a polished arrow, in his quiver he hid me away;
and he said to me, 'You are my servant <   > in whom I will
  be glorified'.
But I thought, I have laboured in vain, spent my strength for
  nothing and vanity.
Yet my right is with Yahweh, and my recompense with my God.
But now Yahweh speaks, who formed me from the womb to be
  his servant,
to bring Jacob back to him, and that Israel might not be cut off.
So I am honoured in the eyes of Yahweh, and my God is my
  strength.
He said : 'It is too light a thing that you are my servant to raise
  up the tribes of Jacob
and to restore the preserved of Israel –
I make you a light to the nations, that my salvation may reach
  to the end of the earth.'

(Isa. 49.1-6)

Here the speaker is the Servant himself. The partner whom he
calls upon to listen to him is the whole body of the nations of
the world. He speaks – exactly in the manner of a prophetic
account in the first person – first of all of his call. Like Jeremiah,

---

[13] We should think of an act such as David's presentation of Solomon as
his successor in I Chron. 28.1ff.
[14] As for example in II Kings 17.27 and Isa. 58.2; cf. Jer. 5.4; 8.7. Our word
'truth' would be closer than 'justice'.

the Servant was called by God before he was born, and before he had been used (while he was still hidden in God's quiver), God had confided to him his plan: he himself was to be glorified in the Servant.[15] When the Servant complained that his efforts were nevertheless vain – the complaint and God's answer which follows are strongly reminiscent of the form in which Jeremiah's Confessions are couched – God renewed his commission, this time in specific terms. On the one hand, the Servant had a mission to Israel. This was to restore those who had been preserved and to raise up again the tribes of Jacob. Behind this mission, however, as yet entirely unaccomplished, already lies a second, namely, to be a light to the Gentiles and to mediate Yahweh's salvation to the ends of the earth. No inner causal connection is apparent between the two, they are indeed far removed from one another. The phrase 'raising up the tribes of Jacob' seems to indicate a re-establishment of the old tribal alliance, and not the organization of the new Israel as a nation.

> The Lord Yahweh has given me a disciple's tongue,
> that I may know how to feed the weary;
> the Lord has opened my ear to know the word.
> Morning by morning he waked my ear, to listen like a disciple,
> and I was not rebellious and I turned not backward.
> I gave my back to those who smote me, and my cheeks to those
>   who pulled out my beard.
> I hid not my face from shame and spitting.
> But the Lord Yahweh helps me, therefore I shall not be confounded,
> therefore I set my face like a flint, and know that I shall not be
>   confounded.
> He who vindicates me is near; who will accuse me?
> Let him come near to me!
> Who has a claim against me? Let him take his stand before me!
> Behold, the Lord Yahweh helps me; who is it who condemns me?
> Behold, all of them wear out like a garment; the moth eats them
>   up.
> (Who among you fears Yahweh, let him hearken to the voice of
>   his servant.
> Who walks in darkness and has no light, let him trust in the
>   name of Yahweh and rely upon his God.
> But all of you who kindle a fire, who set brands alight,
> walk by the light of your fire, by the brands which you have
>   kindled).
>
> (Isa. 50.4-11a)

The form and content of this song is reminiscent of Jeremiah's

[15] We regard 'Israel' in v. 3 as a later interpolation, with the majority of expositors.

Confessions, and it is best defined as a 'prophetic psalm of trust'.
The relationship of the Servant to Yahweh is that of a prophet –
he has an obedient tongue, which finds its special employment in
comforting the weary, and an ear which is unceasingly open to
receive revelation. Since revelations come to him continuously
and without interruption, his experience differs from that of his
predecessors – the Servant's converse with God is constant. His
ministry has certainly brought him sore suffering, but he has never
lost the conviction that he is secure in Yahweh. This gives him
strength to endure and to look ahead to his vindication. The fact
that the language used here is the language of the law courts does
not necessarily indicate that the Servant held a specific legal position; such language forms part of the imagery which is proper to
these expressions of confidence (cf. Job 13.18f.). It is not certain
that vv. 1of. are part of the song, for here suddenly someone else
– probably the prophet, but it may even be Yahweh – speaks about
the Servant. But in view of what they say about the Servant's
suffering and his faith one should not exclude these verses. They
contain an exhortation – or rather, a threat – against those who
ignore the Servant or who are even, perhaps, the authors of his
sufferings.

Behold, my servant shall prosper,
　he is lifted up and will be highly exalted;
even as many were shocked at him,
　his appearance was so marred, beyond human semblance,
　and his form not like that of men,
so he will make expiation for many nations,
　kings shall shut their mouths before him.
For that which has never been told them they shall see,
　that which they have never heard they shall understand.

Who believes what we have heard?
　And to whom is the arm of Yahweh revealed?
He grew up before us like a young plant,
　and like a root out of dry ground.
He had no form, no majesty,
　we saw him, but there was no beauty that we should love him.
He was despised, forsaken by men,
　a man of sorrows, acquainted with grief.
As one from whom men hide their faces
　– he was despised – we esteemed him not.
Yet it was our sicknesses he bore,
　and our pains he carried,
and we reckoned him as stricken,
　smitten by God and afflicted.
But he was wounded for our transgressions,
　bruised for our iniquities.

Chastisement that makes us whole lies on him,
  and with his stripes we were healed.
All we like sheep have gone astray,
  we looked every one to his own way,
But Yahweh laid on him the iniquity of us all.
Racked, he suffered meekly
  and opened not his mouth;
Like a lamb that is led to the slaughter,
  and like a sheep that before its shearers is dumb. . . .
He was taken from prison and judgment,
  and his state, who still thinks of it?
For he was cut off out of the land of the living,
  for our transgressions he was put to death.
And they made his grave with the wicked,
  and his place with evildoers,
although he had done no violence
  and there was no deceit in his mouth.
Yet it was the purpose of Yahweh to smite him [with sickness].
When he makes his life an offering for sin,
  he shall see his offspring, he shall prolong his days.
And the purpose of Yahweh shall prosper in his hand.
After the travail of his life he shall cause him to see light,
  and satisfy him with his knowledge.

My servant . . . makes the many righteous
  and takes their guilt upon him.
Therefore I will give him the many for his portion,
  and he can apportion the strong as spoil,
because he poured out his soul unto death,
  and was numbered with the transgressors,
while he bore the sin of the many,
  and made intercession for the transgressors.
                                        (Isa. 52.13–53.12)

Since the passage is arranged as a sequence – a speech by Yahweh (Isa. 52.13-15), a chorus (Isa. 53.2-10), and another speech by Yahweh (Isa. 53.11-12) – it may be called a prophetic liturgy, though it must be remembered that not only several of its component forms – as, for example, the presentation of the Servant to all the kings of the earth – but also the specific contents of the 'dirge' in particular, go far beyond anything which could have been found in the context of worship. The speech of Yahweh with which the song begins draws attention to the Servant's future, his exaltation. It displays him before all the nations of the world, and it envisages the precise moment at which they will become aware of the true position of the man who has been despised and mutilated beyond human semblance. Greatly astonished, they become acquainted with something 'that had never been told them'. The unusual aspect of this great poem is that it begins with what is really the end of the whole story, the Servant's glorification and the recognition of his significance for the world. This indicates, however, one of the most important factors in the whole song – the events centring on the Servant can in principle only be understood in the light of their end. It is only thus that all the preceding action can be seen in its true colours.

Accordingly, when the chorus which now follows describes the events of which the Servant is the centre, it does so in retrospect; it therefore expresses insights which could only be seen from an eschatological standpoint. There is some dispute about the identity of those who sing the song. If we begin with its context, then it seems that the singers are the contemporary Gentile world: but some commentators believe that because of its resemblance to a lament for the dead the song could only have been sung by Israel.[16] Following the form of a dirge, the chorus launches into a description of the dead man: but what is emphasized here is not the Servant's renown, as in the customary eulogies, but his wretchedness and the contempt in which he is held. The singers accuse themselves of blindness: they had been unable to understand the event which had taken place before their eyes – the Servant suffered for others; the man to whom they had refused fellowship was the man who was truly one with them. The choir never tires of finding new ways with which to reiterate the one fact that the Servant took it upon himself to act vicariously; that submissively and unresistingly, and therefore deliberately, he took this mediating office upon himself even to death, and that in so doing he complied with Yahweh's purpose.[17] Nor does the song spare words in describing the depth of his suffering, though there is no definite information about its nature, because, as is the custom in laments, various afflictions are heaped upon the Servant – his outward

---

[16] The decision is also to some extent dependent on the way in which we understand v. 1b. The question 'to whom is the arm of God revealed?' is probably to be related to the Servant (it therefore has the sense of 'to what sort of a person?'). A different interpretation relates the revelation to a group of people who are for their part opposed to another group to whom Yahweh did not reveal himself. But the idea of a group which pays no heed to the Servant is nowhere suggested in the text.

[17] The statement that the Servant gave his life as 'a sin offering' (v. 10) is another of the variations played on the theme of vicarious suffering. If this alludes specifically to the sacrifices offered in the cult, a special importance would accrue to the expression from the theological point of view; for the suggestion that the Servant's sacrifice surpassed the sacrificial system would certainly be unparalleled in the Old Testament, and it perhaps also contradicts Deutero-Isaiah himself (Isa. 43.22f.). It is perhaps best to understand the word 'sin-offering' in the more general legal sense of 'substitute', 'pledge' (I Sam. 6.3).

appearance, his origin, the disdain in which he was held, sickness (the idea that he was a leper is old), stripes: he was in prison, disfigured, pierced (v. 5a) and bruised, and was given a degrading burial. The song thus endeavours to depict the Servant's sufferings as supreme. At the same time there is an awareness that Yahweh's purpose in appointing the Servant does not fail and that he will have life and 'offspring' (v. 10b) – obviously beyond the grave.[18]

Yahweh's speech at the end of the song introduces a further important concept in describing the Servant's saving work – he 'makes the many righteous', i.e. he brings them back into the proper relationship to God, and does so by 'removing their guilt'. As with his sufferings, so too the Servant's saving function is described in several different ways – he 'cleanses', he 'bears' sicknesses, 'carries' sorrows, chastisement 'is laid upon him', his stripes 'heal', he 'makes' his life 'a substitute', he 'makes righteous', he 'pours out his life', he acts vicariously.

Interpretation of these 'songs' must from the very first be subject to the limits imposed by the very pictorial language in which they are written. The reader is often completely unaware that the author is using metaphor, and even where he uses direct speech he does not become any more precise, for he so piles up his words that, while what he says gains in force and emotion, the terms he uses are not exact, with the result that a certain vagueness still remains. The same is true of the forms he employs. Though the writer certainly uses definite literary categories, he much expands them by the content he gives them. But his method is completely eclectic, so that even the forms have limited usefulness as exegetical guides. They are all to a greater or lesser extent 'disintegrated', i.e. they are divorced from their proper *Sitz im Leben* and broken apart by the special content they are now made to carry. Once this has been noticed, however, it provides a clue for the understanding of the songs as a group. Such extreme language can never have been applied to a living person – or even to one recently dead. If the Servant had been a contemporary prophet, Deutero-Isaiah himself for example, there would have been no need to hark back to forms from the court tradition; and the same holds true of the lavish use made of prophetic forms if he had been a former king. This transcendence of all familiar human categories is characteristic of discourse which foretells the future.

[18] In the song, the 'many' with whom the Servant is contrasted, and for whose sake he suffered, are mentioned on four occasions (Isa. 52.15; 53.11, 12a, 12b). The term is to be understood in the inclusive sense of 'all' (and therefore not as exclusive: many, but not all).

The only way to understand the songs completely is by understanding the nature of the office allotted to the Servant – the title 'Servant of Yahweh' is itself too ambiguous to be much help.[19] The first thing that we can take for granted is that he does hold a definite office, though it may be thought of in an entirely novel way, and, secondly, he is not an imaginary figure standing outside all the familiar and traditional offices. This being so, only two possibilities are open – the Servant's function is either that of a king or that of a prophet. In my judgment, only the second of these can be correct. There are, certainly, one or two expressions (though they are not so numerous as many people think) which are typical kingly predicates, but they can be easily enough explained as incidental expansions of the traditional picture of a prophet.[20] The basic function of a king, that of ruling, is absent. The songs have as their theme proclamation and suffering – the basic prophetic functions at that time. How can the office allotted to the Servant in the 'oracle of presentation' (Isa. 42.1ff.) be understood as anything other than prophetic? In the second song, the Servant's first reference is to his mouth, which Yahweh made into a sword (Isa. 49.2), and in the third – again it is the first thing said – he conceives himself as an obedient speaker and recipient of revelation (Isa. 50.4). We have abundant evidence that by the seventh century the idea of the prophetic role had changed, and the prophet was portrayed as a suffering mediator. Where is there such evidence for a suffering king?

This conception of the Servant's office does not, of course, answer the second question: is the Servant pictured as an individual, or is he a symbol for the whole of Israel in its mission to the world? The second interpretation is a very old one; indeed, as the

[19] The patriarchs, Moses, David, the prophets, and Job are all given the title of Servant of Yahweh in the Old Testament. The idea that Cyrus disappointed Deutero-Isaiah's hopes, and that the latter thereafter transferred the title of Servant to someone quite different, the Servant of God, falls to the ground because of the lack of particularity in the title alone. Did not Yahweh have many servants? Above all, however, this psychological interpretation goes beyond what exegesis can permit. In the case of a prophet of whose personality we know absolutely nothing, we are not in the position to raise such delicate psychological considerations. There may be something in this interpretation; the case may, however, be quite different.

[20] Here belong in particular the presentation by Yahweh (Isa. 42.1ff.), the release of the prisoners (Isa. 42.7) and the exaltation of the Servant before the kings who shut their mouths (Isa. 52.13f.).

interpolation in Isa. 49.3 and the Septuagint's rendering of Isa. 52.1 show, it is the oldest that we know.[21] It is also supported by the fact that Deutero-Isaiah elsewhere applies the term 'Servant of Yahweh' to the nation of Israel,[22] and that much of what he says about Israel is used in the songs to refer to the Servant. Yet this 'collective interpretation' raises insuperable difficulties. The old objection, that according to Isa. 49.6 the Servant has a mission to Israel, is still valid. In addition, there is something forced in assigning to a group such an individualistic literary category as that of prophetic confession (Isa. 49.1ff.; 50.4ff.). Above all, however, it is impossible to identify the lack of faith and unwillingness of Deutero-Isaiah's Israel with the willingness, complete self-surrender, and strength of faith of the Servant of the songs. Deutero-Isaiah did not think Israel's suffering to be innocent (Isa. 40.2; 43.24; 50.1) as in the last song the Servant's is said to be.

Nevertheless, recent research has established that not even a thorough-going individualistic concept of the Servant resolves these difficulties, because the boundaries between the two ideas are fluid at certain points. It can certainly be said that the figure of the Servant embodies all that is good in Israel's existence before Yahweh. There are therefore theological cross-connections between the Servant on the one hand and Israel on the other; Yahweh says of both that he chose them (Isa. 42.1; 41.8), that he upholds them (Isa. 42.1; 41.10), that he called them from the womb (Isa. 49.1; 48.12).

These common features should, of course, be seriously considered by commentators: but they must not be allowed to obscure or veil the fact that the Servant depicted in these songs is a person entrusted with a prophetic mission to the whole world. But to what point in time does he belong? We may rule out those interpretations – some of which are grossly fanciful – that see in the Servant a figure of the past. The idea, long popular, that the Servant is none other than Deutero-Isaiah himself, is also unsatisfactory, because it leaves too many questions open, especially in connection with the last song. This biographical method of interpretation which connects the songs with some individual breaks down on one particular feature which criticism has for too long ignored, because it

[21] In early times, however, this collective interpretation was far from being the only one in the field. In Palestinian Judaism there are instances of the individual and Messianic interpretation.

[22] Isa. 41.8; 42.19; 44.1, 2, 21; 45.4; 48.20.

set the songs in much too narrow a frame – the expressions used go far beyond biography, indeed they go far beyond the description of anyone who might have existed in the past or the present. The picture of the Servant of Yahweh, of his mission to Israel and to the world, and of his expiatory suffering, is prophecy of the future, and, like all the rest of Deutero-Isaiah's prophecy, belongs to the realm of pure miracle which Yahweh reserved for himself.

It is, of course, probable that Deutero-Isaiah included a number of his own experiences during his prophetic ministry in his picture of the Servant. That is not to say that he and the Servant were one and the same person. Jeremiah's suffering and converse with God also played a part in the picture of the Servant, yet Jeremiah is not the Servant. There is, however, one strand of tradition which we must recognize as particularly important for the origin of these songs: that of Moses, especially as he is represented in Deuteronomy. Moses is there designated the Servant of God,[23] indeed, he stands there as the prophetic prototype; and he also had the mission of allotting to the tribes of Jacob the various districts which they were eventually to inhabit (Num. 32.33; Josh. 13.8, 15ff.; 14.1f. [13.32f.]). He, too, acts as mediator between Yahweh and Israel, he suffers, and raises his voice in complaint to Yahweh, and at the last dies vicariously for the sins of his people.[24] 'Chastisement was laid upon him' – are not these traits which all recur in the Servant? And now consider further that the Servant is given the task of raising up the tribes of Jacob and restoring those who have been preserved. Here is struck up the message of the new Exodus, which is of course one of Deutero-Isaiah's main themes. Does not this message actually demand the foretelling – as antitype – of a prophetic mediator who is to be greater than Moses in the same degree as the new Exodus is to outdo the old? He ought not, of course, to be spoken of as a 'second Moses' or a *Moses redivivus*, but as a prophet 'like Moses'. In my opinion, it is very probable that, as with Deuteronomy, Deutero-Isaiah stood within a tradition

[23] In the Old Testament Moses is forty times called a servant of God. Eleven of these references are post-Deuteronomic (they are practically all to be found in the Chronicler's history and are therefore dependent on the Deuteronomic phraseology), and only five are pre-Deuteronomic (Ex. 4.10; 14.31; Num. 12.7, 8; 11.11). Thus, by far the greatest number of references occur in Deuteronomy and the Deuteronomic history. This cannot be a matter of indifference for the interpretation of the almost contemporary texts concerning the Deutero-Isaianic Servant of God.

[24] Deut. 3.23ff.; 4.21; 9.9, 18ff., 25ff. The correspondences between this picture of Moses and the Servant Songs were noticed a long time ago.

which looked for a prophet like Moses.[25] Deutero-Isaiah did not draw upon Deuteronomy. It is much more likely that both used an existing Mosaic tradition, about his office as mediator, and about the prophet who was to come. Deutero-Isaiah, of course, developed it far more fully than did Deuteronomy. The tremendous new factor which he introduced – and it goes far beyond all previous prophecy – was the universal sweep of his prediction; and Deutero-Isaiah adapted the tradition about the prophet who was to come, a tradition which he certainly inherited, to suit this new dimension. Unlike Deuteronomy, what he stresses is the significance of the prophetic mediator for the world. If the interpretation of the Servant of Yahweh as 'a prophet like Moses' is correct, this would also close the uneasy gap which makes itself felt between the Servant songs and the rest of the message of Deutero-Isaiah.

[25] I am increasingly uncertain whether it is correct to understand the well-known verse, Deut. 18.18, in the distributive sense ('a prophet on and on for ever'). Perhaps it rather contains the promise of a new Moses. However, even if the traditional way of taking the verse is the correct rendering of its meaning, a connection can obviously still be made between the Servant songs and this expectation. It can be seen from Jer. 33.17 how the promise of a permanent institution was framed.

18 The New Elements in Prophecy in the Babylonian and Early Persian Period

I

THEIR very succession in time prompts the question of what the three great prophets of the neo-Babylonian and early Persian periods have in common. Ezekiel was a younger contemporary of Jeremiah – the two must have known one another; and at the time when Ezekiel's prophecy ceased (after 571), Deutero-Isaiah may already have been alive. What specially links them, however, is that they lived during the period when the never-ending crisis which began with the birth of the Mesopotamian empires' interest in Palestine had now entered upon its tensest and most acute phase. No one living in Jerusalem about the year 600 could fail to see that world-shaping events were already in preparation. But what was Yahweh's purpose behind them? Was it, indeed, entirely certain that Yahweh was still in control of events? – the element of sense in his control of history, and even his power, had, after all, been questioned. Zephaniah speaks of people who were saying that Yahweh 'does neither good nor evil' (Zeph. 1.12); these were no atheists, but they no longer reckoned with divine action in the present day; and when the storm broke, and the Southern Kingdom suffered the same fate as had the Northern, and saw its upper classes deported to Babylon, the question of Yahweh's relationship to his people became completely uncertain. Indeed, to many of them it seemed already to have received a negative answer (cf. Jer. 44.15ff.). Deutero-Isaiah, too, belongs to this period of acute crisis in that at a time when other answers seemed much more plausible, he came forward with the message of Yahweh's passionate concern for Jerusalem, and with the prophecy that Yahweh was even now about to raise up a world power in order that he might avow his loyalty to his people and glorify himself in history.

On the other hand, in considering the question of the common element in these three prophets, we must remember that they belong to a time when men had become even more detached than before from the ties of religion – a process which left its mark even on the prophets of the day. This does not mean that their prophetic passion was feebler as a result of the contemporary undermining of religious belief, but it does mean that there was some change in their relationship to the traditions of the faith. In the last days of the Monarchy, the individual emancipated himself from the group and asked questions about his rights as a person.[1] Thus, the prophets, too, of the monarchical era are much more of individuals; they are religious and literary personalities to a far greater extent than are Amos and even Isaiah. In short, the specifically human element and all the problems which this entails now claim a much greater place. Accordingly, these three prophets' relationship to the sacral traditions is looser and more eclectic. How arbitrary Ezekiel or Deutero-Isaiah could be in handling a time-hallowed tradition (cf. Ezek. 20; Isa. 55.1ff.)! Jeremiah is generally taken to be the prophet who went furthest along the road of isolation and individuality, and in comparison with him Ezekiel may seem much more bound to tradition. And yet, in his very lavish use of elements taken from tradition, Ezekiel illustrates more than the change in the times in general. Indeed, it is probable that he was ahead of his time in the 'modernity' of his interpretation and his use of a subtly rational and completely novel point of view to master his material. It is Ezekiel who makes it absolutely clear that his thought-world is miles away from the world of traditions which he forces into some sort of relevance for his own day. Therefore, in order to give a proper answer to the question of what these prophets had in common, we have to start from the fact that they had all travelled far along the road towards becoming individuals.

To take an external point first, a new element in these prophets is that, as far as forms are concerned, their preaching stands on a very much broader basis than did that of the earlier prophets. The picture of the prophetic tradition has now far more colours to it. As well as the traditional literary categories (the messenger formula or oracles against foreign nations), we find in the prophets of this age large-scale allegorical compositions (Ezek. 16; 23), a theological

---

[1] As well as the sceptical utterances of the people of Jerusalem: 'the way of Yahweh is not just' (Ezek. 18.25, 29), another saying is quoted in Ezek. 12.22: 'every [prophetic] vision comes to naught'.

excursus (Ezek. 18), a pastoral letter (Jer. 29), dialogues of the prophet with God, long soliloquies of lament, etc. Two things are characteristic here. With Jeremiah and Ezekiel at least, the prophetic 'I' suddenly becomes very much more prominent – indeed, the book of Ezekiel is practically a long prophetic autobiography. These men are actually much more distinct personalities, they are more detached, and in their spiritual and theological aliveness much more self-dependent than were their predecessors.[2] In the same measure, they are also much more free not only in their choice of expression and in the forms in which they clothe their message, but also in their whole dealings with Yahweh. Nothing is more characteristic of the last than the fact that they could sometimes even turn on Yahweh with complaints and reproaches (Habakkuk, Jeremiah). The second feature is unquestionably closely connected with their versatility as individuals – their relationship to the 'thou', the people to whom they spoke, has also changed, for it has become much more intense. Their message enters much more into the hearers' religious situation, indeed, it absolutely pursues them, and this means that the prophets' debate is at a much deeper level. Their audience was largely critical, if not positively sceptical, and if they wanted to be heard at all, they had to adapt themselves to this. Accordingly, their endeavours are directed even more than their predecessors' were towards being really understood by their hearers. They try to correct misconceptions, they are urgent in their efforts to persuade, and they take care that their arguments are cogent. These efforts reach their climax in, for example, Deutero-Isaiah's discussions or his proofs from prophecy, with their broad theological basis (Isa. 41.26f.; 43.9f.; 48.14). This implies that theological reflection played a very large part in giving its characteristic features to the preaching of these prophets. It is certainly no accident that the prophets of this era are the first with whom we see an effort to give an axiomatic definition and explanation of the phenomenon of the word of Yahweh. One notices how engrossed they are not only with each separate 'word' which they have to deliver, but also with the phenomenon of the word of Yahweh in general. In the context of a purely abstract considera-

---

[2] The direct result of this individualization of prophecy was the increase in the number of collisions with those who saw the same situation with different eyes, and whom we call 'false prophets'. The collisions must have grown more and more in proportion as this individualizing process progressed. It was only in this period that the latent problem of the authority of the prophetic word appeared in all its final acuteness.

tion of the value which belongs to different modes of revelation, Jeremiah calls 'the' word of Yahweh a hammer that breaks the rocks in pieces, and he contrasts it with the less authoritative form of revelation by means of dreams (Jer. 23.28f.). Again, Deutero-Isaiah's statements on the word of Yahweh are demonstrably those of a theoretical theologian. There is something almost schematic about the way he divides the empirical world into two realms. On the one side is the world of flesh and the transience of everything in it; on the other, the word of Yahweh, the only thing creative and productive of blessing (Isa. 40.6-8; 45.10f.). This unsurpassable value which is accorded to the word of Yahweh naturally increased these prophets' self-confidence. As the bearers and spokesmen of this word they occupied an absolutely key position between Yahweh and his government of the world.

2. One of the central subjects upon which they reflected was God's 'justice', that is to say, the question of how Yahweh's faithfulness to the covenant was made effective. It was a question which had not only become a source of serious perplexity to the people of the day: it was also one which even the prophets were no longer able to answer in the same way as Israel had hitherto done. With Habakkuk it was the arbitrary action and arrogance of stronger political powers that raised doubts as to whether Yahweh was still gracious to his people. Jeremiah and Ezekiel faced the same problem from a different angle – how did Yahweh's will to save work out in practice for the individual? Did not his actions prove that he paid no heed to the individual, and that he was indifferent both to his guilt and his devotion and obedience? Did Yahweh's actions afford a reasonable basis for faith? It is not surprising that the prophets' answer to this perplexing contemporary problem do not follow any set pattern – why, different prophets even framed the question in different ways! Ezekiel countered the complaint that Yahweh lumped the generations together in wholesale acts of judgment by roundly asserting the contrary – each individual stands in direct relationship to God, and Yahweh has the keenest interest in the individual and the decisions which he takes, because he wants to preserve his life (Ezek. 18). In advancing this view, Ezekiel abandoned the old collective way of thinking. How modern and revolutionary the prophet appears here, this very prophet whose thinking is at the same time so conditioned by sacral orders! Jeremiah too has heard it said that the children had to bear their fathers' guilt, and he, too, used what was a radically individualistic view to

counter the saying (Jer. 31.29f.). The answer that Habakkuk and
Jeremiah received to the question 'why' was different from that
received by Ezekiel. Whereas Ezekiel had no hesitation in speaking of a clearly perceptible logic in the divine action in the case of
an individual's responsible decision, with Jeremiah and Habakkuk
the answer to the question why there should be such great and
mysterious suffering is so remarkably veiled and obscure that it
makes one feel as if Yahweh were retreating before the question,
and withdrawing into ever deeper seclusion. At all events, both
cases are alike in that they give no answer to the question 'why',
but only disclose horizons of still greater sufferings and trials.
Jeremiah has to learn that he is still at the very start of his road,
and that Yahweh can make no use of him if he is already failing in
'a land that is safe' (Jer. 12.5). While this oracle confines itself to
directing the prophet's troubled eyes to greater problems and
suffering, the one received by Habakkuk contained more comfort:
it speaks of the promise that accrues to perseverance in faith on
the part of the righteous (Hab. 2.4).

There was another respect in which the relationship between
men of this time and Yahweh had been called in question. Not only
had Yahweh's faithfulness to the covenant become a problem
for them, but there must also have been many who came increasingly to doubt whether it was possible for Israel, that is, for the
human partner, to maintain the covenant relationship offered her
by Yahweh. For these people, therefore, what we call 'assurance
of salvation' had been shaken by doubts as to the possibility of
men's faithfulness to the covenant. This brings us to the deeply
perplexing questions which Jeremiah answered with the message
of the new covenant and Ezekiel with that of the new heart.

In this connection, we must first of all say something more about
the great theological contexts to which these belong. For in this
matter Jeremiah and Ezekiel were, of course, far from being lone
voices crying in the wilderness. On the contrary, it can be easily
shown that, in certain circles at least, religious thinking was very
much alive during these years, and that it apparently concentrated
on the question of the covenant, on how far men might rely upon
it and how much it could bear. Here we must first mention Deuteronomy and the people who gave it its final form; for Deuteronomy
is, of course, the outline of a comprehensive covenant theology,
directed solely towards making the people of the time believe that
the covenant had a meaning for their own day and generation. It

covers a huge time-span, from Moses and the events at Sinai down to its own day, and it cries out to this late generation: now is the accepted time, now is the day of salvation! Here we must particularly consider the two passages Deut. 5.2f. and 29.4ff. [3ff.], for they reveal more clearly than anything else the effort to make the 'contemporaneousness' of the Sinai covenant plausible for the present. The way in which Deuteronomy presses this offer of salvation also shows a concern lest Israel should reject what was almost an ultimatum (Deut. 30.15ff.); nevertheless, Deuteronomy still has a lively confidence that, if Israel harkens to the voice of Moses and obeys the commandments, she will have 'life'.

3. Some decades after the great occasion of the publication of Deuteronomy, in the reign of Josiah, saw the birth of the Deuteronomic history. This splendidly conceived theology of history does not, it is true, deal particularly with the problem of the covenant, but it works out, with a fascinating theological precision, that it was on Yahweh and his commandments alone that Israel, along with her kings, came to grief. Nowhere is this crushing verdict so forcefully expressed as in the words put into the mouth of Joshua at the assembly at Shechem, with which he cuts clean through Israel's declaration that she is prepared to serve Yahweh:

'You cannot serve Yahweh, for he is a holy and a jealous God' (Josh. 24.19).

Like the sentence passed by the Deuteronomic history, these words – which are quite without parallel in the Hexateuch – must in some way link up with the verdicts passed by the prophets, particularly those of Jeremiah and Ezekiel; they are in line with what Jeremiah says about the Ethiopian who cannot change his skin (Jer. 13.23), and with Ezekiel's understanding of man. No one in Israel had yet realized with such clarity as Ezekiel the incapacity of human beings to live with and belong to God. His representation of the saving history as a series of entirely fruitless attempts on God's part (Ezek. 20) is almost blasphemous, and it, too, is connected with Josh. 24.19.

It is clear, therefore, that a radically new factor had at this time entered into men's understanding of the will of Yahweh, a factor which specially affected the prophets. The change in their outlook as compared with that of the earlier prophets is shown by the fact that Jeremiah and Ezekiel made the concept of the will of God addressed to Israel into something concrete by speaking summarily of Yahweh's *Torah* or of *the* statutes.[3] They no longer judge single transgressions in the light of single commandments, but measure Israel against the whole body of Yahweh's will, and to this degree they recognize Israel's complete incapacity to obey. For these prophets the hardest problem lies in the realm of anthropology – how can this 'rebellious house', these men 'of a hard forehead and a stubborn heart' (Ezek. 2.3f.), who are as little able to change themselves as an Ethiopian can change the colour of his skin (Jer. 13.23) – how can these be Yahweh's people? Here, then, Yahweh's commandments have turned into a law that judges and destroys. The change can be clearly seen in a prophetic utterance which may well come from this time. It is couched in the form of a liturgy of the gate, that is to say, the ritual of question and answer which took place on entering the precincts of a shrine. Now, however, the usual question runs in a completely different way – it has almost become a rhetorical question answered by 'the sinners' themselves:

> Who can dwell with the devouring fire?
> Who can dwell with everlasting burning?
>
> (Isa. 33.14)

What was once a ritual used in worship has become an insoluble problem.

If we are to understand the prophets' answer to this, the hardest question they faced, we must once again reflect on the idea of Yahweh's covenant with Israel, so clearly and impressively presented in Deuteronomy, for the Israel which Moses addresses is actually the Israel of the last days of the monarchy. Deuteronomy sets the scene in the past, but it is really Josiah's Israel which had just made the covenant with Yahweh and which was still looking forward to the fulfilment of his great promises; this Israel had certainly not as yet found rest, which means that the redemption of the great promise of blessing was still to come. A comparison between this basic concept in the theology of Deuteronomy and Jeremiah's prophecy of the new covenant immediately reveals their similarity. Deuteronomy also looks forward to the future, to a time when Israel, obeying the commandments, is to live in the

---

[3] Characteristic examples of these summary quotations of *the* Law are Jer. 6.19; 8.8; 9.12 (13); 16.11; 31.33; 32.23; Ezek. 5.6; 11.12, 20; 18.5ff.; 20.5ff.; 36.27. With some of these references, of course, account has to be taken of the Deuteronomic stamp given to the prophet's words.

promised land. Neither Deuteronomy nor Jeremiah expect there
to be any miraculous change in the outward conditions of Israel's
future life. According to Deuteronomy, Israel is to be a true nation
and to enjoy Yahweh's blessings in the realms of history and
nature alike. According to Jeremiah, Jerusalem is to be rebuilt,
there is again to be buying and selling, people will again go on
pilgrimages, and the laughter of those who rejoice will again be
heard in the villages (Jer. 24.5ff.; 33.4ff.; 30.18f.); this corresponds
line for line with the picture in Deuteronomy even down to the
latter's injunction to rejoice (Deut. 12.7, 12, 18; 14.26; 16.11, etc.).
There is only one point of difference: Jeremiah speaks of a new
covenant, while Deuteronomy preserves the old one and goes to
the limits of theological possibility as it extends its force to apply
to contemporary conditions – the final period of the Monarchy.
The difference highlights the crucial feature in the prophetic
teaching; for Jeremiah places his entire confidence in the expectation of a new saving act with which Yahweh is to eclipse the Sinai
covenant: but Deuteronomy hopes that Yahweh is now to give
effect to the promises of the old covenant. Here is a remarkable
and deep distinction which must be linked, as we have already
seen, with the fact that for Deuteronomy the question of Israel's
obedience had not yet become a problem, whereas Jeremiah and
Ezekiel take Israel's total inability to obey as the very starting-point
of their prophecy.

We have already seen, of course, that the new thing looked for
by Jeremiah did not mean that the Sinai covenant and its contents
became obsolete. The prophet did not expect Yahweh to put his
relationship to Israel on an absolutely new basis. The new thing is
part of something else, for Jeremiah believed that Yahweh's old
offer to Israel, that she should be his people and obey his commandments, was still valid. Here his view of the fulfilment of the
Sinai covenant is exactly the same as Deuteronomy's. The new
thing lies in the human sphere, in a change in the hearts of men.

Ezekiel's ideas are so much his own that it is unlikely that his
pericope about Israel's spiritual renewal was taken directly from
Jer. 31.31ff. It is therefore all the more significant that the climax
of his forecasts in Ezek. 36.25ff. should correspond almost exactly
to Jeremiah. The only difference is that Ezekiel's description of the
process of man's re-creation is very much more precise and detailed.
He goes further than Jeremiah in that for him Yahweh's work of
re-creation is divided into a whole series of separate divine acts, and

the first of these is the promise that Israel will be cleansed from her sins – something which Jeremiah only includes as an appendix. Yahweh is next to give Israel a heart of flesh instead of a stony heart; and finally he is to give her the most important gift of all, the gift of his spirit so that she can keep his divine commandments.

We may notice in passing that Deutero-Isaiah, too, speaks of a new covenant which Yahweh is to make with Israel. Isa. 55.3 clearly shows that this future event is not seen as the actualization of an already existing covenant. Here it is the covenant with David which in its new form is to embrace the whole people and bring glory to it (Isa. 55.3ff.). Though Deutero-Isaiah differs from Jeremiah and Ezekiel, we can see how much the problem of the covenant was exercizing men's thoughts during this whole period, and how the prophets also felt themselves challenged to define their attitude to it.

We have still to consider the revolutionary significance of the amazing new factor which the message of Jeremiah, Ezekiel, and Deutero-Isaiah must have contained for its hearers. The adjective 'new' in Jer. 31.31 implies the complete negation of the saving events on which Israel had hitherto depended. Such a judgment was infinitely harsher than any previous one, for it was an out-and-out challenge to the validity of the basis of salvation on which Israel relied. It is as though these prophets had changed the outlook of faith by 180 degrees. The saving power of the old ordinances is abolished, and Israel can only find salvation in new, future saving appointments on Yahweh's part.

Now, the message of the end of the old and the need to turn to a future act of Yahweh was not itself new – it is also to be found in the eighth-century prophets. With the prophets of our period, however, the gulf between the old and the new has become much wider, the new beginning, which is the future saving event, is much more sharply, and indeed aggressively, marked off from the end of the old – consider words such as 'not like the covenant which I made with their fathers' (Jer. 31.32), or 'remember not the former things!' (Isa. 43.18), or the mention of a time when the confession 'as Yahweh lives who brought up Israel out of the land of Egypt' will be done away with (Jer. 23.7). Jeremiah's comments on the ark are also properly to be brought in here (Jer. 3.16f.). Evidently the creation of a new ark was being considered. Jeremiah abruptly rejects the proposal, however, for he envisages a time when 'people shall no more say, "The ark of the covenant of Yahweh"'; it will

no longer be remembered, far less remade, for Jerusalem, and not
the ark, will be called 'Yahweh's throne'. When we remember that
for centuries the ark had been the sacral focal-point of Israel's
worship, we can see again the gulf between past and future in the
saving history. In this matter, as well as in the words 'they shall
not remember', the oracle links up with Isa. 43.18. How could the
prophets' hearers countenance such words, which blasphemously
challenged everything that they held most sacred? Yet the men
who spoke in this fashion were zealous devotees of Yahweh and
spoke of him more seriously and with greater fervour than did
any of their contemporaries.

The perplexing element in the message of these prophets was
therefore what they said about a deep gulf in Yahweh's saving
action towards his people, a gulf in whose depths God's people lay
dead (Ezek. 37). Theologically speaking, they consigned their audience, and all their contemporaries, to a kingdom of death where
they could no longer be reached by the salvation coming from
the old saving events. In this state, nothing remained for them but
to cast their whole being on the future saving act which was already imminent. The task confronting such a man as Deutero-
Isaiah was to use every means in his power – tender invitations,
comfort, or theological argument – to overcome their scepticism
and lack of faith. None of the prophets of this period was his equal
in showing quite clearly, from an interpretation of history, the
gulf between the old and the new that was to come (Isa. 41.22;
42.9; 43.9, 18f.; 44.6-8; 45.21; 46.9-11; 48.3-6). Yet behind this apparently irresolvable contrast of the 'former things' on the one hand
with the 'new things' (which are already 'springing forth' like new
shoots! Isa. 42.9; 43.19) one can detect the difficult question of the
continuity of God's history with Israel, which seemed to have
reached its end with the divine judgment on Judah and Jerusalem
in 587. In the last resort, the question was whether the contemporaries of this prophet could still understand themselves as the Israel
which had once been brought to life by God. God's history with
his people did not continue automatically, once it had begun.

At first sight, Deutero-Isaiah in fact seems to pass a negative
verdict on the continuity of the divine history, with his blunt
contrast of the 'former things' and the 'new things'. But the very
fact that he is constantly engaged in argument with the 'former
things', that he needs the statements of earlier history because it,
too, prophesied and was proved right, shows that his answer to the

question of continuity is not just a simple 'no'. It would therefore be wrong to say that Deutero-Isaiah and the other prophets of this period see a complete break in salvation history, dividing it into two unrelated parts. According to their prophecies, the 'new things' will follow the pattern of the 'old' – a new Exodus, a new covenant, a new David, etc. The old is thus renewed; it is present in the new, in the enigmatic dialectic of valid and obsolete. The prophets obviously set great store by this typological correspondence, for they work it out in their prophecies, and in so doing they are very careful to show how the new overtakes and surpasses the old. The new covenant will be better than the first, the new Exodus more glorious, and the suffering of the eschatological servant greater and, just because of this, also more effectual, than that of Moses.

4. The prophets of this period deal in a remarkable way with the Davidic promise and therefore with the ideas associated with the Messiah. Here, too, these ideas seem to be kept quite separate from the prophetic preaching which is based on other traditions. This is striking. Who, for example, would imagine that the wide-ranging view of the future in Ezek. 36.16ff. could stand side by side with a quite different perspective on the future, the messianic one contained in Ezek. 17.22-24; 34.23f.; 37.24f.? Despite their astonishing freedom in re-presenting the old tradition, a freedom which goes beyond anything that was possible for the prophets of the eighth century, these prophets still keep the strains of the Exodus-Conquest tradition and the Davidic tradition quite distinct. They do not seem to have felt the need, so obvious to us, to put them together to form one picture.

Nevertheless, the prophecy of this period has a special affinity with the messianic hope, for these prophets saw the Davidic monarchy, in the form it had then, disappear from the historical scene. Jeremiah witnessed the successor to the family of David, Gedaliah (Jer. 40f.). But he had been appointed by the king of Babylon, whose rule, according to Jeremiah, was not a legitimate one. Yahweh himself had delegated the rule of the world to Nebuchadnezzar, and even the people of Judah had to submit to him (Jer. 27.6). The independent sovereignty of Judah and its king was over.

One can see how a considerable crisis developed over messianic expectations. How was the rule of the world by Babylon or by Cyrus (II Chron. 36.23) to be reconciled with that which had been long promised to the family of David? The fact that Yahweh had

entrusted – as Jer. 27.7 says quite explicitly – the rule of the world
to a worldly power until its term came to an end had introduced
a completely new conception of history alongside the messianic
one. Interest is now attached much less to individual rulers than
to world-empires and their succession. This conception of history
can be seen developed to its greatest extent in apocalyptic (cf.
Dan. 2; 7). Deutero-Isaiah drew the simplest conclusions from this
subordination of Israel to a world power: he reinterpreted the
messianic tradition completely by transferring the promises of the
Davidic covenant to the people. Jeremiah and Ezekiel adopted a
different course. In order to understand their messianic preaching
it must be realized that in the period between 597 and 587 there
was some uncertainty as to who was the legitimate ruler. Was the
exiled Jehoiachin or was Zedekiah the legitimate king? Both
Jeremiah and Ezekiel attack all hopes pinned on existing possibilities.[4] Both believe that the Davidic dynasty is coming to a
complete end. So here, too, the breach has become much wider than
Isaiah imagined, for the collapse of the house of David is a final
one. The dirge which Ezekiel sings over the house of David (Ezek.
19) says clearly that what still remains will perish. It should, however, be noticed that despite this Jeremiah, and more particularly
Ezekiel, spoke of a messianic future. If one remembers first the
finality of the death on which Ezekiel so inexorably insists, and
then the duration which Jeremiah assigns to the present world
order (Jer. 25.11; 29.10), there is no alternative but to speak of a
messianic expectation for the distant future, as opposed to the
imminent coming contemplated by the eighth-century prophets.

5. In order to understand the last of these concepts, the prophetic
Servant of Yahweh, we must add something to our previous summary. Though the picture of the suffering Servant of God portrays
a man of almost superhuman qualities, there are still one or two
things to say about its origin, for it is not so completely isolated
in the prophet's message as might at first sight appear. Let us take
as our starting point the fact that the Servant's office is manifestly
prophetic. He proclaims the divine will and is entrusted with a
ministry of mediation which can only be called prophetic. Although our knowledge of Deutero-Isaiah is very slight, we can still
be sure that he must have been specially competent to paint such
a picture of the Servant's office. He had in fact to describe his own
office raised to the ultimate degree; it was from his own experi-

[4] Cf., for example, Jer. 22.24-30.

ences and suffering that he formed the description of one greater than himself. The time was now long past when to be a prophet was something which carried with it its own evidence and required no justification, when a man prophesied because Yahweh had spoken (Amos 3.7). In the period to which Jeremiah, Ezekiel, and Deutero-Isaiah belonged, the prophetic office itself had become the subject of theological reflection. If we are correct in regarding the preaching of the eighth-century prophets as in some sense a continuous dialogue with tradition, the same thing is certainly true of the prophets of the Babylonian and early Persian period. There is, however, one difference. In the interval the tradition had been enriched by a new factor, a store of experiences, and also of problems, which from generation to generation had attached themselves to the office and its representatives like a growing burden. The tradition in question must have been unique, and it was actually formed in unfavourable circumstances, for, as we are firmly convinced, the prophets under discussion should be regarded as an independent body of men and not as duly authorized officials. The best proof that there was such a tradition of the prophetic office at the end of the monarchical period, and that it in turn would have moulded the prophets of this age, is the presence of a relatively fixed – indeed, by now almost conventional – picture of the prophet which is to be found in various contemporary versions.

One of the most important factors affecting the prophets of this time is the way in which their office increasingly invaded their personal and spiritual lives. Here again one must guard against exaggerating the difference from earlier prophecy into a difference in principle. Elijah and Amos, too, must have been keenly affected in their own persons by the opposition and vexation they encountered. Nevertheless, anyone who reads Jeremiah feels that at one vital spot something has broken. The very forms which he uses proclaim this – he expands his message into lyrics into which a new element enters: in these poems the prophet opens up a dimension of pain. It is a twofold suffering, the suffering of those upon whom judgment has come, but at the same time also God's grief over his people. And then – and this is the really important thing – Jeremiah himself enters into this twofold suffering; it weighs upon him, and he speaks of it as his own personal affliction. There is a difference here compared, for example, with Amos, for in his case we may unreservedly assume that his innermost spiritual and personal being remained less impaired. Jeremiah shifted the ground, and came over in sympathy to the side of the men under judgment. Indeed, Jeremiah's Confessions particularly showed us how, as a result, his prophetic office went to pieces, how the fragments of this utterly fruitless office fell away from him, and how then, simply as a human being vulnerable at every point, he was step by step led nearer to the terrifying night of abandonment by God. Baruch then gave an objective account of this suffering and failure, and the main purpose of his writing was probably to counter any doubts as to Jeremiah's work as a prophet. The catena of mounting suffering and increasing failure is not evidence against Jeremiah's prophetic role. On the contrary, just because Jeremiah was a genuine prophet of Yahweh, his path inevitably ended in the way it did. His failure and collapse prove beyond doubt that he was a genuine prophet. Was Baruch in this passion story only describing, almost as a modern writer might, what he actually observed in Jeremiah, or did he have some preconceived idea about the suffering prophet which Jeremiah seemed to him to fulfil? Whatever the answer may be, he, too, expresses a very changed idea of the prophetic office.

Yet we meet the same idea in Ezekiel also. His very appointment as the responsible watchman resulted in his having to discharge his office at the risk of his own life (Ezek. 33.1f.); on one occasion Yahweh even gave him the strange command to lie for a long time on the one side to bear the guilt of the house of Israel, and then on the other to bear that of the house of Judah (Ezek. 4.4-8). The prophets had from the first performed symbolic actions: but here is something much more than the realistic demonstration of a tremendous guilt: it is the imposition of this guilt on one man whose task it is to bear it. Here again, then, the office with which the prophet is charged deeply affects the sphere of his personal life, and causes him to suffer; and here the suffering is expressly vicarious. The difference is significant. In the case of the earlier symbolic acts, the sign was something exterior to the soul and spirit of the prophet concerned (wearing horns, breaking jars, etc.). Now, however, the prophet himself becomes a sign (Ezek. 12.6), and this consists in the fact that he has been drawn by God himself into enduring the judgment sooner than all others and by way of example (cf. also Ezek. 21.11 [6]). We also meet this greatly changed conception of what is incumbent on a prophet in the judgment which Ezekiel passes on the false prophets. He reproaches them for not building a wall round Israel and not going up into the breaches when Yahweh threatened the nation (Ezek. 13.5), that is to say, they ought to have protected Israel, taken up their posts in her defence. Without question Ezekiel is thinking of omission to plead for the nation in prayer, though perhaps he may also have had some other form of intercessory work in mind. We are taken a stage further by a verse in Ps. 106.23, which sings Moses's praises for entering into the breach when Yahweh was resolved to destroy the people for the sin of idolatry, and was only deflected from his purpose by Moses's intercession (Ex. 32.9ff.). Intercession was, to be sure, one of the particular functions of a prophet from the earliest times. Yet, what a change must have come over this ministry now that it was exercised by a prophet who was ready to throw his own life into the breach between God and Israel! Nevertheless, this was the way in which later prophecy, the subject of the present section, understood the prophetic office. In the case of Jeremiah, his suffering had still no particular relationship to his office as intercessor. Jeremiah cannot, in fact, explain his suffering, and it obviously never occurred to him that there could be something vicarious about it, or that Yahweh had imposed it upon him actually for Israel's salvation.

There is, however, a picture of a suffering intercessor which must be almost contemporary with Jeremiah, a picture whose dimensions surpass the merely human. This is Deuteronomy's picture of Moses. Moses makes himself the intercessor for Israel. He speaks of his fear (Deut. 9.19), of the wrath of Yahweh which drove him to make intercession for the people and for Aaron, and recounts the words of the prayer which he then spoke. Yet, he made entreaty for himself as well, for Yahweh had cast his wrath against Israel upon him ('he was angry with me for your sake'), and had laid on him a terrible punishment for Israel's sake – he was not himself to set foot on the promised land, but was to die before it was reached. His plea that Yahweh should avert this fate was peremptorily silenced – he had to acquiesce in this hard decree (Deut. 3.23-8; 4.21-7). The detailed way in which the whole story is told, with the prayers and answers set forth at length, shows how keen an interest there was at this time in this aspect of the prophetic office. Here, indeed, the act of intercession is more than just mentioned – Deuteronomy wants to move its readers with the picture of a man who, while greatly afraid, took God's wrath on himself, and who was to die vicariously outside the promised land. And if we consider with this the expectation Moses gave voice to that Israel should expect just such a prophet as himself in the future (Deut. 18.18), then we are at once brought face to face with Deutero-Isaiah's prophecy of the suffering Servant, for God himself is to bear witness before the whole world 'that he bore the sins of the many, and espoused the cause of the transgressors [making intercession for them]' (Isa. 53.12). This is not meant to imply that Deutero-Isaiah took Deuteronomy's picture of a prophet as his immediate starting-point and went on to build upon it. It does mean, however, that his ideas about the nature of the prophetic office were familiar at the time and held by definite theological schools. Isa. 53 is not as isolated and unrelated in the prophetic message as it has often been supposed to be. On the contrary, what it says was prepared long beforehand. The formula of its theological prehistory may be said to rest on two antecedents. The first is the intercessory office, which from the very first the prophets knew was entrusted to them. The other is that inroad which the prophet's role made upon his soul and spirit which we have already mentioned. It is only by seeing Isa. 53 in its proper context that we can see how unique it was. There are five specific points which separate the prophecy of Isa. 53 from the current ideas of the time. 1. What is said about the depth and comprehensiveness of this prophetic suffering far surpasses all that had ever been said before. 2. Where, however, the Servant songs go especially far beyond all that had been said before them is their description of the Servant's readiness to suffer and of his paradoxical confidence of his safety in God. 3. Isa. 53 foretells the Servant's advance into a realm beyond suffering where he is glorified before the whole world. 4. In Isa. 53 the people for whom the Servant suffered overcome their initial blindness and acknowledge him. Their actual words are given. 5. The songs speak of the Servant as having a significance which reaches far beyond Israel. He confronts all the nations of the world. Kings are to shut their mouths before this Servant of God (Isa. 52.15).

19 The Prophets of the Later Persian Period:

Trito-Isaiah, Haggai, Zechariah, Malachi and Jonah

D E U T E R O - I S A I A H had spoken of the imminent restoration of the exiles, led by Yahweh in person, but we do not possess any document which gives us information about the actual return itself. It took place, but we do not know how, or even when. There are reasons which make it probable that the first move to the homeland only took place in the reign of Cambyses and not as a result of the edict of Cyrus. It is remarkable, however, that the event made no particular impact either on its own or on future generations. The return was obviously not accompanied by miraculous events – indeed, those who took part in it did not in any way regard it as a saving event. If they had done so, they would never have allowed it to fall into oblivion as if it were of no particular significance. It was obviously not celebrated as the fulfilment of a great prophetic prediction. Deutero-Isaiah's prophecies had therefore still to be fulfilled. None the less, Israel's situation had altered. The great hardship of the deportation had given way to the lesser ones of the resettlement and reconstruction. Yet for this era, too, Yahweh had raised up prophets who carried on the message of his advent. The theological judgments passed on these prophets of the later Persian period are usually guarded, if not actually negative. There can, of course, be no question of comparing messages of such matchless depth and range as those of Jeremiah, Ezekiel, and Deutero-Isaiah, each one of whom represents a whole world of prophecy and theology, with those of Trito-Isaiah, Joel, Haggai, Zechariah, and Malachi. None the less, we ought to be more chary of such summary judgments as 'men of the Silver Age'. To say nothing of the fact that these involve the setting up of an idea of spiritual originality which was unknown to Israel in general and to the prophets in particular, the only proper question is whether these prophets, in giving the message they did, were true ministers to their own day, or whether, in the light of all the understanding of Israelite prophecy we think we have reached, they failed in their task. No one can detract from the greatness of a Jeremiah or an Ezekiel, but this does not at all mean setting up the concept of 'greatness' as a theological norm and measuring the later prophets by it. Because of the inevitability of the approaching disaster, the final years before the fall of Jerusalem were not without greatness, and in the same way, because its hardships were so clear, the situation of the exiles in Babylon had greatness. The period after the return was neither clear nor great. Yet it and all its problems were what concerned these prophets, and their only success could lie in the way in which they dealt with them.

The situation of the community in Jerusalem towards the end of the sixth century – obviously by no means a clear one – is reflected in the messages which are subsumed under the name of *Trito-Isaiah* (Isa. 56–66). This prophet's call certainly speaks quite clearly of an office of comfort entrusted to him which has a very strong pastoral stamp upon it, namely 'to bind up the broken-hearted, to proclaim liberty to the captives' (Isa. 61.1). Yet, as prophet he had also to deal with grave abuses, with almost catastrophic social and legal conditions (Isa. 57.1ff.), and with the failure of the ruling class to do its duty (Isa. 56.9ff.). Here the keenness of his insistence on justice and righteousness hardly falls short of the charges made by the pre-exilic prophets. This is particularly true of the prophetic criticism which he levelled at the vain cultic observances, which, he says, are far less pleasing to Yahweh than compassion for others would be (Isa. 58.1ff.). Unlike the pre-exilic prophets, however, the people with whom Trito-Isaiah was concerned were not outwardly arrogant: rather, they were men of little faith. He therefore discusses with them whether Yahweh's arm is too short (Isa. 59.1); he uses theological arguments to make the delay in the coming of salvation intelligible as due to the community's mounting guilt: 'Therefore [Yahweh's] justice is far from us' (Isa. 59.9). Indeed, Yahweh actually protests by his lips that he was ready to be sought out and found by those who did not seek him; he spread out his hands all the day to his people. Yet, a terrible retribution will overtake those who still repulse these hands (Isa. 55.1ff.). Thus, like the old prophets, Trito-Isaiah tears open a gulf where one was not hitherto seen, and separates

Israel from Israel. Unfortunately, we know too little about the cultic conditions of the time to be able to be more precise about those who 'provoke' Yahweh (Isa. 65.3) – the offences in question must have been grave cultic abominations. These sinners are contrasted with the servants of Yahweh whom the prophet addresses in rapturous terms and to whom he promises Yahweh's salvation. In his proclamations of salvation he not only takes up central themes of Deutero-Isaiah's message, but he also shows himself to be so strongly influenced even by the latter's diction and emotions that we are right in guessing that Trito-Isaiah's relationship to Deutero-Isaiah is something like the close one of pupil or disciple. Thus, such phrases as 'build up', 'make the way plain' are re-echoed in Trito-Isaiah (Isa. 57.14; 62.10), and so is the saying about Mother Zion's astonishment at the abundance of her children (Isa. 66.7f.=49.21). The tradition is followed particularly strongly in the rapturous words which describe the city of God which Yahweh has again taken in his care, and the arrival of the first pilgrims (Isa. 62). Nevertheless, it is easy to see how the phraseology taken over from Deutero-Isaiah has here been adapted to meet a situation which had changed considerably both externally and internally. With Deutero-Isaiah, Zion is the climax of the prediction, the goal of the eschatological restoration; here, however, Zion is the starting-point of the prophet's thoughts, and she is Zion unredeemed, still waiting, forced to importune Yahweh, constrained to give him no peace, begging him to give effect to that glorification of the city of God which still tarries. This is not the language of Deutero-Isaiah. The background to Trito-Isaiah's message was a dangerous situation – characterized by the feeling that a divine promise was long overdue. Yet Trito-Isaiah calmly takes up the oracle of Yahweh's imminent advent to his city. Indeed, the climax of his message comes with his attempt to warn his contemporaries and make them see that Yahweh's transfiguration of his city by his coming, despite its delay, is a genuine and world-shaking event (Isa. 56.1; 58.8, 10f.; 62.1-3, 11, etc.).

The prophetic message of *Haggai* and Zechariah also culminates in the approaching advent of Yahweh and the imminent establishment of his kingdom, but, to the great embarrassment of not a few of the commentators, this message is linked most closely to the rebuilding of the Temple in Jerusalem which had been destroyed by the Babylonians; the link is, indeed, so close that for these two prophets the rebuilding of the Temple is actually the necessary

precondition of Yahweh's advent and of his kingdom. It is perfectly true that no such idea can be found in Isaiah or Jeremiah.
The reason can hardly be that these prophets were so much 'spiritual' than Haggai and Zechariah, for the pre-exilic prophets, too,
had very down-to-earth ideas about the eschatological salvation and
its fulfilment. The difference is explained simply by the completely
different spiritual condition of the people to whom the later prophets were sent. In the earlier period, Israel was faced with the
alternatives of political alliance or trust in Yahweh; failing these,
the question of proper justice in the gate was made *status confessionis*; these were the factors which determined whether or not
Israel still belonged to Yahweh. Now, the people of Jerusalem
were living in a state of 'resigned security', and because of their
concern with economic matters, which prevented them from looking any higher, the question of the rebuilding of the Temple had
become *status confessionis*. The Temple was, after all, the place
where Yahweh spoke to Israel, where he forgave her her sins, and
where he was present for her. The attitude taken towards it therefore determined the attitude for or against Yahweh. People, however, had no great interest in the place; because of economic hardship they kept putting off rebuilding it – it was 'not yet the time'
for it, they said (Hag. 1.2). Haggai completely reverses this scale
of priorities: Israel is no longer Israel if she does not seek first
the kingdom of God; if she does this, then the other thing, the
blessing of Yahweh, will be given her as well (Hag. 1.2-11; 2.14-19).
What he said and demanded was not in principle different from
Isaiah's call for faith during the Syro-Ephraimitic war. Haggai's
only reason for saying what he did was his belief that the eschatological Israel was to have a sacral centre, and that this alone would
guarantee her existence. It is very doubtful whether Isaiah would
have opposed him. Is it not better to see the genuineness of Haggai's prophecy in the fact that against all the evidence he interpreted the period as one of salvation and that even in the poor
conditions of his time he saw Yahweh beginning something new,
and begged his followers to prepare for the event which Yahweh
was to accomplish for them and to place themselves at his disposal? Had he thought otherwise, he would have admitted that
the prevailing despondency was justified, and that it was right to
assume that Yahweh could naturally have nothing to do with such
wretched conditions. When in the end a start was made to the
rebuilding of the Temple, and when the foundations already gave

some idea of its area, Haggai addressed the older people and expressed the sentiments which their own hearts probably did not
dare even to admit: 'Is it not in your sight as nothing?' (Hag. 2.3).
There is a prophetic grandeur in this little scene and its blunt
words about the insignificance of God's new start. Haggai did not
narrow Israel's world by binding her once more to the Temple;
rather he enlarged it by wresting from his contemporaries some
acknowledgment of Yahweh's eschatological work.

One thorny problem was still, however, unanswered. Who were
to be the future participants in Temple worship and who were
therefore to have a part in rebuilding the Temple? Was it not
arguable that, like all pagan temples, it should throw open its doors
to everyone who felt himself drawn to worship within them? It
was, after all, the Persian government which arranged for the rebuilding and supplied the necessary materials. But Samaria was at
that time still the seat of the provincial government in whose
jurisdiction Jerusalem lay. It is therefore not surprising that, once
the building was in process, official circles there became interested,
and wished to have a share in it, even if only to have a finger in
the pie. It is also perfectly possible that on plain economic grounds
this desire found support even in the Jerusalem community itself.
Using the form of a prophetic parable, Haggai gave a blunt No in
answer to this question. For the present the Temple is built solely
for and by Israel; not everyone who offers gifts within the framework of its cult will be 'well-pleasing' to Yahweh. To us today it
sounds a harsh decision; many would rather that the prophet had
given the opposite verdict. But it ought not to be difficult to see
that Haggai was only being true to the first and second commandments, and that he insisted upon a separation such as Elijah or
Deuteronomy had also battled for in their time. Yahwism was
not a religion of which one could become an adherent at will,
while possibly still maintaining other cultic connections; it went
back to a divine act of election and remained tied to a definite
national entity. Thus Haggai's importance lies in the fact that he,
like a second Elijah, saw in the difficult question of religious ex-
clusion a question which had disturbed Israel in days gone by
also, a clear cut 'Either – Or' at exactly the point where his contemporaries were no longer aware of it. We must stress again that
had he made a different decision, he would have denied Isaiah's
whole struggle against the policy of alliances, a struggle which
Isaiah hoped would detach the relationship between Yahweh and

Zion from all political stratagems and standards of judgment.
Neither Isaiah nor Haggai saw their decision as a spiritual one; for
them it was a question of keeping an appointed historical place
free for Yahweh's action.

It was Haggai himself who envisaged the time when all the
nations were to worship Yahweh and bring him their treasures,
and, surprisingly enough, he believed that this time was already
imminent (Hag. 2.6-9). It was for this time, when Yahwism would
throw off its national limitations and become a universal religion
– the time of the Messiah – that the Temple had to be built. It is
to be preceded by a fearful shaking of the heavens and the earth;
the nations are to wage internecine war, and Yahweh is to destroy
the weapons of war – it is a 'day of Yahweh'. Thereafter, however,
the anointed one is to enter upon his office as the signet-ring of
Yahweh, i.e., as the one who gives effect to Yahweh's decrees.
When Haggai made this prophecy, he was not thinking vaguely of
some unspecified anointed one. He clearly and unequivocally designated as the coming anointed one David's descendant Zerubbabel, the grandson of the unfortunate Jehoiachin.

It is common to point out that Haggai here differs radically from
the pre-exilic prophets by naming a living member of the house of
David as the coming anointed one; and this raises the question
whether he so showed himself to have been a dreamer. Since we
know nothing of the contemporary circumstances, it is quite possible to reconstruct a plausible picture of a great freedom movement breaking out in Judah, connected with the convulsions
shaking the Persian empire, and finding a spokesman in Haggai,
though Zerubbabel's participation would remain uncertain. But,
quite apart from the fact that the little Book of Haggai does not
give the slightest impression that the prophet was carried away by
a popular movement, our sources are simply not adequate for any
such reconstructions. All we can do is acknowledge that Haggai
regarded Zerubbabel as the coming anointed one, but that in fact
Zerubbabel never came to the throne. If this leads to a derogatory
judgment of Haggai's prophecy, how then is, say, Deutero-Isaiah
to be exempt from the same verdict, when we remember his prophecy of the returning exiles' miraculous journey through the
desert? We must also remember the situation revealed in the royal
psalms. Did not the writers of these psalms in each case regard
the subject of their praises as Yahweh's anointed one? And were
those to whom they were first addressed still on the throne of
David when, in the post-exilic age, these poems were read and
handed on with a mounting Messianic interest? (Cf. e.g., 1 Chron.

16.7ff.; II Chron. 6.41f.). The differences between these men and Haggai was that Haggai was thinking of a throne which no longer existed. But in any case, is it so very important that Haggai included a contemporary historical figure in his predictions? Isaiah must have believed that the anointed one whose coming he foretold was also in some respects an historical figure. And even such an anointed one as Haggai's is only a vice-gerent for him in whom all Old Testament predictions are Yea and Amen.

How are we to decide whether a prediction is visionary or factual? Is it not possible that a prediction which was defined as 'visionary' at the time of its delivery afterwards became absorbed in the great complex of prophetic tradition, because like other such predictions it was applied, after the failure of its first objective, to a future act of God?

The message of the prophet *Zechariah* is very similar to that of Haggai. His preaching, too, is closely co-related to the Temple, now in process of re-erection, and to the Davidic Zerubbabel, for whom, as he looks for the imminent eschatological saving event, Zechariah also holds out the prospect of a Messianic office. Zechariah appeared on the scene in 520, only a few months after Haggai, and, according to the dates given in his book, he prophesied for two years longer than Haggai. Thus, when he first began to preach, the rebuilding of the Temple was already under way. It has been pointed out, quite correctly, that Zechariah does not, as one might easily have expected, reiterate Haggai's summons to persevere in this work without slackening. Zechariah never admonishes or drives when he speaks; rather, his words about the completion of the Temple are most usually in the indicative mood. For example, those adverse factors which look like towering mountains will be levelled out and 'the hands of Zerubbabel will complete this house' (Zech. 4.6-10). Of course, Haggai and Zechariah do not contradict each other, for in spite of his admonitions Haggai too regarded Yahweh himself as the real initiator of the work which was to be undertaken – it is the spirit of Yahweh that authorizes the community to rebuild and gives it the strength to do so (Hag. 1.14; 2.5), while in an oracle with a keen polemical edge Zechariah opposed any idea of bringing in human or political means to defend the new Jerusalem :

Not by might and not by power, but by my spirit, says Yahweh of hosts.

(Zech. 4.6)

This was Israel's old watchword when she waged holy wars: it was also to apply when the final saving event came to pass.

As with Haggai, the subject of Zechariah's message is the pro-clamation of the imminent advent of Yahweh (Zech. 2.14[10]; 8.3). It is characteristic of both that they try to bring their hearers to a right understanding of the signs of their time. This time had been one of calamity, and, since the Temple was a complete ruin, it may also actually have been reckoned, from the viewpoint of the cult, as a time of fasting. The blessing of Yahweh had been withheld, and men's labours met with no success (Hag. 1.5f.). From now on, however, – and the way in which they exactly fix the 'now' is characteristic of the realism of the two prophets' thoughts about saving history (Hag. 2.15, 18; Zech. 8.11) – from now on it is a time of salvation. These two prophets therefore regard themselves as placed exactly at the point of the sudden great critical change. Trito-Isaiah was still almost completely in the dark – think of the moving prayer of lament in Isa. 63.7–64.11, and also Isa. 59.9-15. The hour in the saving history at which Haggai and Zechariah speak is under different auspices – the night is far spent, the day is at hand. The building of the Temple brought the dawn of the time of salvation. The time of adversity is at an end, and blessing – understood in a completely material way as agricultural prosperity – will begin immediately (Hag. 2.15-19), and has indeed begun already (Zech. 8.10-12). It is important that the great turning-point for these prophets which brings the final saving act had its way prepared by an historical event to which particularly limited sacral significance was attached. Neither the edict of Cyrus nor the return of the exiles were happenings which were given any special dignity as saving events.

We have just seen that Zechariah envisaged the early advent of Yahweh to his dishonoured city. The cycle of his *night visions* reveals many details connected with the eschatological new order which precedes this advent.

As the first vision (Zech. 1.7-15) makes clear, the outward con-dition of the world gives as yet no indication of the advent of Yahweh and his kingdom. The heavenly messengers who have patrolled the earth and observed it carefully can only bring back to heaven's gate the depressing report that they found the earth at peace and the nations living in security. It would, however, be a mistake to conclude that nothing is now to be looked for from Yahweh. He is in fact exceedingly jealous for his city, and his imminent salvation is already prepared, even down to the last detail. This is still unknown on earth; but it will soon be experienced. For – this is the second vision (Zech. 2.1-4 [1.18-21]) – the powers which are to smite those empires opposed to Yahweh are already drawn up. The third vision (Zech. 2.5-9 [1-5]) is full of dramatic excitement. The prophet sees 'a man with a measuring line in his hand', who is about to measure the new Jerusalem, clearly in order to prepare in advance for the building of her walls. However, an angel excitedly recalls him, for the new city of God is actually to be without defences; her sole protection is to be the wall of fire provided by the glory of God. This vision undoubtedly reflects certain plans of the returned exiles to rebuild the demolished walls. Zechariah opposed them. History, of course, came to ignore this prophetic protest, as it did others, for the wall was in fact later rebuilt, at the particular instigation of Nehemiah (Ezra. 4.6ff.; Neh. 3). The fourth vision (Zech. 3.1-7) sketches a court action in heaven over which the angel of Yahweh presided, and in which the accuser ('Satan') appeared against the high priest Joshua. The crime of which the latter is accused is not specified, but the fact that he appeared clothed in mourning suggests that the charge was a just one. However, it is better to see Joshua here as the representative of the community which is guilty in the eyes of Yahweh than to think of personal transgression on his own part. Here again there is an episode – the angel of Yahweh dismisses the charge with a sharp rebuke to the accuser. Joshua is invested anew; jurisdiction over the Temple and the offering of sacrifice in the forecourts are put under his charge; indeed, he is even given free access to the company of the heavenly beings. (How real the divine world is, and how near to human beings: if Yahweh so authorizes it, it is but a step!) In contrast to this vision, in the fourth (Zech. 4.1-6a, 10b-11, 13-14) Joshua is shown a picture in which there is no movement at all. A lampstand with forty-nine lights is flanked by two olive trees. These are 'the two anointed' – Joshua and Zerubbabel – 'who stand before the lord of the whole earth'. Zechariah thus sees – and this is unique in prophecy – the new Israel constituted as a dyarchy; the representative of the priestly office stands with equal rank next to the representative of the royal office. Later, in the fifth vision (Zech. 5.1-4), thieves and those who swear falsely have been driven out of the community and evil itself (this is the sixth vision, Zech. 5.5-11) has been removed; the seventh vision (Zech. 6.1-8) reverts to the picture given in the first. In the meantime morning has come; the heavenly chariots are ready to go out into the world. Nothing is divulged of the duties assigned to them except that those going towards the north – and this certainly means Babylon – have to 'lay down' Yahweh's spirit in the north country, obviously to encourage the Diaspora there to return home and enter into the Messianic kingdom.

After these pictures had appeared to his spirit during the course
of a single night, Zechariah awakened. What had they done for
him? He learned that at a time of calm in the world's history,
when the nations believed themselves secure in their own powers
alone, the kingdom of God was already prepared in heaven. He
became aware that Yahweh was jealous for Jerusalem and that
he had already made all the preparations for his own advent –
he had appointed his representatives and provided for and overcome all complications and opposition. The clear-cut way in which
the heavenly world is differentiated from the earthly is important.
The eschatological saving orders and offices are already present in
the world above. Indeed, even the events which must necessarily
precede the advent of the kingdom of God – as, for example, the
removal of evil – are already accomplished in the sight of the
world above, so that they have anticipated the course of events
on earth. This is not how either Isaiah or Jeremiah regarded the
eschatological event. Isaiah was, of course, aware of a world above
which was the abode of Yahweh and his heavenly court; but the
emphasis now placed upon the archetypal existence of the final
things in heaven is something new. Ezekiel shows the change beginning; he received his message in the form of a heavenly book (Ezek.
2.8ff.). Deutero-Isaiah hears how the processional road for Yahweh's return to Jerusalem is already prepared in the world above
(Isa. 40.3ff.), and this brings him quite close to Zechariah. In this
late period Israel apparently gave a greater place to certain ideas
common to the whole of the east; for in the Babylonians' sacral-
mythical picture of the world, it was an established fact that
everything on earth, particularly if it had sacral value, had its
corresponding archetype in the world above. In the same way also,
according to the Priestly Document, the tabernacle was modelled
on a heavenly pattern (Ex. 25.9, 40). In apocalyptic these age-old
concepts were once again expressed in a completely new way.

The little book of the anonymous prophet which bears the name
of *Malachi* only contains six oracles. The man who addresses us is
exclusively concerned with abuses practised by the community.
He attacks priests who are careless in ritual matters, divorce, and,
above all, blasé scepticism in religious matters. This suggests that
he was writing after the religious revival under Haggai and Zechariah and the completion of the rebuilding of the Temple. It is
remarkable that this prophet's message contains practically no
clues which might determine the tradition to which he belongs.

He gives less of a broad exposition of eschatological ideas than any other prophet, perhaps because he uses the form of the polemic dialogue. He mentions God's eschatological action in only two of his oracles (Mal. 2.17–3.5; 3.13-21 [3.13–4.3]). Yahweh is to come unexpectedly, and his day is to bring judgment upon the godless; but for those who fear God, 'the sun of salvation' will shine forth. The idea that Yahweh will send a messenger before his own final advent (Mal. 3.1) is only found in Malachi. There is debate about whether the prophet thought of a heavenly or an earthly messenger – did he perhaps think of himself as this messenger? In an appendix to the little book the return of Elijah, who had been taken up to heaven at his death, is expected immediately before the terrible day of Yahweh : he is to turn the hearts of the fathers and the hearts of the children towards one another (Mal. 3.23f. [4.5f.]).

The little *Book of Jonah*, perhaps more than any other in the Old Testament, calls for special appreciation of the literary form in which its message is clothed.[1] At all events, the straightforward message contained in this book has been distorted ever since people began to be puzzled by Jonah's sojourn in the belly of a fish. The minor detail whether this could be accepted as an event that actually happened became the all-important matter of contention, and it was left to modern criticism, which has been able to restore to so much of the Old Testament its pre-scriptural form, to explain the story properly. Quite obviously, it is a story with a strong didactic content, and should not be read as a historical account. It deals with a man of God who – from the narrator's standpoint – lived in times so remote as to be almost legendary, the time of Jeroboam II (II Kings 14.25).

The material of the book is laid out with great artistry, for it falls into two exactly corresponding halves, Jonah in the ship and Jonah at Nineveh. In both cases the heathen appear in a much better light than the prophet. It was they who took the initiative during the storm and who saw that Jonah was the cause of the trouble; and how happily things turned out through them in Nineveh! They are simple and transparent in God's presence, but Jonah is an unknown quantity, and psychologically complex. He is at his worst when he speaks of his faith in confessional and cultic

---

[1] The text seems to be seriously disturbed at one point only; v. 5 in ch. 4 is wrongly placed; it should be put after 3.4. The psalm of thanksgiving in 2.3-10 [2-9] is a later addition.

terms – witness on the one hand when he talks religion in the ship's cabin ('I am a Hebrew, and fear Yahweh, the God of heaven . . .' Jonah 1.9), and on the other his words with God about forgiveness. At the end of the first section comes the sacrifice which the sailors offer to Yahweh. That they become believers in the God of Israel means that one of God's aims has already reached its goal. Yet this was, of course, merely a prelude to what was afterwards to be repeated on a grand scale in the deliverance of Nineveh.

The story of Jonah thus falls within the literary category, which we have already met, of a story told about a prophet, with the difference that this has now actually become didactic narrative to a greater degree than the earlier stories were. Indeed, it seems to have been the last and strangest flowering of this old and almost extinct literary form. Consider how the story is told – with a grace and ease unmatched in the prophetic literature. And yet, it deals with grave matters, with a city whose days are numbered in the sight of God, with evil men, and above all with a prophet whose attitude to his office was outrageous. Of course, even in the earlier narratives about prophets, the 'hero' of the story was never the prophet himself, but rather Yahweh, who was glorified through the prophet. In this respect there is really no great change; the only difference is that God is here glorified not through his ambassador, but in spite of his ambassador's complete refusal. The ridiculous, stubborn Jonah, grudging God's mercy to the heathen, but filled with joy at the shade of the castor-oil plant, and then wanting to die when he sees it withering away, is unable to impede God's saving thoughts – they achieve their goal in spite of everything. Indeed, this constitutes the particular enigma of the book – for all his disobedience Jonah is nevertheless a figure whom God used as a king might a subject: it was because of him that the sailors' attention was drawn to Yahweh and the men of Nineveh repented. Thus, there is no indignation or complaint over the prophet's refusal. Considering God's victorious work, even a refusal like this could be related in these non-tragic, and even gay, terms.

It is best not to let conjecture about the contemporary causes of the book cloud our interpretation of it. We have no knowledge of any 'universalistic' opposition to the 'particularist' measures taken by Ezra and Nehemiah, and the book itself contains no evidence to support such a theory. Moreover, polemical and tendentious writings usually wear a different appearance. Further it is wrong to suggest that the book's universalism wished to see covenant and election finally severed from their restriction to Israel; it addresses those who know covenant and community; and it is these men whom it warns against the temptation of using their peculiar position in God's sight to raise claims which compromise Yahweh's freedom in his plans for other nations. It is not at once obvious why the story portrays a prophet as the embodiment of such a grudging faith, for the great prophets did try to open their fellow-countrymen's eyes to the fact that Yahweh's plans embraced the whole world of nations. For all his orthodoxy the really bad thing about Jonah is his aloofness. This was displayed on board ship, and also before Nineveh : when life and death were at stake, he remained withdrawn, in a very sinister position. It would certainly be wrong to interpret the story as a final judgment on prophecy in Israel. This would be to misjudge prophecy entirely. Yet the prophetic proclivity for self-questioning – one of the best aspects of its spirit – once again sprang to life in this little book. It is worth noticing that one of the last utterances of Israelite prophecy is so devastatingly self-critical; for in the way in which in this book it strips itself of all honours, and turns men's gaze away from itself in order to give the honour to him to whom alone this is due, it reveals something of the 'he must increase, but I must decrease' spoken by the last in the line of these ambassadors (John 3.30).

20 The Prophecies of the New Jerusalem

THE subject of Haggai's and Zechariah's prophecies of salvation was the eschatological restoration of the Temple and of the city of God. The outward form given by Zechariah to what we may properly call eschatological Israel was that of a city state, and this undoubtedly reflects the historical situation of the time : for at that time Jerusalem was the scene of everything that was vital and concrete in Israel, whether hope or despair. If the prophets wanted to speak at all relevantly to the men of their time it had to be within the frame of reference of this restricted area; and they had to declare that, in spite of everything, this was not too narrow a basis for Yahweh to begin his eschatological saving work.

This also explains why Deutero-Isaiah speaks of Jerusalem or Zion so often, while clearly meaning the people.[1] No wonder that it was the Zion tradition which came back to life just at the time when 'Israel' was being confined to so narrow a political sphere. Originally this Zion tradition was one 'election tradition' among others.[2] When the idea of election was transferred in name to Jerusalem and the Zion tradition was closely associated with the David tradition, it was clearly made more systematic and its special character was somewhat dulled. This first happened with the Deuteronomist, in the promise that Yahweh wanted his grace to prevail 'for the sake of David and for the sake of Jerusalem, which I have chosen' (I Kings 11.13, 32). There was never a fusion of the two traditions; for a long time the David tradition and the Zion tradition led separate existences side by side, for the Zion tradition was indissolubly bound up with the idea of the reign of Yahweh.[3] So this Zion tradition was unexpectedly developed in the post-exilic period. In fact, all the detailed pictures associated with it belonged

[1] Isa. 40.2, 9; 49.14; 51.3, 16, etc.
[2] Exodus and Zion traditions are combined in Ex. 15.17f.
[3] E.g.: Micah 4.7; Zeph. 3.15; Obad. 21; Zech. 14.9.

to it from the beginning: the high mountain of God,[4] the dwelling-place of God,[5] the kingdom of God, the streams of water;[6] even the idea of the pre-existence of the city of God in heaven, first attested in apocalyptic, goes back to a very old mythological approach.[7] Details of two different complexes of ideas may be detected in the preaching of the post-exilic prophets about the glory of Zion.

1. The announcement of the failure of a hostile attack on Zion apparently forms part of the oldest traditions of pre-exilic Jerusalem; indeed, there are indications that this tradition derives from the pre-Davidic Jerusalem. We have already seen how it was suddenly developed by Isaiah, and how he used it like the theme of a fugue, making ever-new variations on it as he applied it to his own day. No other prophet employed this range of concepts at such length. In comparison, the brevity of Micah's presentation (Micah 4.11-13) makes him seem to belong really to the past, an impression which is strengthened by the fact that here Zion is herself summoned to fight against the enemy, a feature which is absent in the later variations of the theme. The picture which portrays the eschatological assault by the nations on the largest scale is the prophecy of the coming of Gog and Magog and of their destruction 'on the mountains of Israel' (Ezek. 38f.). Though the poem enters into great detail in other respects, it says practically nothing about the battle itself, particularly about the disposal of the dead and the collection of the weapons that is to keep Israel busy for seven years. Interestingly enough, this prophecy expressly appeals to earlier predictions (Ezek. 38.17); it regards itself as based on an earlier prophetic tradition. In Joel 4.9-17 [3.9-17], too, we meet with the idea earlier expressed in Isaiah that the nations advancing against Zion do not in the least come by their own initiative and choice, but because they are summoned by Yahweh (cf. Ezek. 38.4, 39.2). Here again what comes in question is a day of Yahweh with earthquake and darkness (v. 14). Yahweh is to judge the nations in the valley of Jehoshaphat; Zion will be preserved. The final development of these variations on the theme of the foreign nations' assault on Zion comes in Zech. 12 and 14, where the basic component parts of this cycle of concepts – Yah-

[4] Ps. 48.3; Isa. 2.2; Ezek. 17.22; 40.2; Zech. 14.10.
[5] Ps. 46.5f.; 76.3; Joel 3.21; Isa. 8.18, etc.
[6] Ps. 46.5; Isa. 47.1ff.; Isa. 33.21; Joel. 3.18; Zech. 14.8.
[7] Syr. Baruch 4.2-6.

weh's assembling of the nations, the battle, and the preservation of
Zion – are set out in full side by side. A unique feature here is the
idea that the enemy will actually force their way into the holy
city itself and work dire havoc within her; the text also gives
many grisly details about the chastisement of the enemy (Zech.
14.12). Another unique feature of this text is the interweaving of
motifs which derive from entirely different eschatological concepts
– from henceforward, the survivors of the foreign nations will
make pilgrimage to Zion and worship Yahweh. External conditions
are to be miraculously changed – the whole land is to become a
plain, only Jerusalem will remain aloft on the mountain, and living
waters are to flow out from it. There is to be no alteration of light
and darkness in the city: there is to be perpetual daylight. This
elaboration of the usual cycle of concepts by means of a number
of different ideas of what was expected to happen shows that the
passage is of late composition. But since there are certain gaps in
the picture, we have also to reckon with the possibility that later
interpolations may have been added to it.

   2. The other cycle of concepts which is attached to the eschatological city of God, and is also frequently taken up and transformed
in a variety of ways by the prophets, is that of the pilgrimage of
the nations to the city on Mount Zion. This concept differs from
the one just considered in that it describes a peaceful event: its
subject is the salvation of the nations, and not their judgment. In
the oldest version in which we have it, Isa. 2.2-4, the first stage
in the eschatological event is a miraculous change in physical geo-
graphy. At the end-time, the mountain of the house of Yahweh is
to rise aloft and be exalted high above all the hills round about it,
so that it will be visible to all nations. These will immediately set
out and stream to it from every side, because they can no longer
endure the desperate condition in which they live. They therefore
come as pilgrims to Yahweh, 'for out of Zion goes forth instruction'. Just as the bands of Israel's pilgrims year by year made the
journey to Zion where, at the climax of the festival, Yahweh's will
as expressed in law was proclaimed to them, so the prophecy ex-
pects that 'at the end of the days' the nations will present themselves on Zion for a final settlement of all disputes, and to receive
those fixed rules for living by which Yahweh grants salvation, and
that thereafter – once they have returned home again – they will
reforge their weapons of war into the implements of peace. If this
passage had been the only reference to the concept, we should

have been blind to the fact that Isaiah only selected some features from what is obviously a rich and living cycle of concepts.

In Deutero-Isaiah, too, only parts of the total range of concepts are in each case actualized. None the less, it is characteristic of the importance and independence which attached to these ideas that, when the prophet makes use of such prophecies, he does not confine himself to incidental allusions, but always fills up a whole unit with them. It is interesting to see the way in which he transposed the traditional material into the situation of his own day. In Isa. 49.14-21 he turned it into an oracle of comfort for despairing Jerusalem. Those who stream to her from round about are her own children! In the following unit (Isa. 49.22-3), the prophet takes up the traditional *motif* – he foretells the coming of the nations. This time, however, it is Yahweh himself who gives them the signal to come. Yet, here again Deutero-Isaiah wove something of his own into the material: the nations are to come and bring the sons and daughters of Zion in their arms. 'Kings shall be your foster-fathers.' In Isa. 45.14-15 it is again the foreign nations who come, bringing their precious treasures. The special feature of this passage, however, which makes it unique among all the adaptations of the material, is the confession which Deutero-Isaiah puts into the mouth of the nations who are brought to worship the God of Israel:

'God is with you only, and there is no other, no god besides him' (Isa. 45.14).

The fullest development of this traditional material is to be found in Trito-Isaiah (Isa. 60), and this makes the chapter very important for the correct evaluation of others which are related to it. Like the beginning of Isa. 2, it speaks of a transfiguration of the city of God, the 'coming of a light', as a result of which Jerusalem emerges from her previous insignificance and thus sets in train the pilgrimage of the nations.[8] Here the poet did not miss the chance of giving a magnificent description of this coming of the nations. On the sea the sailing ships can be seen hastening like flights of doves from the west, and from the east the caravans and camels of Midian and other Arabian tribes. They bring sheep for sacrifice, gold and incense for the Temple – they even bring the exiles from

---

[8] This command 'to become a light' has a precursor in Isa. 52.1: 'Awake, awake, put on your strength, O Zion; put on your beautiful garments, O Jerusalem.'

among God's people. Thereafter lawlessness and social oppression
will cease. Peace will be the overseer and righteousness the governor in the city of God; the days of her mourning will be at an
end.[9]

The briefest mention of the pilgrimage of the nations is in Haggai (Hag. 2.6ff.). Yahweh is to shake the nations, then they will
arise and bring all their precious things to Zion, for 'the silver is
mine, and the gold is mine', says Yahweh. Haggai really took only
one feature from the whole range of concepts, that of the solemn
conveyance of the treasures of all the nations to Yahweh. Yahweh
alone has a rightful claim to all the valuables which now lie scattered among the nations; only at the *eschaton*, once the Temple
has been prepared, will the treasures which are his by right, and
which have meanwhile been apportioned amongst the nations,
revert to Yahweh's possession. On the other hand, Isaiah also took
only one detail from the complex. His interest is concentrated not
upon the cultic aspect of the event, the entry of the nations into
the worship of Yahweh and the presentation of their offerings, but
upon the reception of Yahweh's ordinances, on which basis alone
there can be lasting peace among the nations in the latter days.
The expectation of a feast, which Yahweh is to prepare for the
nations on Zion, probably also belongs in this context of the pilgrimage of the nations, as does the expectation that 'on this
mountain' Yahweh will destroy the covering that is cast over all
peoples, death itself (Isa. 25.6-8; cf. also Jer. 3.17; Zech. 8.22).

This belief in a future pilgrimage of the nations to Zion is thus
seen to be a very fluid tradition, which the prophets could actualize
in quite different ways. The author of Zech. 9–14 apparently connected it with the wars of the nations.[10] He, too, knows of the land
being changed into a plain and the holy city being exalted above
it, of the pilgrimage of the nations 'who survive' to worship Yahweh, and also of the perfect holiness of the city of God (Zech. 14.10,
11, 16, 20).[11]

[9] Cf. also Isa. 56.7; 66.18, 23.
[10] Similarly Zeph. 3.8ff.
[11] The vision of the new temple and the new city of God in Ezek. 40–48
also fits in here. Traditio-historically, it can be set alongside Zech. 14.10,
where the city set aloft (cf. Ezek. 40.2) and its gates are again mentioned.
The traditional element, the waters that issue from the temple, is also found
in Zech. 14.8 and Ezek. 47. The difference, of course, lies in the fact that
Ezek. 40ff. took the description of the structural features and the institutions
of the new temple as almost its sole theme, and in consequence goes into
much fuller detail concerning what it depicts.

The theme of the eschatological pilgrimage of the nations to Zion is also found several times in the apocryphal literature, as for example Tobit 13.9ff.; 14.5ff.; Enoch 90.28-33; and Syb. Or. 3. 703-31. Finally, in apocalyptic there arose the idea that the new Jerusalem in all its perfection would come down from heaven to earth (Rev. 21.2; IV Ezra 7.26; 13.36).

21 The Prophetic Word and History

Retrospect

APART from some lesser units, prophecy in Israel ended with Malachi and Trito-Zechariah. There is, especially in Malachi, an impression that prophecy was flagging: but the subsequent silence inspires several questions. Was it the sign that eschatological expectations had actually become extinct – that is to say, did it indicate that the line of those who carried on the prophetic tradition had come to an end? The psychological concept of exhaustion does not altogether cover all the data concerned. A more valid reason might be that in the period after Alexander the Great, Palestine was left untouched by any events of world-wide scale, and it was always in the shadow of such events that the prophets operated. Above all, however, we must remember the internal religious structure of the post-exilic community. Haggai and Zechariah saw the rebuilding of the Temple wholly within the perspective of a great eschatological event. But, as a result of the Priestly Document, which may have been brought to Jerusalem by the returned exiles, and its non-eschatological cultic theology, this vision must have become lost. As time went on, the consolidation of the post-exilic community, which apparently corresponded to the restoration which many of the returned exiles hoped for, had become more and more bound up with an increasingly consistent elimination of eschatological ideas. This does not mean that these ideas were no longer represented: but the ruling priestly aristocracy in Jerusalem tended to push eschatological expectation more and more on one side, and finally forced it into separation. It is indeed hard to believe that the writer of, say, Zech. 14 held the same faith, and worshipped in the same way, as did the author of Chronicles, who was in all likelihood his contemporary. It is possible that this was the time when the prophets' eschatological expectation broke for ever with the theocracy. Thereafter the latter developed into the service of a law which, now divorced from the saving history, itself became an absolute entity.

At this point, however, we must again introduce a brief theological consideration. At the very beginning of this book we considered the question of the proper designation of the new element which prophecy constituted in Israel. In earlier exegesis of the prophets two basic ideas in particular were constantly brought forward. The first was that in the prophetic preaching ethical monotheism came to the fore for the first time. Amos was regarded as almost 'the incorporation of the moral law', and Isaiah as the preacher of 'the universal moral order'. The other was the appearance of the spiritual man who stood in a direct religious relationship to God. This whole way of looking at prophecy, which tried to make an over-hasty break-through to basic religious and philosophical truths, has now been abandoned, for what is peculiar to prophecy comes neither from the peculiarity of its spiritual experiences and encounters nor from its religious ideas taken by themselves. In all probability, the questions considered by earlier criticism will one day require to be taken up again, though under different theological presuppositions. Our particular concern has been to put the prophets back into the saving history and to pay heed to the aspects of prophecy which result from this. We began with a fact already established by exegetical investigation – each of the prophets occupied a place of his own in the history of the relationship between God and Israel. This place was a determining factor in their message, and is the only standpoint from which to understand their whole discourse. They are conscious of being placed inside a historical continuum with wide perspectives over both past and future. Within it, however, each prophet stands as it were at the cross-roads where God's dealings with Israel, which have been almost stationary, suddenly and dramatically begin to move again. The place at which they raise their voices is a place of supreme crisis, indeed almost a place of death, in so far as the men of this period of crisis were no longer reached by the saving force of the old appointments, and were promised life only as they turned to what was to come. All the prophets shared a common conviction that they stood exactly at that turning point in history which was crucial for the existence of God's people. This is the standpoint from which one has to understand their passionate demolition of the old, in particular of all false means of security before God, as well as what they say of the approach of entirely

new and terrifying divine acts of salvation. Yet, they also shared
a common certainty that the new thing which they expected was
already prefigured in the old, and that the old would be present
in the new in perfect form. Thus, the old actually seems to have
had a prophetic significance for them, at least to the extent that
they were certain that Yahweh was not going to nullify what he
had himself begun and established, but would link on to it, in
order to bring it the more splendidly to completion. Or, to put it
in another way, they shared in a common, spell-bound watching
for the new thing, and along with it in a denial of the saving
power of Yahweh's old appointments, though the latter was not
of course expressed in its full consistency until Jeremiah, Ezekiel,
and Deutero-Isaiah. For them, Israel's life and death depended solely
on the meeting with the Lord who was to come. Western man,
with his philosophical equipment, has here to remember that this
recourse to, and actualization of, old traditions was much more than
merely an effective rhetorical device. Projecting the old traditions
into the future was the only possible way open to the prophets of
making material statements about a future which involved God.

In my opinion, the most effective way of making this aspect
of Old Testament prophecy once more central – and I judge it to
be prophecy's most important specific content – is still the way of
taking the prophets and their message individually. (This does not,
of course, imply that this is the only possible way of presentation.)
Any 'systematic' treatment of the prophets has to face the gravest
difficulties inherent in the expressly charismatic character of practically all their utterances. Such a treatment must also in no case
obscure their position in the saving history. For during its course
of more than three centuries, prophetic teaching developed in very
varied ways. The message of each prophet was exactly directed to
meet a specific time, and it contained an offer which was never
repeated in precisely the same form as it had with the original
speaker. In the matter of God's requirements and offers, the time
of Nebuchadnezzar was completely different from that of Sennacherib. Therefore, in the time of Jeremiah – indeed any time after
the disaster of 701 – no one could any longer argue for the safe-
guarding of Zion in the sense that Isaiah had foretold it. The Jerusalem of the day did not recognize the hour; the waves of history
rolled over Zion. Deutero-Isaiah's prophecy that Yahweh would
lead his people home was valid in that precise form only for the
exiles of Babylon. Even Trito-Isaiah could only take it up in a

considerably altered form, because the historical situation had altered. Thus, the message of every prophet was closely bound up with the point in history at which it was delivered, and after this point no message could be repeated exactly in its original sense. This is where creative interpretation begins.

One question in this survey may not, however, be evaded, the question of the fulfilment of all these prophecies. True, the prophets did not always speak of events in the future. But they often did so, and not infrequently prophesied quite definite events in the political sphere. If one remembers their display of rhetoric and the passion in their remarks, it would be trivial to dismiss this side of the picture as inconsequential. Even where the prophecies seem less precise, we still find wide-ranging developments in the political sphere which the prophets regarded with the utmost concentration.

Of course, the exegete must not forget the difficulties which confront him at this point. How can he expect to establish that a prophecy was fulfilled? There are, indeed, a handful of cases in which one can speak of the fulfilment of a prophetic threat, in which an event can be indicated which to some extent corresponds to what has been prophesied.[1] But only to some extent! For anyone who is familiar with the question knows how events are simplified over a considerable interval of time and how many aspects of a particular event which are clear to its contemporaries remain hidden from the historian. Who can know the horizons of the understanding of the people of the time? How did they regard a prophecy? What was there in it that attracted their attention, i.e., to what extent did they take it literally?[2] It is fatal to deal with a question without having some idea of the chief participants, the prophet's audience. There was, of course, a time when the question of fulfilment was really open to discussion – that of Jeremiah. Indeed, one might almost say of the few instances which present themselves here (Jer. 28.7ff.; Deut. 18.21f.) that Jeremiah's whole career as a prophet was dogged by the temptation to see Yahweh as 'a deceitful brook, like waters that fail' (Jer. 15.18). Ezekiel had to resist the undisguised scepticism of his contemporaries, who

[1] One could say that e.g. Isa. 7.7; Jer. 22.10-12, 24-30; 28.15-17; 25.11-12 were fullfilled and e.g. Isa. 20.1-6; Jer. 22.18f.; 36.20-31; 44.29-30; 43.8-13; Ezek. 29.17-20 were not fulfilled.
[2] Was the uncannily accurate account of the approach of the Assyrians in Isa. 10.27-32 meant to be taken literally? Or was the message understood by the audience of the time as a form of prophetic poetry?

taunted him with the saying 'The days grow long, and every vision comes to naught' (Ezek. 12.22). Here not only the prophet, but also his audience, were faced with the problem of non-fulfilment. From then on the problem seems to have remained, and so we see later prophets fighting against resignation and scepticism with greater or lesser success. The great Exodus prophesied with tremendous excitement by Deutero-Isaiah did not take place under the personal leadership of Yahweh, accompanied by all its consequent miracles. The same is true of the great pilgrimage of the peoples to Zion, of which Isaiah may already have spoken. Even if, as has been pointed out, the number of fulfilled prophecies is about the same as those which were not fulfilled, there is a considerable problem here, and the very seriousness of the statements of the prophets does not allow us to minimize it. In the present context it is only possible to offer a few remarks on the question of how Israel dealt with the problem of a delay.

The difficulty of ascertaining fulfilment or non-fulfilment lies, as we have said, in our present position. We can only approach the problem from our point of view, as it is presented to us by historical scholarship. That means that we see a particular historical event which might be regarded as the fulfilment of a prophetic forecast only in extreme isolation, quite removed from all connotations which it might have for the religious audience of the time. As a result, the question of fulfilment threatens to become a simple matter of calculation, which either works out or does not work out. Here, however, it is clear that we are departing from both the spirit of the word of the prophets and the capabilities of their audience. A fact of history which, it is believed, can be taken in isolation and in the abstract as a prediction which has been proved correct – is that the same thing as a fulfilment brought about by Yahweh? The predictions of the prophets were only part of what Israel experienced day by day from the hand of Yahweh. Neither they nor the fulfilments which could be ascertained stood by themselves; to be what they claimed to be they needed a larger context in which and from which they had to be understood. This was faith in Yahweh. What was already present here – though it is difficult to calculate more exactly – was a general knowledge, a general experience of Yahweh and his rule, a knowledge of the only possible attitude of man to Yahweh. In short, it was established that all Yahweh's dealings with Israel demanded faith and not calculation. (And here is the limit of our historical understanding!) The reason why the delay of the fulfilment of the promises experienced by Israel (like the 'delay of the Parousia' in the early church) did not develop into a deep-seated crisis was simply that Israel knew well enough that Yahweh was the master, and not the servant, of his words. In the end, therefore, the question could never be one of fulfilment, taken by itself; it was a question of Yahweh and his lordship. That is the meaning of the so-called 'formula of acknowledgment' which occurs so frequently in the words of the prophets, and particularly those of Ezekiel, '. . . that they may know that I am Yahweh'. It cannot be said more clearly than this that the divine demonstration of saving acts in history is not an end in itself, but a means to an end; it leads to the acknowledgment and worship of Yahweh. (In this way, after a long digression we have returned once again to the statements with which this book began, that the message of the prophets was rooted deeply in the experiences of Yahweh which ancient Israel had already had, and that without this foundation they would be incomprehensible not only to us, but also to their contemporaries.)

If one considers the characteristics of faith in Yahweh, it does not appear so surprising that Israel was unconcerned that there was a delay in the fulfilment of promises or that they were not fulfilled at all. Nor do we feel that the standing of a prophet was seriously affected by this sort of thing. We have numerous indications of revisions of earlier prophecies, of their adaptation to different circumstances, and nowhere does this seem to have been thought to be embarrassing or humiliating. It was embarrassing and humiliating suddenly to be given no answer by Yahweh (Micah 3.7), and it was embarrassing and ridiculous if a prophet showed himself incapable of allowing for a sudden change of intention on Yahweh's part (Jonah 4).

However, the problem should not be limited to that of unfulfilled prophecies. It extends far more widely, for even prophecies which *had been* fulfilled were handed down to subsequent generations as the prophetic word. Even they did not cease to point to the future. Was it less surprising that a prophetic message which was once directed precisely to a particular audience should suddenly be detached from this immediate point of reference and addressed to a quite different time without any explanation and without consideration of its earlier context? *Here we touch on the riddle of the way in which Yahweh dealt with Israel throughout her history – on the one hand the utmost seriousness with which Yahweh bound himself to history and a particular present, and on the other the ease with which he withdrew himself, to claim another present in a new way.* This sudden change in a prophetic prediction, which was at one time directed towards a particular political situation and all of a sudden applied to a quite different period, can often be observed in the Old Testament. The greatest metamorphosis takes place, however, when the texts are set in the context in which they must eventually be seen, that of the New Testament saving event.

22 Apocalyptic

Apocalyptic and Wisdom

E V E N after prophecy had ceased, Israel continued to look into the future and to speak of the eschatological events still to be realized. She had learned much from the prophets, and a number of their predictions were absorbed into the language in which she expressed her hope, as for example the hope for a new Jerusalem (Tobit 13f.) or the hope for the coming of a Messiah (Ps. Sol. 17). But quite apart from the fact that the themes of this already somewhat standardized hope had become rather monotonous, with nothing like the fullness and vividness of the prophets' view of the future, the eschatology here was quite different from that to be found in the prophets. The horizon on which a totally new saving act of God dawns is no longer that of an ultimate crisis between Yahweh and Israel; the pleasant prospect of this hope looks for a time when Israel leads her life in obedience to the commandments. The elements of the eschatological hope which were still preserved in the proclamation of the prophets are now incorporated within the pattern of a conservative piety based on the Law. One might regard this as a kind of distant expectation, a phenomenon which is otherwise alien to the Old Testament. In an astonishing way, however, the religious hope of Israel was expressed once again, this time on the basis of quite different presuppositions and with the vision of a universalism unconceived hitherto, in apocalyptic.

In speaking of apocalyptic, it is necessary to remember that no satisfactory definition of it has yet been achieved. There are good reasons for this. We find some help in determining the background and characteristics of apocalyptic if we consider the titles adopted by the apocalyptic writers. as indications of the traditions on which apocalyptic is based can be seen in these designations. It is clear that Daniel was trained for the life of the court (Dan. 1.3ff.) and was even regarded as a wise man (Dan. 2.48), though a wise man of quite a different stamp from his pagan counterparts. Enoch, too, is described as a 'scribe', 'scribe of righteousness' (Enoch 12.3f.; 15.1; 92.1); he is a learned man whose wisdom exceeds the wisdom of all men (Enoch 37.4). Finally, Ezra is termed 'scribe of the knowledge of the Most High' (IV Ezra 14.50). Indeed, were they not scientists in the strict sense of the word, as concerned with astronomical and cosmological problems as with the question of the ordering of history? As a result, their learning is always book-learning. Again and again the reader is referred to books in which this comprehensive knowledge is written down.[1]

This first brief survey thus already shows quite a clear picture: the roots of apocalyptic seem primarily to be in the wisdom tradition. If apocalyptic were a continuation of prophecy (it has even been called the child of prophecy), apart from anything else it would be most striking that it does not take up the traditions attached to the great names of prophecy, but goes back to the ancestors of wisdom, to Daniel, Enoch, Ezra and others. At the end of the book of Daniel is what amounts to a glorification of the teacher of wisdom (Dan. 12.3). But there are still weightier grounds for not seeking the roots of apocalyptic in prophecy.

One decisive factor is the impossibility of reconciling its view of history with that of the prophets. There is no way from the message of the prophets, specifically based on the saving history, i.e. on particular traditions of election, to the apocalyptic picture of history or to its idea that the events of the end-time have been laid down since the beginning of the world. There is no mention of Israel's history in the two great dream-visions in Daniel, the vision of the image of the kingdoms and the vision of the four beasts. Here God is alone with the kingdoms of the world; even the Son of Man does not come from Israel, but 'with the clouds of heaven'. This picture of history seems to lack any credal character. It no longer reveals any knowledge of the saving acts of God from which a historical picture had formerly been constructed. When they made their predictions, the prophets had always openly taken their standpoint in their own day and age; it was from that point that they saw the vistas of history roll back into the past or forward into the future. In contrast, the apocalyptic writer veils his own standpoint in time. Scholars are generally able to deduce it from a number of indica-

[1] E.g. Enoch 14.1; 33.4; 72.2; 81.1; 82.1; 93.1; 108.1; IV Ezra 14.24, 44; Ass. Mos. 1.16f., etc.

tions with a reasonable degree of accuracy, but the writer himself is concerned to offer a survey of history in which everything turns upon the fact that the epochs of world history are predetermined from the beginning. The question thus arises whether such a conception is not the sign of a great loss of historical sensitivity, whether history has not been excluded from this idea of epochs which can be known and calculated. At any rate, the question of the existential relationship of apocalyptic to history, the question whether it is not rather gnosis or speculation, becomes very pressing here. It arises particularly in connection with the conception of the unity of world history which is already to be found in Daniel's picture of the kingdoms (Dan. 2.31ff.) and in the vision of the four beasts (Dan. 7.2ff.). The kingdoms of the world have an origin, a character and a destiny, and what unfolds in them has been determined from the very beginning. The movement of world history represented so vividly in these symbolic pictures shows an increase of evil. This view of history is thus extremely pessimistic. A negative goal must be reached in world history, the measure of wickedness (Dan. 8.23). World history leads to an 'abyss', to a great destruction (Enoch 83.7). This increasing evil evidently lies in the nature of man and the kingdoms which he establishes, though it manifests itself in different ways.

Though apocalyptic surrenders the view of a saving history to be found in the earlier interpretation of history – as we have seen, the saving event is concentrated on the end-time – , history is not, of course, entirely removed from God's control. On the contrary, the apocalyptic writers were consoled by the fact that it was completely under the control of God. What particularly interested them was the question of the divine ordering of the course of history. We see that they find the answer in the recognition of a strict predetermination of history. In their conviction, nothing new ever happens; 'the Holy One determined days for all things' from the very beginning (Enoch 92.2; cf. Jub. 32.21). How differently the prophets speak of Yahweh's guidance of history! From time to time something new and unexpected is revealed to them; in any case, no trace can be found in their preaching of the human question of the meaning and significance of the course of history. It is a 'strange work', to which Yahweh applies himself. Isaiah's picture of Assyria fluctuated because Yahweh's plans fluctuated. Israel might 'repent', Yahweh might 'repent himself' of his doom. According to Jeremiah, at one time Yahweh decided to build up his people and at another to tear them down: 'Behold, like the clay in the potter's hand, so are you in my hand' (Jer. 18.5ff.). Contrast with that the view of apocalyptic:

(God) with measure has measured the time and by number has numbered the seasons. Neither will he move nor stir things till the measure appointed be fulfilled (IV Ezra 4.37).

We thus have to say that with apocalyptic, on the basis of quite different theological presuppositions, a conception of the divine rule in history appeared on the scene which was basically different from that of the prophets. Whether this conception of history is to be understood as a necessary counterbalance and a breakthrough to a new theological perspective or whether it is a fatal distortion of Yahwistic faith is a question which is still far from finding an answer.

What has been said does not, of course, mean that there is no connection at all between apocalyptic and the legacy of prophecy. This connection existed by virtue of the simple fact that the apocalyptic writers concerned themselves with the books of the prophets as they did with many other spheres of learning, and occasionally contributed in their own way to the solution of particular exegetical problems. Such careful study could not have been without its effect. Thus we see how apocalyptic to an increasing degree makes use of prophetic forms (accounts of visions, speeches by God, etc.). But predicting the future was no monopoly of the prophets. We hardly ever see them concerned with the art of interpreting dreams, which was a privilege of the wise men throughout the ancient East and is practised to a great extent in apocalyptic. On the other hand, it is clear that the apocalyptic writers also draw on prophetic forms in their accounts of visions. The adoption of prophetic forms is at its strongest in the Syrian Apocalypse of Baruch.

23 Daniel

W E now come to Daniel! In view of what has just been said, no one will expect a prediction based, like that of the prophets, on definite election traditions. In fact, the traditions connected with the patriarchs, Exodus, or Zion all seem to lie quite outside Daniel's thought.[1] The songs of praise which occur here and there in the text (Dan. 2.20-3; 3.33 [4.3]; 4.31-4 [34-7]; 6.27-8 [26-7] are markedly different from the earlier ones which, as is well known, had as their chief subject Yahweh's wonderful works in creation and in the saving history. Here, the speaker's religious horizon has almost no connection with the actual events of history; he extols the greatness of God's power, which can make and unmake kings, deliver men and set them free. God's enlightening wisdom is also praised, and so is the indestructibility of his kingdom. This does not mean, of course, that in Daniel's time Israel had completely severed her links with the tradition of salvation history. Even for Daniel, the ground of Israel's well-being is loyalty to the traditional commandments, and her greatest danger anything which prevents this loyalty. These commandments themselves are now set forth, however, in a surprisingly absolute way, and their old connection with the saving history is broken. They have a clear meaning which is for all time. God's will is therefore no longer to be reinterpreted to meet new situations, as had been the usual practice in the past.

The legends of Daniel (chs. 1–6), the oldest traditional material in the book, very clearly illustrate the way in which Israel remained bound by the commandments, as they also do all the possibilities of conflict which this entailed. They depict the members of God's people as quite separated and isolated from the community in which they lived: yet they are quite sure that it was possible for the Israelites and their heathen neighbours to co-exist in a pagan empire. They make their heroes compete successfully

---

[1] Only in the prayer in Dan. 9.4ff. is there reference to the law of Moses and to the Exodus. This passage has, however, to be regarded as a secondary interpolation and in any case it is not a prophecy.

in the difficult career of state officials – Daniel accepts the educational facilities of the land (Dan. 1), as he does the honours which were Nebuchadnezzar's to confer (Dan. 2.48f.; 6.29 [28]). The Nebuchadnezzar or the Darius of these stories can never have been intended to represent the terrible Antiochus IV who set up the 'abomination that makes desolate'. The confident loyalty to Nebuchadnezzar shown by Daniel and his friends reflects a much more peaceful time than that of the Maccabean revolt. These legends, with their manifest didactic purpose, were originally addressed to the Jews of the Persian diaspora. The message they brought to their own age was an exhortation to obey the commandments of their own God precisely within the narrow limits of co-existence with the worshippers of other gods. It was also a warning: they were to be on their guard, and ready, if need be, to face very bitter hostility. For hatred of the chosen people and of their way of worship could spring up spontaneously from the very heart of these empires – their cult. Three of these six stories (Dan. 1; 3; 6) give examples of this hostility which would completely have destroyed the chosen people had not God himself carried them through every danger. Here is the other aspect of the message of these legends – the exiled Jews must know that they are not alone; despite all appearances, they have not been abandoned to the control of a despotic world-empire. Divine help rewards their persistence in obedience (Dan. 3; 6). Here there is a widening of the theological horizon: for behind the problem of the threat to the chosen people and their deliverance can be seen the hand of the God who directs world history, who is not mocked (Dan. 5), and who has power to depose and reinstate even emperors (Dan. 4). This message was a vital one for a people so closely involved in the life of a pagan empire. The confidence reflected by these legends is based on the conviction that God will keep faith. They bring not only a warning but also a message of comfort.

It seems paradoxical that these same stories which so confidently emphasize the possibility of co-existence with pagans should on the other hand speak openly of the final consequence of obedience, namely martyrdom. The right to apply this term to pre-Christian martyrs has been questioned: it is alleged that we may only speak of martyrdom where the suffering is expressly related to the idea of witness-bearing (and not to loyalty to the Law), and, in particular, only where the martyr is conscious that 'a part of God's final discourse with mankind is being fulfilled in him', that is to

say, where the martyr is aware of being involved in the eschatological Christ event (H. von Campenhausen, *Die Idee des Martyr-
iums*, 1936, p. 3 and in particular pp. 106ff.). This is certainly a
correct definition of Christian martyrdom, and is one which we
ought to keep in mind, for it points to features in martyrdoms
which only became definitive with the coming of Christ and with
his passion. On the other hand, the passion of Jeremiah and of the
Servant, and even the conflicts described in Dan. 3 and 6, come
very close to Christian martyrdom; for even in Israel it became
more and more apparent that loyalty to Yahweh logically would
lead to suffering. The people who were affected by this paradox
did not regard suffering as a sign that their fellowship with God
was ended, nor did they refuse to accept its consequences. Here
it is important that the three young men do not rely on the
miracle, but concede that God is free to allow even his own followers to perish (Dan. 3.18). Further, it cannot be said that the
idea of bearing witness is only of secondary importance in Dan.
3; for by their obedience to the commandments the youths do
bear witness to the God of Israel, and they also say that this is
what they are doing. The connection between witness-bearing and
suffering is, of course, still closer and more logical in the case of
Jeremiah; it is he, and not the three youths of Daniel, who is the
martyr *par excellence* of the Old Testament.

In the legends, the proper theme of the later apocalypses, the
consummation of history, is no more than hinted at. The problem
of the world-empires, their immense power, their disappearance,
and the emergence of new empires to take their place, is already
present; the dimensions of history are still, however, this world. It
is only in the visions of the night in Dan. 2 and 7 that the writer
carries us to that farthest margin where history touches the realm
of the transcendent; indeed, his gaze passes over into the transcendent world itself. In the vision of the four kings, very ancient ideas
about a series of world ages (such as occur in Hesiod and others)
have been fused with similar ideas about a series of four empires
in the political world (which are later found in Latin writers). It
can easily be seen that the reference to Antiochus Epiphanes was
only brought about by means of an extension of the schema in
which the kingdoms are represented by four metals; for, in what
may be presumed to be its earliest form, the picture of the four
kingdoms probably referred to the empire of Alexander. The process of adjustment to apply it to Antiochus IV and the great tribu-
lations which he caused is not itself a unity, because the text lent
itself to increasingly wider interpretations – this is particularly true

of the dream's interpretation (Dan. 2.36-45). The main point is, of course, perfectly clear: with the terrible fourth kingdom into which the empire divides, world history will come to an end. The stone which is to be cut 'by no human hand', and which is to destroy the kingdom and itself to become a great mountain, is an image of the kingdom of God that fills the whole earth. The same is true of the vision of the four beasts; here, too, what is obviously older material has been made – though not without some difficulty – to refer to the persecution of Israel for her faith by Antiochus IV.[2] Of course, in this vision the scene is changed. We are shown a throne room in heaven, and the description of everything that takes place here goes far beyond what is said in the vision of the kings. In the first part of the vision of the four beasts it is clear that some power is controlling the kingdoms. This is signified by the indeterminate passives, 'its wings were plucked off', 'it was made to stand' (v. 4), 'it was given' (v. 6). But in the vision of the throne the realm from which this controlling power comes is made visible. It is the throne room of Yahweh, in which a court of judgment is held, and in which the final transference of dominion over the world is solemnly made to the 'man'. Apocalyptic ideas are far removed from the tradition of the Davidic Messiah – the anointed one of the prophets comes from the line of David and from Bethlehem (Micah 5.1 [2]), and not down from heaven; but at the same time there can be no doubt that the son of man described in Dan. 7.13 is initially presented as a Messianic figure in the wider sense of the term.

We still do not know the origin of this concept, but we can say this much: the vision speaks of an individual who comes from the heavenly world, and whom God authorizes to take 'dominion and glory and kingdom' over all the nations of the world.[3] Oddly enough, this figure of the 'man' which, as we have just said, was

[2] Like the four rivers in Gen. 2.10ff. or the four horns in Zech. 2.1 [1.18], the four beasts represent the world in general. In Dan. 7.3 an idea that the four beasts came up contemporaneously out of the sea is still clearly visible. This would then completely correspond to Zechariah's picture of the four horns.

[3] Of the countless attempts to determine the origin of the Son of Man concept, the one which seems to me to merit special consideration is that in which the idea of the man who comes with the clouds of heaven is connected with that of the coming of the 'glory of Yahweh', especially as this worked out in Ezek. 1.26. Ezekiel too sees 'something like a man' come down from heaven. Besides, the coming of the divine 'glory' with the cloud is already characteristic of the account given in the Priestly Document.

quite certainly understood initially as an individual, is given a collective interpretation in the passage which explains it (Dan. 7.17-27): the 'man' is the incorporation of 'the saints of the Most High'. The view – hitherto almost unchallenged – that 'the saints of the Most High' refers to the people Israel, has recently been shaken; in face of both the linguistic usage of the Old Testament and of extracanonical texts, we should more probably understand them as heavenly beings; that is to say, the reference is to the idea that at the end of the ages dominion over the world is to be put into the hands of the angels.[4] However this may be, the subject matter of this dream vision has a greater width than any of the visions of the prophets, for it embraces all that takes place from creation down to the coming of the kingdom of God. The kingdoms come up out of the realm of chaos; their nature and behaviour is pictured in bizarre fashion. Apart from the excesses of the fourth beast, they are passive rather than active, and over them all, even over the havoc wreaked by the 'horn', Yahweh bears sovereign and unending sway. All that is needed to strip the horn of its power and to destroy it is a sentence passed by the court. On the other hand, the 'man' does not come from the realm of the unformed, but from the divine world on high. All this is described as from a spectator's point of view; the vision is not conceived as projected from its recipient's own historical standpoint, he does not stand within the events he beholds, but outside, and as he looks, all world history passes before his spirit like a film.

Where, in v. 25, it comes to its climax and refers to Antiochus Epiphanes, the vision of the four beasts itself cryptically named a period up to which the persecution would continue. It is, however, only in the latest material in the Book of Daniel, Dan. 8-12, that this desire to give precise times for the duration of the persecution and the beginning of the turning of the tide towards salvation becomes prominent. It is not at all surprising that the various calculations set forth in these chapters do not completely agree, for at that time the Wisdom teachers had different ways of going about their involved calculations. One particular desire was to determine the time of the end on the basis of the exposition of older prophetic texts. The exegesis of the seventy years prophesied by Jeremiah (Jer. 25.12; 29.10) is certainly only one of many examples, and it shows the way in which the prophetic books were read at the time. This method of interpreting old and valued

[4] Only one reference, Dan. 7.21, cannot be fitted into this interpretation.

texts gave the apocalyptic writers a completely new understanding of them. For it gave such texts a possible second meaning in a perfectly clear form. The seventy years were interpreted as 'seventy weeks of years' (Dan. 9.24), that is, as a time span of 490 years.

This is probably the first instance of that form of scriptural exegesis which was to become so important for both Judaism and early Christianity. It is entirely probable that the three-and-a-half times which play such a part in the calculation of the end (Dan. 7.25; 12.7) also derive from some old tradition, though, of course, the source upon which Daniel here drew has not yet been discovered. In other places too, the statements made about the future are simply exegesis of older words of scripture. Thus, in Dan. 9.26, in the prophecy of the end of Antiochus Epiphanes, the term 'flood' occurs. This is certainly not a random choice, but goes back to Isa. 10.22; for the very next verse to that (Isa. 10.23) is used in the same passage in Daniel, the only difference being that the 'decreed end' is now made to refer to the Seleucid king (Dan. 9.27), and the 'rumours' which terrify him and impel him to his final effort are taken from Isa. 37.7. In Dan. 11 criticism has always noted the transition from v. 39 to v. 40 as the break where *vaticinium post eventum* passes over into genuine foretelling. To think of it in this way is, however, to obscure what the writer wanted to suggest, for for him the whole thing is foretelling. Both history which was (for him) already in the past and the future looked forward to in the old prophetic writings were alike revealed as a complete course of historical events foretold by God. Without any doubt, a delicate exegetical touch was necessary in order to interpret the old prophetic books in such a way; for the expositors presupposed that these books only contained as it were an initial revelation, which still required the proper key-revelation which apocalyptic exegesis gave.

Where the course of history is predestined to such a degree, man's power of choice can only have a subordinate significance; men are only in a limited sense agents in what takes place, and therefore the pictures in apocalyptic literature lack the genuine tension of history. The oppressor must 'fill his measure full' (Dan. 8.23), and the oppressed are ordered to wait for 'the end of the indignation' (Dan. 11.36). Here, it is true, the writer distinguishes between the unfaithful who 'violate the covenant' and those who 'know their God' (Dan. 11.32). Among those who stand firm, the 'wise men' have a leading part to play – they 'help many to understand' (Dan. 11.33), 'they lead them to righteousness' (Dan. 12.3); indeed, their very death has a purifying and cleansing effect, reminding one of the atoning function of the Servant (Isa. 53.11). Without any doubt, the apocalyptist sides with those who endure persecution rather than those who take up arms against it, and in so doing he is only being true to his own basic conviction that what must be will be. He is far removed from the Maccabees and their policy of active resistance; their large following is actually suspect in his eyes. There is something almost sublime about the way in which, as he tells the story, he sets down a whole series of their amazing victories simply as something relatively unimportant, 'a little help' which the oppressed receive at this time (Dan. 11.34). His gaze is imperturbably fixed on the goal which God has appointed for history, and this forbade him to glorify the Maccabean revolt as an upsurge of human fortitude.

24 The Book of Expectation

T H E writings of ancient Israel, both those which were concerned with her past relationship to God and those which dealt with her future one, were seen by Jesus Christ, and certainly by the Apostles and the early Church, as a collection of predictions which pointed to him, the saviour of Israel and of the world. How could they do this – for the Old Testament never mentions Jesus Christ, nor does it visualize such a man as appears in the Gospels and Epistles? The Old Testament can only be read as a book of ever-increasing expectation which had first been aroused by the promise of a land to the pre-Mosaic patriarchs. Of this, however, there was, oddly enough, never any satisfactory historical fulfilment and consummation. The conquest under Joshua which was in fact its historical fulfilment was described and documented in great detail : but the Conquest was clearly never regarded as the full and final realization of this divine promise. Even as late as Deuteronomy – about 600 years after Joshua – Israel believed that this promise concerning the land was still in abeyance, and only in the future did she expect it to be realized in a way truly appropriate to God's word. In the interval Yahweh had brought new saving institutions into being : Zion had been 'founded', and David 'chosen'.

These new foundations were at first celebrated in Israel's praise in the form of statements made about the past, but they suddenly led to predictions about a new saving action for Israel. We have seen this in the case of the prophets' Messianic predictions and their predictions of the new city of God. The history of Yahwism is thus characterized by repeated breaks. God appoints new institutions and fresh starts which inaugurate new eras of tradition. Yet scarcely had Israel come to terms with these before she was again startled by being pointed to new acts of God, and by being forced to leave behind ideas in which she had just made herself at home. This shows us once again how completely different Israel's religious ideas were from those of other countries of the ancient East. In Egypt or Babylon the only possible salvation after any political or religious disturbance – of which there were many – was that the nation should return to these primeval sacral orders which found expression in myth and the cycle of the festivals: but Israel emphasized the unique character of what had occurred. Consequently a survey of the great movements of her history gives us the impression of a lack of repose – the nation is always on pilgrimage – and the constant emergence of new religious ideas seems to leave her a stranger in time. The impression that she was travelling along a road which could not be retraced is undoubtedly strengthened by the self-portrait drawn in her surviving literature. Her cultic life probably contained rather more constant and recurrent elements – that is, more of the 'cyclic' – than is evident here:[1] but Yahwism achieved its fullest self-expression precisely in this concentration upon the uniqueness of each of God's new saving acts.

Yahweh's covenant with the patriarchs, the revelation of his name, the events at Passover, the miraculous crossing of the Red Sea, the making of the covenant at Sinai, the establishment of Zion, the covenant with David, Yahweh's entry into the temple with his Ark, are all points of departure into a new form of Israel's existence, and all from the very start contained far-reaching divine promises. As we have seen, however, in the predictions of the prophets some of them were, as archetypes of mighty predictions, projected into the future. Israel's expectations thus continually grew wider. It is amazing to see how she never allowed a promise to come to nothing, how she thus swelled Yahweh's promises to an infinity, and how, placing absolutely no limit on God's power to fulfil, she transmitted promises still unfulfilled to generations to come.

Even those writings which actually have no kind of eschatological expectations whatsoever, as for example the Deuteronomic history or the Book of Job, nevertheless still have something that points mysteriously to the future. Were the acts of guidance and chastisement, the saving orders which were so strong a feature of the monarchical period, finally justified when an unhappy king was at last allowed to put off his prison clothes and to sit as a vassal at the table of the king of Babylon (II Kings 25.27ff.)? Was the great issue to be decided between Job and God resolved when

---

[1] Behind texts like Ex. 12 (the institution of Passover), II Sam. 6, Ps. 24. 7-10 or Ps. 132 (the bringing of the Ark into the Temple) lie cultic observances which were repeated in the cycle of the festivals.

the rebel was silenced before God, when an old man had children and herds given him again? This peculiar discrepancy between such endings and the themes which had been raised before them compel us to read the Old Testament as a book in which expectation keeps mounting up to vast proportions. This attempt to understand the prophets of Israel also makes it possible to see the incorporation of the Old Testament in the New as a process which was already heralded in the Old Testament itself. For the prophets, in whose relationship to the saving traditions of Israel a great gap could be discerned, were in their turn very free in their use of these elements of tradition. The freedom of the apostles and evangelists in accepting, changing, or rejecting the tradition was no less than that which Ezekiel had already claimed for himself. We can therefore see how there was again a degree of 'regularity' in the way in which the last new interpretation of the saving event was made.

Attempts have often been made to understand the Old Testament in the light of the New, and they are still legitimate. But the opposite course must also be undertaken, that of outlining the way from the Old Testament to the New. It is true that the New Testament saving event was the 'guideline' by which the first Christian communities attempted to come to terms with the Old Testament and by which they were led to a completely new perspective on it. But the reverse is equally true : the Old Testament saving history and the Old Testament revelation of God was a guideline which enabled them to understand and preach the Christ event, as can be seen, say, from the account of the Passion with its many references back to the Old Testament or in the theological argument of many of the apostolic letters. The two Testaments legitimate each other. The first principle – that the Old Testament is to be interpreted in the light of Christ – does not seem to be disputed as much today as the second, that we need the Old Testament to understand Christ. But is it really the case that we know who Jesus Christ is so well that we only have a secondary problem to solve, that of finding the relationship between the Old Testament and this Christ whom we already know?

Index of Biblical References